The Best of the Huckleberry's Chuckleberries
A Compilation of Volumes 1, 2, and 3

By Victoria Caudle

Cover concept by Victoria Caudle

Copyright © 2018 Victoria Caudle
All rights reserved.

ISBN-10: 1729705960
ISBN-13: 978-1729705964

Dedication

This book is dedicated to my parents, Charles and Olivia Cook, who taught me by example speaking words that edify and lift up really does make a better world -- and to my husband, Doug Caudle, the crazy Norwegian I love who taught me to look at things differently and laugh through everything.

- Victoria Caudle

"Laughter is the sun that drives winter
from the human face."
~ Victor Hugo

CONTENTS

Acknowledgments   i

Volume 1   Pg 3

Volume 2   Pg 101
Volume 3   Pg 198

ACKNOWLEDGMENT

You, the loyal readers of Huckleberry Press, were the inspiration for my beloved Chuckleberries and I thank you all. From their humble beginnings in the Huckleberry Mountains of Fruitland Valley, Chuckleberries became the legacy of Huckleberry Press and the personified diplomat you readily welcomed into your homes each print edition. Chuckleberries tied us together to form Huckleberry Country. Thank you to all who joyfully took the time and thoughtfulness over the years to contribute material. Your emails and letters kept me company working many late nights to make deadline. I gratefully acknowledge and celebrate you for sharing the love of laughter.

100% of the Profits of the Purchase of this Book Support Our Ministry in Costa Rica

A Message from the Author:

Each book purchase is appreciated beyond words. Doug and I fund our own way to volunteer for outreaches in Costa Rica. Your purchase allows us to directly help impoverished families keep their children in school and enables Doug to volunteer as the tuition-free electrical apprenticeship training instructor at Hope Fellowship in Guanacaste, Costa Rica to help adults lift themselves out of poverty with the skills that will provide them with better paying jobs. Please keep buying the books as gifts for others and please encourage others to buy the book and we promise to be your hands and feet to help others so they can help themselves. All because of you, the people we help will know the love, compassion, and grace of Jesus – and you!

Love and Friendship,
Victoria and Doug Caudle

Volume 1

I really love my furniture. Me and my recliner go way back.

Q & A
Q: What goes "Ooh ooh"?
A: A cow with no lips.

Mime School
Every year, hundreds of kids are shipped off to mime school never to be heard from again.

Q & A
Q: Where is happiness made?
A: At the satisfactory.

It's Up In The Air
Did you hear about the mother who gave birth to her baby while she was on a flight? I guess you can say the baby was airborne.

Farmer milks a cow
    A farmer was milking his cow. He was just starting to get a good rhythm going when a bug flew into the barn and started circling his head. Suddenly, the bug flew into the cow's ear. The farmer didn't think much about it, until the bug squirted out into his bucket. It went in one ear and out the udder.

Now, That's Really Low!
Someone broke into my apartment last night and stole my limbo stick.
How low can you go?

Knitting Sheep
I read an article earlier that said it actually takes three sheep to make one sweater.
That's so cool! I didn't even know they could knit!

Naptime
If a child refuses to sleep during nap time, are they guilty of resisting a rest?

Lawnmower Man
I just saw a man slumped over a lawn mower crying his eyes out.
He said he'll be fine. He's just going through a rough patch.

Faster Than Light
If light travels faster than the speed of sound, how come I can hear the guy in the BMW behind me honk before the light turns green?

That Fell Flat!
The only thing flat-earthers fear is sphere itself.

Elvis Tribute Act
I called to buy tickets for an Elvis tribute act.
It was an automated phone system, "Press 1 for the money, 2 for the show…"

CAPITAL JOKE
I WRITE ALL MY JOKES IN CAPITALS…
THIS ONE WAS WRITTEN IN PARIS.

That's Just Nuts
What did the nut say when it was chasing the other nut? … "I'm a cashew!"

Something Not To Do
Don't ever take a sleeping pill and a laxative at the same time.
But, if you do, you'll sleep like a baby.

Q & A
Q: What do you call an unshaven British Spy?
A: Stubble-07.

That's Confusing
I asked a librarian for a book about Pavlov's dog and Schroedinger's cat.
She said it rang a bell, but she wasn't sure if it was there or not.

Possession
Who decided to call it "marijuana possession" ... and not "joint custody?"

Suspicious
Three conspiracy theorists walk into a bar.
Now, you can't tell me that's just a coincidence.

Banned!
Do you ever wake up, kiss the person sleeping beside you, and be glad that you are alive? I did and apparently I won't be allowed on this airline again.

Caged!
At the zoo I noticed a slice of toast in one of the enclosures.
I asked the keeper, "What is that toast doing in the cage?"
She said, "It was bread in captivity."

Quick! Warn Him!
Edgar Allen Poe is about to walk into a tree and you only have enough time to say one word before he hits it. What should you say to him?
"Poetry!"

The Color Purple
I was forced to swallow purple food coloring. I feel violated.

Beyond Rescue
Why could the lifeguard not save the hippie? Because he was too far out, man.

Q & A
Q: How do you know if a sniper likes you?
A: He misses you.

I Miss My Ladder
I recently got a step ladder. It hurts not being able to see my real ladder anymore.

Internet Flowers
I accidentally sent my friend flowers over the internet. Whoops, E-Daisies!

Cloud Computing
I never knew how technologically advanced Moses was.
But, today I learned he had the first tablet that could connect to a cloud.

Orange
I dreamed I drowned in an ocean made of orange soda.
When I woke I realized it was just a Fanta sea.

Speechless
The doctor told me my voice box is damaged and I may never speak again. I can't tell you how upset I am.

Czech The Sound
I have a Polish friend who's a sound technician.
Oh, and a Czech one too. Czech one too. Czech one too.

Good Outlook Now
I was feeling bad about the future today, but then I installed the new version of Office. It improved my outlook.

That Bad!
I didn't ever realize how bad of a driver I was until yesterday when my GPS Navigation System said, "In 400 feet, do a slight right, stop, and let me out."

All That Time
My friend has been a limo driver for 25 years and hasn't had a single customer. All that time and nothing to chauffeur it.

Seaweed Addiction
I'm addicted to seaweed. There's no denying that I must seek kelp.

Workplace Violence
Today at work I beat my boss over the head with a pie chart.
I've been charged with "a graph-aided assault."

Bank Robber
A young man robbed a bank wearing a suit made of many mirrors.
But, he turned himself in after taking some time to reflect.
Luckily, the judge was lenient as he saw a lot of himself in the young man.

"What comes from the heart, goes to the heart." ~ Samuel Taylor Coleridge

My Car Phone
I drove my car into a river and watched it turn into a mobile phone.
One minute, a Kia. Next minute, Nokia.

No School For Garbage Men
Did you know there's no official training for garbage men? They just pick it up as they go along.

Fish cost a fortune
Two Virginia rednecks go on a fishing trip. They rent all the equipment – the reels, the rods, the wading suits, the rowboat, the car, and even a cabin in the woods. They spend a fortune!

The first day they go fishing, they don't catch anything. The same thing happens on the second day, and on the third day. It goes on like this until finally, on the last day of their vacation, one of the men catches a fish.

As they're driving home they're really depressed. One guy turns to the other and says, "Do you realize that this one lousy fish we caught cost us fifteen hundred bucks?"

The other guy says, "Wow! Then it's a good thing we didn't catch anymore!"

Pessimist and a dog
An avid duck hunter was in the market for a new bird dog. His search ended when he found a dog that could actually walk on water to retrieve a duck. Shocked by his find, he was sure none of his friends would ever believe him.

He decided to try to break the news to a friend of his, the eternal pessimist who refused to be impressed with anything. This, surely, would impress him. He invited him to hunt with him and his new dog.

As they walked by the shore, a flock of ducks flew by, they fired, and a duck fell. The dog responded and jumped into the water. The dog, however, did not sink but instead walked across the water to retrieve the bird, never getting more than his paws wet. This continued all day long; each time a duck fell, the dog walked across the surface of the water to retrieve it.

The pessimist watched carefully, saw everything, but did not say a single word.

On the drive home the hunter asked his friend, "Did you notice anything unusual about my new dog?"

"I sure did," responded the pessimist. "He can't swim."

You Know They're Growing Up, When…
Children: You spend the first 2 years of their life teaching them to walk and talk. Then you spend the next 16 telling them to sit down and shut-up.

The following are some of the oldest original riddles. How many can you solve?

1. What goes round the house and in the house but never touches the house?
2. What is it that you can keep after giving it to someone else?
3. What walks all day on its head?
4. What gets wet when drying?
5. What comes once in a minute, twice in a moment, but never in a thousand years?
6. The more you take, the more you leave behind. What are they?
7. He who has it doesn't tell it. He who takes it doesn't know it. He who knows it doesn't want it. What is it?
8. Who spends the day at the window, goes to the table for meals and hides at night?
9. There are four brothers in this world that we all born together. The first runs and never wearies. The second eats and is never full. The third drinks and is always thirsty. The fourth sings a song that is never good.
10. A cloud was my mother, the wind is my father, my son is the cool stream, and my daughter is the fruit of the land. A rainbow is my bed, the earth my final resting place, and I'm the torment of man.

Answers to Riddles: 1. The sun. 2. Your word. 3. A nail in a horseshoe. 4. A towel. 5. The letter "M." 6. Footsteps. 7. Counterfeit money. 8. A fly. 9. Water, fire, earth, wind. 10. Rain.

Where is my goat?

There were these two guys out hiking when they came upon an old, abandoned mine shaft. Curious about its depth they threw in a pebble and waited for the sound of it striking the bottom, but they heard nothing. They went and got a bigger rock, threw it in and waited. Still, nothing. They searched the area for something larger and came upon a railroad tie. With great difficulty, the two men carried it to the opening and threw it in. While waiting for it to hit bottom, a goat suddenly darted between them and leapt into the hole!

The guys were still standing there with astonished looks upon their faces from the actions of the goat when a man walked up to them. He asked them if they had seen a goat anywhere in the area and they said that one had just jumped into the mine shaft in front of them! The man replied, "Oh no. That couldn't be my goat; mine was tied to a railroad tie."

The only reason some people get lost in thought is because it's unfamiliar territory. ~ Paul Fix

If you can keep your head about you when all about you are losing theirs, it's just possible you haven't grasped the situation. ~ Jean Kerr

The Two Bear Hunters From Seattle

Two hunters from Seattle were driving through Stevens County to go bear hunting. They came upon a fork in the road where a sign read "BEAR LEFT" so they went home.

I have a question

A father and son went fishing one day. While they were out in the boat, the boy suddenly became curious about the world around him. He asked his father, "How does this boat float?"

The father replied, "Don't rightly know son." A little later, the boy looked at his father and asked, "How do fish breath underwater?"

Once again the father replied, "Don't rightly know son." A little later the boy asked his father, "Why is the sky blue?"

Again, the father replied, "Don't rightly know son." Finally, the boy asked his father, "Dad, do you mind my asking you all of these questions?"

The father replied, "Of course not, if you don't ask questions, you never learn nothin'."

10 THINGS TO THINK ABOUT

1. The dictionary is the only place where success comes before work.
2. The best way to realize your dreams is to wake up.
3. Some come to the fountain of knowledge to drink, some prefer to just gargle.
4. Remember the tea kettle; though up to its neck in hot water, it continues to sing.
5. People who complain about the way the ball bounces usually dropped it.
6. People who think they know everything upset those of us who do.
7. People will accept your idea much more readily if you tell them Benjamin Franklin said it first.
8. People will believe anything if you whisper it.
9. The more an item costs, the farther you have to send it for repairs.
10. The idea is to die young as late as possible.

"The easiest way for your children to learn about money is for you not to have any." ~ Katherine Whitehorn

"The different between winners and losers is that winners do what losers don't want to do." ~ Dr. Phil McGraw

BRAINTEASERS

1. Here is a quotation with all the spaces and vowels removed. What is the quotation?

MNCNNTBTCRFLNTHCHCFHSNMS

2. Here are the names of four flowers with the vowels removed. What are the four flowers?

GRNM   GRDN   CLMBN   CLNDN

3. Rearrange the letters of the following phrase to give the name of a U.S. state:
VIEWING A STIR

4. Which of the following words is the odd-one-out?
IBIS   IBEX   ORYX   SIKA   ZEBU

5. What do the words below have in common?
ADAM   CLAIM   GALL   BUOY   FOND   RAMP

ANSWERS: 1. A man cannot be too careful in the choice of his enemies, (Oscar Wilde). 2. Geranium, Gardenia, Columbine, Celadine. 3. West Virginia. 4. The Ibis is a bird, the others are mammals. 5. Each can have ANT appended to form a new word.

Go on a hiking trip

Sherlock Holmes and Matthew Watson were on a camping and hiking trip. They had gone to bed and were lying there looking up at the sky. Holmes said, "Watson, look up. What do you see?

"Well, I see thousands of stars."

"And what does that mean to you?"

"Well, I guess it means we will have another nice day tomorrow. What does it mean to you, Holmes?"

"To me, it means someone has stolen our tent."

I marked the spot

Two friends rented a boat and fished on a lake every day. One day they caught 30 fish. One guy said to his friend, "Mark this spot so that we can come back here again tomorrow."

The next day, when they were driving to rent the boat, the same guy asked his friend, "Did you mark that spot?"

His friend replied, "Yeah, I put a big 'X' on the bottom of the boat."

The first one said, "You fool! What if we don't get that same boat today!?!?"

Flying in the plane

Two hunters got a pilot to fly them into the far north for elk hunting. They were quite successful in their venture and bagged six big bucks. The pilot came back, as arranged, to pick them up. They started loading their gear into the plane, including the six elk. But the pilot objected and he said, "The plane can only take four of your elk; you will have to leave two behind." They argued with him; the year before they had shot six and the pilot had allowed them to put all aboard. The plane was the same model and capacity. Reluctantly, the pilot finally permitted them to put all six aboard. But when they attempted to take off and leave the valley, the little plane could not make it and they crashed into the wilderness.

Climbing out of the wreckage, one hunter said to the other, "Do you know where we are?"

"I think so," replied the other hunter. I think this is about the same place where we landed last year!"

Catching Many Fish

A fisherman returned to shore with a giant marlin that was bigger and heavier than he. On the way to the cleaning shed, he ran into a second fisherman who had a stringer with a dozen baby minnows. The second fisherman looked at the marlin, turned to the first fisherman and said, "Only caught one, eh?"

Actually appeared in a church bulletin or announced in a service:

* This afternoon there will be a meeting in the South and North ends of the church. Children will be baptized at both ends.
* Tuesday at 4 P.M. there will be an ice cream social. Will ladies giving milk, please come early?
* Wednesday the Ladies Literary Society will meet. Mrs. Johns will sing "Put Me In My Little Bed" accompanied by the Pastor.
* Thursday at 5 P.M. there will be a meeting of the Little Mothers Club. All wishing to become Little Mothers will please meet the Minister in his study.
* This being Easter Sunday, we will ask Mrs. Jackson to come forward and lay an egg on the altar.
* The service will close with "Little Drops of Water." One of the ladies will start quietly and the rest of the congregation will join her.
* On Sunday a special collection will be taken to defray the expenses of the new carpeting. All wishing to do something on the carpet, please come forward and get a piece of paper.
* The ladies of the Church have cast off clothing of every kind. They may be seen in the basement on Friday afternoon.

* This evening at 7 P.M. there will be a hymn sing in the park across from the Church. Bring a blanket and come prepared to sin.

[From Richard Lederer's *Anguished English*]

"If it's a penny for your thoughts and you put in your two cents worth, then someone, somewhere is making a penny." ~ Steven Wright

Farmer's Son

The school of agriculture's dean of admissions was interviewing a prospective student, "Why have you chosen this career?" he asked.

"I dream of making a million dollars in farming, like my father," the student replied.

"You father made a million dollars in farming?" echoed the dean, much impressed.

"No," replied the application. "But he always dreamed of it."

SILLY JOKES

Q: Did you hear about the cowboy who got a dachshund?
A: Everyone kept telling him to get a long, little doggie.

Q: It is good manners to eat fried chicken with your fingers?
A: No, you should eat your fingers separately.

Q: Why do hens lay eggs?
A: If they dropped them, they'd break.

Q: Why do seagulls live near the sea?
A: Because if they lived near the bay, they'd be called bagels.

Q: Diner: Do you serve chicken here?
A: Waiter: Sit down, sir. We serve anyone.

Working in a Small Town

Joe grew up in a small town, then moved away to attend college and law school.

He decided to come back to the small town because he could be a big man in this small town – a big fish in a small pond. He did everything he could to impress everyone. He opened his new law office in the nicest location in town, though he had little prospect for income early on.

One day, he saw a man coming up the sidewalk, and Joe was desperate to make a good impression on this new potential client. So, as the man came to the door, Joe picked up the phone. He motioned the man in, all the while talking, "No. Absolutely not. You tell those clowns in New York that I won't settle this case for less than one million. Yes. The Appeals Court has agreed to hear that case next week. I'll be handling the primary argument and the other members of my team will provide support. Okay. Tell the DA that I'll meet with him next week to discuss the details."

This sort of thing went on for almost five minutes. All the while the man sat patiently as Joe rattled "instructions." Finally, Joe put down the phone and turned to the man. "I'm sorry for the delay, but as you can see, I'm very busy. What can I do for you?"

The man replied, "I'm from the phone company. I came to hook up your phone."

SILLY BUMPER STICKERS

On the back of an SUV in Eastern Washington: "Save Our Dams – Remove the Lockes." *(pre-Gregoire)*

"Hug a Logger – You'll Never go Back to Trees."

"Suburbia: where they tear out the trees and then name streets after them."

"It's Not Hard to Meet Expenses, They're Everywhere."

"Time is what keeps everything from happening at once."

"I didn't fight my way to the top of the food chain to be a vegetarian."

"Lead Me Not Into Temptation, I Can Find It Myself."

"What happens if you get scared half to death twice?"

"Don't bother me. I'm living happily ever after."

"I started out with nothing and still have most of it left."

On the back of a VW owned by an anesthesiologist: "The Ether Bunny."

Huh? Oh, Right!

Said a boy to his teacher one day, "Wright has not written write right, I say."
And the teacher replied as the blunder she eyed, "Right! Wright, write "write" right, right away!"

LETTER FROM A FARM KID NOW AT THE MARINE CORPS RECRUIT DEPOT IN DIEGO

Dear Ma and Pa:

I am well. Hoe you are. Tell Brother Wait and Brother Elmer the Marine Corps beats working for old man Minch by a mile. Tell them to join up quickly before maybe all of the places are filled. I was restless at first because you got to stay in bed till nearly 6 a.m., but am getting so I like to sleep late.

Tell Walt and Elmer all you do before breakfast is smooth your cot and shine some things. No hogs to slop, feed to pitch, mash to mix, wood to split, fire to lay. Practically nothing. Men go to shave but it is not so bad, there's warm water.

Breakfast is strong on trimmings like fruit juice, cereal, eggs, bacon, etc., but kind of weak on chops, potatoes, ham, steak, fried eggplant, pie and other regular food. But tell Walt and Elmer you can always sit by the two city boys that live on coffee. Their food plus yours holds you till noon when you get fed again.

It's no wonder these city boys can't walk much. We go on "route" marches, which the Platoon Sergeant says are long walks to harden us. If he thinks so, it is not my place to tell him different. A "route march" is about as far as to our mailbox at home. Then the city guys get sore feet and we all ride back in trucks. The country is nice, but awful flat. The Sergeant is like a schoolteacher. He nags some. The Capt. Is like the school board. Majors and Colonels just ride around and frown. They don't bother you none.

This next will kill Walt and Elmer with laughing. I keep getting medals for shooting. I don't know why. The bulls-eye is near as big as a chipmunk head and don't move. And it ain't shooting at you, like the Higgett boys at home. All you got to do is lie there all comfortable and hit it. You don't even load your own cartridges. They come in boxes.

Then we have what they call hand-to-hand combat training. You get to wrestle with them city boys. I have to be real careful though, they break real easy. It ain't like fighting with that ole bull at home. I'm about the best they got in this except for that Tug Jordan from over in Silver Lake. He joined up the same time as me. But I'm only 5'6" and 130 pounds and he's 6'8" and weighs near 300 pounds dry. Be sure to tell Walt and Elmer to hurry and join before other fellers get onto this setup and come stampeding in.

Your loving daughter,
Gail

White Hair

One day, a little girl is sitting in the kitchen, watching her mother do the dishes at the kitchen sink. She suddenly notices that her mother has several strands of white hair sticking out in contrast to her brunette hair. She looks at her mother and inquisitively asks, "Why are some of your hairs white, Mom?"

Her mother replied, "Well, every time that you do something wrong and make me cry or unhappy, one of my hairs turns white."

The little girl thought about this revelation for a while and then asked, "Momma, how come ALL of grandma's hairs are white?"

Where's Bill?

A group of friends went deer hunting and paired off in two's for the day. That night one of the hunters returned alone, staggering under the weight of an eight point buck.

"Where's Bill?"

"Bill had a stroke of some kind. He's a couple of miles back up the trail."

"You left Bill laying out there and carried the deer back!?!"

"A tough call," nodded the hunter, "but I figured no one is going to steal Bill."

Hunting Dogs

A young man from the city went to visit his farmer uncle. For the first few days, the uncle showed him the usual things – chickens, cows, crops, etc. After three days, however, it was obvious that the nephew was getting bored, and the uncle was running out of things to amuse him with.

Finally, the uncle had an idea. "Why don't you grab a gun, take the dogs, and go hunting?"

This seemed to cheer the nephew up, and with enthusiasm, off he went, dogs in trail. After a few hours, the nephew returned.

"How did you enjoy that?" asked the uncle.

"It was great!" exclaimed the nephew. "Got any more dogs?"

Chicken Farming

A life-long city man, tired of the rat race, decided he was going to give up the city life, move to the country, and become a chicken farmer. He found a nice, used chicken farm, which he bought. Turns out that his next door neighbor was also a chicken farmer. The neighbor came for a visit one day and said, "Chicken farming isn't easy. Tell you what. To help you get started, I'll give you 100 chickens." The new chicken farmer was thrilled. Two weeks later the new neighbor stopped by to see how things were going. The new farmer said, "Not too good. All 100 chickens dies." The neighbor said, "Oh, I can't believe that.

I've never had any trouble with my chickens. I'll give you 100 more." Another two weeks went by, and the neighbor stops in again. The new farmer says, "You're not going to believe this, but the second 100 chickens died too." Astounded, the neighbor asked, "What went wrong? What did you do to them?" Well, says the new farmer, "I'm not sure whether I'm planting them too deep or not far apart enough."

The Sick Duck

A man took his old duck to the Doctor, concerned because the duck wouldn't eat. The Doctor explained to the man that as ducks age their upper bills grown down over their lower bills which makes it difficult for the animal to pick up its food.

"What you need to do is gently file the upper bill down even with the lower bill. But you must be extra careful because the duck's nostrils are located in the upper bill and if you file down too far, when the duck takes a drink of water it'll drown."

The man goes about his business and about a week later the Doctor runs into his patient. "Well, how is that duck of yours?" the Doctor inquires.

"He's dead," declared the heartbroken man.

"I told you not to file his upper bill down too far! He took a drink of water and drowned didn't he?" insisted the Doctor.

"No." lamented the man. "I think he was dead before I took him out of the vise."

Dog Breeds that Failed...
* Collie + Lhasa Apso – Collapso, a dog that folds up for easy transport
* Newfoundland + Basset Hound = Newfound Asset Hound, a dog for financial advisors
* Collie + Malamute = Commute, a dog that travels to work
* Pekingese + Lhasa Apso = Peekasso, an abstract dog
* Labrador Retriever + Curly Coated Retriever = Lab Coat Retriever, the choice of research scientists
* Bloodhound + Labrador = Blabador, a dog that barks incessantly
* Malamute + Point = Moot Point, owned by ... oh, well, it doesn't matter anyway
* Deerhouse + Terrie = Derriere, a dog that's true to the end

Points to Ponder
* How come we choose from just two people for President and fifty for Miss America?

* Wouldn't it be nice if when we messed up our life we could simply press 'Ctrl Alt Delete' and start all over?
* Why is it that our children can't read a Bible in school, but they can in prison?
* If money doesn't grow on trees, then why do banks have branches?

Learning From History

A father noticed that his son was spending way too much time playing computer games. In an effort to motivate the boy into focusing more attention on his schoolwork, the father said to his son, "When Abe Lincoln was your age, he was studying books by the light of the fireplace." The son replied, "When Lincoln was your age, he was The President of the United States.

The Price of a Cow

A car dealer with a reputation for taking advantage of his customers called a local farmer and said he was coming over to buy a cow. When he arrived, he found the farmer had affixed this "sticker" to the cow:

COW BASE MODEL	$499.95
Shipping and Handling	35.75
Extra Stomach	79.25
Two-tone exterior	142.10
Produce storage compartment	126.50
Heavy-duty straw chopper	189.60
Four spigot/high-output drain system	149.20
Automatic fly swatter	88.50
Genuine cowhide upholstery	179.90
Deluxe dual horns	59.25
Automatic fertilizer attachment	339.40
4-by-4 traction drive assembly	884.16
Pre-delivery wash and comb	69.80
FARMER'S SUGGESTED LIST PRICE	2,843.36
Additional dealer adjustments	300.00
TOTAL PRICE (including options)	$3,143.36

What Kind of "Taters" are You Having for Thanksgiving Dinner?

There are many different kinds of "taters." When the family and friends gather for Thanksgiving this year, see how many different "taters" you're having at dinner. I hope all you have are sweet taters. You'll see what I mean when you read on:

Some people never seem motivated to participate, but are just content to watch while others do the work. They are called "Spec Taters."

Some people never do anything to help, but are gifted at finding fault with the way others to the work. They are called "Comment Taters."

Some people are very bossy and like to tell others what to do, but don't want to soil their own hands. They are called "Dick Taters."

Some people are always looking to cause problems by asking others to agree with them. It is too hot or too cold, too sour or too sweet. They are called "Agie Taters."

There are those who say they will help, but somehow just never get around to actually doing the promised help. They are called "Hezzie Taters."

Some people can put up a front and pretend to be someone they are not. They are called "Emma Taters."

Then, there are those who love others and do what they say they will. They are always prepared to stop whatever they are doing to lend a helping hand. They bring real sunshine into the lives of others. They are called "Sweet Taters."

So, when you have the family and friends for Thanksgiving Dinner next week, let everyone know how much you love the "Sweet Taters."

It's All Relative

A man is trying to understand the nature of God and asked him: "God, how long is a million years to you?" God answered: "A million years is like a minute." Then the man asked: "God, how much is a million dollars to you?" And God replied: "A million dollars is like a penny." Finally the man asked, "God, could you give me a penny?" And God says, "In a minute."

"The Rules of Chocolate"
("Confectionately" dedicated to Marilynn Newbill, Fruitland, Washington!)
* If you have melted chocolate all over your hands, you're eating it too slowly.
* Chocolate covered raisins, cherries, orange slices, and strawberries all count as fruit, so eat as many as you want.
* The program: How to get 2 pounds of chocolate home from the store in a hot car. The solution: Eat it in the parking lot.
* Diet tip: Eat a chocolate bar before each meal. It'll take the edge off your appetite and you'll eat less.
* A nice box of chocolate can provide your total daily intake of calories in one place. Isn't that handy?
* If you can't eat all your chocolate, it will keep in the freezer. But if you can't eat all your chocolate, what's wrong with you?

* If calories are an issue, store your chocolate on top of the fridge. Calories are afraid of heights, and they will jump out of the chocolate to protect themselves.
* If you eat equal amounts of dark chocolate and white chocolate, is that a balanced diet? Don't they actually counteract each other?
* Money talks. Chocolate sings.
* Chocolate has many preservatives. Preservatives make you look younger.
* Question: Why is there no such organization as Chocoholics Anonymous? Answer: Because no one wants to quit.
* If not for chocolate, there would be no need for control top pantyhose. An entire garment industry would be devastated.
* Put "eat chocolate" at the top of your list of things to do today. That way, at least you'll get one thing done.

Children's Letters to God
* Dear God, Instead of letting people die and making new ones, why don't you just keep the ones you have? – Johnny
* Dear God, Maybe Cain and Abel would not kill each other so much if they had their own rooms. It worked with my brother. – Larry
* Dear God, If you watch me in church on Sunday, I'll show You my new shoes. – Mickey
* Dear God, I bet it is very hard to You to love all of everybody in the world. There are only four people in our family and I can never do it. – Nan
* Dear God, In Sunday school they told us what You do. Who does it when you are on vacation? – Jane
* Dear God, I read the Bible, what does the "beget" mean? Nobody will tell me. – Love, Allison
* Dear God, Are You really invisible or is it just a trick? – Lucy
* Dear God, Is it true my father won't get into Heaven if he uses his bowling words in the house? – Anita
* Dear God, Did You mean for the giraffe to look like that or was it an accident? – Norma
* Dear God, Who draws the lines around the countries? – Nan
* Dear God, I went to this wedding and they kissed right in church. Is that okay? – Neil
* Dear God, Did You really mean "do unto others as they do unto you?" Because if you did, then I'm going to fix my brother. – Darla
* Dear God, Thank you for the baby brother, but what I prayed for was a puppy. – Joyce

* Dear God, Please send me a pony. I never asked for anything before. You can look it up. – Bruce
* Dear God, If we come back as something – Please don't let me be Jennifer Horton because I hate her. – Denise
* Dear God, I want to be just like my Daddy when I get big but not with so much hair all over. – Sam
* Dear God, I think the stapler is one of Your greatest inventions. – Ruth
* Dear God, I think about You sometimes even when I'm not praying. – Elliott
* Dear God, Of all the people who work you You I like Noah and David best. – Rob
* Dear God, My brother told me about being born but it doesn't sound right. They're just kidding, aren't they? – Marsha
* Dear God, I would like to live for 900 years like that guy in the Bible. – Love, Chris
* Dear God, We read Thomas Edison made light. But in Sunday school they said you did it. So I bet he stole Your idea. – Sincerely, Donna
* Dear God, I didn't think orange went with purple until I saw the sunset You made on Tuesday. That was cool. – Sara

House Painting

A man was painting his house when a poorly dressed fellow approached and said he was down on his luck. He asked whether he could do something to earn a meal or a few dollars.

The homeowner thought for a minute. "Sure," he said. "Take this can of yellow paint, go around back, and paint my porch."

An hour later the man returned.

"Finished already?" asked the homeowner.

"Yeah," the bum said. "But I have some news for you. That's not a Porsche, it's a Mercedes."

If you ever find yourself in a horror movie…

* When it appears that you have killed the monster, NEVER check to see if it's really dead.
* Never read a book of demon-summoning aloud, even as a joke.
* Do not search the basement, especially if the power has gone out.
* If your children speak to you in Latin or any other language which they should not know, shoot them immediately. It will save you a lot of grief in the long run. However, it will probably take several rounds to kill them, so be prepared. This also applies to kids who speak with somebody else's voice.
* As a general rule, don't solve puzzles that open portals to hell.

* If you find a town which looks deserted, there's probably a good reason for it. Don't stop and look around.
* Don't fool with recombinant DNA technology unless you're sure you know what you're doing.
* If you're running from the monster, expect to trip or fall down at least twice. Also note that, despite the fact that you are running and the monster is merely shambling along, it's still moving fast enough to catch up with you.
* If your car runs out of gas at night on a lonely road, do not go to the nearby deserted looking house to phone for help. If you think that it is strange because you thought you had half of a tank, shoot yourself instead. You are going to die anyway, and most likely be eaten.
* AND MOST IMPORTANTLY: When trying to escape from a serial killer, never run UPstairs.

When it rains...

A newcomer to Seattle arrives on a rainy day. When she gets up the next day, it's raining. It also rains the day after that, and the day after that. She goes out to lunch and sees a young kid and, out of despair, asks, "Hey, kid, does it ever stop raining around here?"

The kid says, "How should I know? I'm only 6."

Warden Learns a Lesson

A man is walking from the lake carrying two fish in a bucket. He is approached by the Game Warden who asks him for his fishing license. The fisherman says to the warden, "I did not catch these fish, they are my pets. Every day I come down to the water and whistle and these fish jump out and take them around to see the sights only to return them at the end of the day."

The warden, not believing him, reminds him that it is illegal to fish without a license. The fisherman turns to the warden and says, "If you don't believe me then watch," as he throws the fish back into the water.

The warden says, "Now whistle to your fish and show me that they will come out of the water."

The fisherman turns to the warden and says, "What fish?"

Teacher Learns a Lesson

At a special school birthday party, a kindergarten teacher was receiving gifts from her pupils. The florist's son handed her a gift. She shook it, held it overhead, and said, "I bet I know what it is, some flowers."

"That's right," the boy said, "but how did you know?"

"Oh, just a wild guess." She said.

The next pupil was the daughter of the candy store owner. The teacher held it overhead, shook it and said, "I bet I can guess what it is, a box of candy."

"That's right, but how did you know?" asked the girl.

"Oh, just a wild guess," the teacher said.

The next gift was from the son of the liquor store owner. The teacher held it overhead, but it was leaking. She touched a drop of the leakage with her finger and tasted it. "Is it wine?" she asked.

"No," the boy replied, obviously delighted that he had stumped her.

The teacher touched another drop of the liquid and placed it to her tongue. "Champagne?" she asked.

"No," the clearly delighted boy answered.

"I give up, what is it?"

The boy enthusiastically replied, "It's a puppy!"

Let's Teach Osama Bin Laden a Lesson

Little David comes home from first grade and tells his father that they learned about the history of Valentine's Day. "Since Valentine's Day is for a Christian saint and we're Jewish," he asks, "will God get mad at me for giving someone a valentine?"

David's father thinks a bit, and then says "No, I don't think God would get mad. Who do you want to give a valentine to?"

"Osama Bin Laden," David says.

"Why Osama Bin Laden?" his father asks in shock.

"Well," David says, "I thought that if a little American Jewish boy could have enough love to give Osama a valentine, he might start to think that maybe we're not all bad, and maybe start loving people a little bit. And if other kids saw what I did and sent valentines to Osama, he'd love everyone a lot. And then he'd start going all over the place to tell everyone how much he loved them and how he didn't hate anyone anymore."

His father's heart swells and he looks at his boy with newfound pride. "David, that's the most wonderful thing I've ever heard."

"I know," David says, "and once that gets him out in the open, the Marines could have a clear shot at him."

Kids on Marriage
How do you decide who to marry?

You got to find somebody who likes the same stuff. Like, if you like sports, she should like it that you like sports, and she should keep the chips and dip coming. – Alan, age 10

No person really decides before they grow up who they're going to marry. God decides it all way before, and you get to find out later who you're stuck with. – Kirsten, age 10

What is the right age to get married?
Twenty-three is the best age because you know the person FOREVER by then. – Camille, age 10
No age is good to get married at. You got to be a fool to get married. – Freddie, age 6

How can a stranger tell if two people are married?
You might have to guess, based on whether they seem to be yelling at the same kids. – Derrick, age 8

What do you think your mom and dad have in common?
Both don't want any more kids. – Lorie, age 8

What do people do on a date?
Dates are for having fun, and people should use them to get to know each other. Even boys have something to say if you listen long enough. – Lynnette, age 8
On the first date, they just tell each other lies and that usually gets them interested enough to go for a second date. – Martin, age 10

What would you do on a first date that was turning sour?
I'd run home and play dead. The next day I would call the newspapers and make sure they wrote about me in all the dead columns. – Craig, age 9

When is it okay to kiss someone?
When they're rich. – Pam, age 7
The law says you have to be eighteen, so I wouldn't want to mess with that. – Curt, age 7
If you kiss someone, then you should marry them and have kids with them. It's the right thing to do. – Howard, age 8

Is it better to be single or married?
I'm never going to have sex with my wife. I don't want to be all grossed out. – Theodore, age 8
It's better for girls to be single but not for boys. Boys need someone to clean up after them. – Anita, age 9

How would the world be different if people didn't get married?

There sure would be a lot of kids to explain, wouldn't there? – Kevin, age 8

How would you make a marriage work?

Tell your wife that she looks pretty even if she looks like a truck. – Ricky, age 10

Afraid of the Dark

A little boy was afraid of the dark. One night his mother told him to go out on the back porch and bring her the broom.

The little boy turned to his mother and said, "Mama, I don't want to go out there. It's dark."

The mother smiled reassuringly at her son. "You don't have to be afraid of the dark," she explained. "Jesus is out there. He'll look after you and protect you."

The little boy looked at his mother real hard and asked, "Are you sure he's out there?"

"Yes, I'm sure. He is everywhere, and he is always ready to help you when you need him," she said.

The little boy thought about that for a minute and then went to the back door and cracked it a little. Peering out into the darkness, he called, "Jesus? If you're out there, would you please hand me the broom?"

Drawing God

A kindergarten teacher was observing her classroom of children while they drew. She would occasionally walk around to see child's artwork. As she got to one little girl who was working diligently, she asked what the drawing was.

The girl replied, "I'm drawing God."

The teacher paused and said, "But no one knows what God looks like."

Without missing a beat, or looking up from her drawing, the girl replied, "They will in a minute."

Job Interview

Stephanie goes to a job interview. The boss says, "I'll give you 8 dollars an hour starting today, and in three months, I'll raise it to 12 dollars an hour. So, when would you like to start?"

Stephanie replies, "How about 3 months from now?"

When you were born, everyone around you was smiling and you were crying. Live your life so that when you die, you're smiling and everyone around you is crying.

Importance of a raise

"I have to have a raise," the man said to his boss. "There are three other companies after me."

"Is that so?" asked the manager. "What other companies are after you?"

"The electric company, the telephone company, and the gas company."

The Secret

A mother was showing her boy how to zip up his coat.

"The secret," she said, "is to get the left part of the zipper to fit in the other side before you try to zip it up."

The boy looked at her quizzically... "Why does it have to be a secret?"

"Heart Surgeon"

A mechanic was removing a cylinder head from the motor of a Harley, when he spotted a world-famous heart surgeon in his shop. The heart surgeon was waiting for the service manager to come take a look at his bike. The mechanic shouted across the garage, "Hey Doc, do you mind if I ask you a question?"

The famous surgeon, a bit surprised, walked over to the mechanic working on the motorcycle.

The mechanic straightened up, wiped his hands on a rag and asked, "So Doc, look at this engine. I also can open it up, take valves out, fix them, and put in new parts and when I finish this will work just like a new one. So how come I get a pittance and you get the really big money; when you and I are doing basically the same work?"

The surgeon paused, smiled and leaned over, and whispered to the mechanic, "Try doing the job while the motor is running!"

The Trade

A preacher was making his rounds to his parishoners on a bicycle, when he came upon a little boy trying to sell a lawnmower. "How much do you want for the mower?" asked the preacher.

"I'm just trying to make enough money to buy a bicycle," said the little boy.

After a moment of consideration, the preacher asked, "Will you take my bike in trade for it?"

The boy said, "You got a deal."

The preacher took the mower and tried to crank it. He pulled on the string a few times with no response from the mower.

The preacher called the little boy over and said, "I can't get this mower to start."

The little boy said, "That's cause you have to cuss at it to get it started."

The preacher said, "I'm a minister, and I can't cuss. It's been so long since I've been saved that I don't know if I even remember how to cuss."

The little boy looked at him happily and said, "Just keep pulling on that string. It'll come back to ya!"

The Ranch of His Dreams

The Seattleite had always dreamed of owning his own cattle ranch, and finally made enough money to buy himself the spread of his dreams in Eastern Washington.

"So, what did you name the ranch?" asked his best friend when he came out to visit.

"We had a heck of a time," admitted the new cowboy. "Couldn't agree on anything. We finally settled on the Double R Lazy L Triple Horseshoe Bar-7 Lucky Diamond Ranch."

"Wow!" his friend was impressed. But looking around he saw no cattle.

"So...where are all the cows?"

"None of 'em survived the branding."

Noun Gender

From the Washington Post Style Invitation, in which it was postulated that English should have male and female nouns. Readers were asked to assign a gender to nouns of their choice, and explain their reasons. The best submissions:

SWISS ARMY KNIFE – Male. Even though it appears useful for a wide variety of work, it spends most of its time just opening bottles.
KIDNEYS – Female. They always go to the bathroom in pairs.
TIRE – Male. It goes bald and often is over-inflated.
HOT AIR BALLOON – Male. To get it to go anywhere, you have to light a fire under it...and, of course, there's the hot air part.
SPONGES – Female. They are soft, squeezeable, and they retain water.
WEB PAGE – Female. It is always getting hit on.
SHOE – Male. It is usually unpolished, with its tongue hanging out.
COPIER – Female. One turned off, it takes a while to warm up. It is an effective reproductive device when the right buttons are pushed. And it can wreak havoc when the wrong buttons are pushed.
ZIPLOC BAG – Male. They hold everything in, but you can always see right through them.
SUBWAY – Male. It uses the same old lines to pick up people.
HOURGLASS – Female. Over time, the weight shifts to the bottom.
HAMMER – Male. It hasn't evolved much over the last 5,000 years, but it's handy to have around.

Contributed by a Friend Who's a "Keeper"

"Keepers. It was a way of life, and sometimes it made me crazy. All that re-fixing, reheating, renewing, I wanted just once to be wasteful. Waste meant affluence. Throwing things away meant you knew there'd always be more. But then my Father died, and on that clear summer's night, in the warmth of the hospital room, I was struck with the pain of learning that sometimes that isn't any more. Sometimes, what we care about most gets all used up and goes away…never to return. So, while we have it, it's best we love it…and care for it…and fix it when it's broken…and heal it when it's sick. This is true for marriage…and old cars…and children with bad report cards…and dogs with bad hips…and aging parents…and grandparents. We keep them because they are worth it, because we are worth it. Some things we keep. Like a best friend that moved away, or a classmate we grew up with. There are just some things that make life important, like people we know who are special…and so, we keep them close!"

Learning Important Lessons

A priest is walking down the street one day when he notices a boy trying to press a doorbell on a house across the street. However, the boy is very small, and the doorbell is too high for him to reach. After watching the boy's efforts for some time, the priest decides to help. The priest steps smartly across the street, walks up behind the little fellow and, placing his hand kindly on the child's shoulder, leans over and gives the doorbell a solid ring.

The child looks over his should and smiles at the priest. "Thank you father," he says, "Now we run!"

Pet Appreciation Week

* Lick you dog's face.
* Bring your cat a dead bird.
* Get your dog a bone and bury it for him.
* Make a concerted effort to learn to purr.
* Eat supper on the floor.
* Spend quality time with your pet rolling around in something really awful.

Child's Perspective

Grandpa and granddaughter were sitting talking when she asked, "Did God make you, Grandpa?"

"Yes, God made me," the grandfather answered.

A few minutes later, the little girl asked him, "Did God make me too?"

"Yes, He did," the older man answered.

For a few minutes, the little girl seemed to be studying her grandpa, as well as her own reflection in the mirror, while her grandfather wondered what was running through her mind.

At last she spoke up. "You know, Grandpa," she said, "He's getting a lot better at it."

The Gift

Fresh out of gift ideas, a man bought his mother-in-law a large plot in an expensive cemetery as a birthday gift. On her next birthday, he bought her nothing. She was quick to comment loud and long on his thoughtlessness. The man said only one thing – "Well, you haven't used the gift I gave you last year."

Praying for Presents

Two young boys were spending the night at their grandparents the week before Christmas. At bedtime, the two boys knelt beside their beds to say their prayers when the youngest one began praying at the top of his lungs. "I PRAY FOR A NEW BICYLCE...I PRAY FOR A NEW PLAY STATION...I PRAY FOR A NEW DVD PLAYER..."

His older brother leaned over and nudged the younger brother and said, "Why are you shouting your prayers? God isn't deaf."

To which the little brother replied, "No, but Grandma is!"

A Night on the Town

A couple was going out for a rare night on the town. They dressed up in their finest clothes, called a cab and put the cat out. The taxi arrived, and as the couple walked out of their home, the cat shot between their legs, back into the house and up the stairs. They did not want the often rowdy cat to have the run of the house while they were gone, so while his wife waited in the taxi, the husband went upstairs to chase the cat back out. Not wanting the cab driver to know that the house would be left empty, the woman explained to him, "My husband is just going upstairs to stay goodbye to my mother."

A few minutes later, the husband got into the taxi and said, "Sorry I took so long. Stupid old thing was hiding under the bed and I had to poke her with a coat hanger to get her to come out!"

Mothers & Their Sons

So, the first Catholic woman tells her friends, "My son is a priest. When he walks into a room, everyone calls him 'Father'." The second Catholic woman chirps, "My son is a bishop. Whenever he walks into a room, people call him 'Your Grace'." The third Catholic woman says, "My son is a cardinal. Whenever he walks into a room, he's called 'Your Eminence'."

As the little old Jewish lady sips her coffee in silence, the first three give her this subtle "Well...?" look, so she says, "My son is 6'5:; he has broad square shoulders, lean hips and is very muscular; he's terribly handsome, has beautiful hair, dresses very well and always smells wonderful. Whenever he walks into a room, women say, 'Oh, my God...'

KIDS!

A man in Florida, in his 80s, calls his son in New York one November day. The father says to the son, "I hate to tell you, but we've got some troubles here in the house. Your mother and I can't stand each other anymore, and we're getting a divorce. I've had it! I want to live out the rest of my years in peace. I'm telling you now, so you and your sister shouldn't go into shock later when I move out." He hangs up, and the son immediately calls his sister in the Hamptons and tells her the news.

The sister says, "I'll handle this."

She calls Florida and says to her father, "Don't do ANYTHING till we get there! We'll be there Wednesday night."

The father agrees, "All right." The old man hangs up on the phone and hollers to his wife, "Okay, they're coming for Thanksgiving. Now, what are we going to tell them for Christmas?"

Swiss Army Tactics

The Swiss have an interesting army. Five hundred years without a war. Pretty impressive. Also pretty lucky for them. Ever see that little Swiss Army knife they have to fight with? Not much of a weapon there. Corkscrews. Bottle openers. Can you see it now? "Come on, buddy, let's go. You get past me, the guy in back of me, he's got a spoon. Back off. I've got the toe clippers right here!"

Relatives of Vincent Van Gogh

His obnoxious brother: Please Gogh
His dizzy aunt: Verti Gogh
The brother who ate prunes: Gotta Gogh
The brother who worked at a convenience store: Stopn Gogh
The grandfather from Yugoslavia: U Gogh
The brother who bleached his clothes white: Hue Gogh
The cousin from Illinois: Chica Gogh
His magician uncle: Wherediddy Gogh
His Mexican cousin: Amee Gogh
The Mexican cousin's American half brother: Grin Gogh
The nephew who drove a stage coach: Wellsfar Gogh

The ballroom dancing aunt: Tan Gogh
The bird lover uncle: Flamin Gogh
His nephew psychoanalyst: E Gogh
The fruit loving cousin: Man Gogh
An aunt who taught positive thinking: Wayto Gogh
The little bouncy nephew: Poe Gogh
A sister who loved disco: Go Gogh

15 Totally Useless Facts & Statistics
1. Coca-Cola was originally green.
2. Each day more money is printed for Monopoly than for the U.S. Treasury.
3. Smartest dogs: 1) border collie; 2) poodle; 3) golden retriever.
4. Hawaiian alphabet has 12 letters.
5. Men can read smaller print than women; women can hear better.
6. Chances an American lives within 50 miles of where they grew up: 1 in 2.
7. Amount American Airlines saved in '87 by taking out 1 olive from each salad served in first class: $40,000.
8. City with the most Rolls Royce's per capita: Hong Kong.
9. State with the highest percentage of people who walk to work: Alaska.
10. Percentage of Africa that is wilderness: 28%.
11. Percentage of North America that is wilderness: 38%.
12. Estimated % of American adults who go on a diet each year: 44%.
13. Barbie's measurements if she were life size: 39-23-33.
14. Only President awarded a patent: Abe Lincoln, for a system of buoying vessels over shoals.
15. Cost of raising a medium-size dog to the age of eleven: $6,400.

Scary Storms
    One summer evening, during a violent thunderstorm, a mother was tucking her small frightened boy into bed. She was about to turn off the light when he asked with a tremor in his voice, "Mommy, will you sleep with me tonight?"
    The mother smiled and gave him a reassuring hug, "I can't dear," she said, "I have to sleep with Daddy."
    A long silence was broken at last by a shaken little voice saying, "The big sissy."

The First Drive
    Martin has just received his brand new driver's license. The family troops out to the driveway and climbs in the car where Martin is going to take them for a ride for the first time. Dad immediately heads for the back seat, directly behind the newly minted driver.

"I'll bet you're back there to get a change of scenery after all those months of sitting in the front passenger seat teaching me how to drive," says the beaming boy to his father.

"Nope," comes Dad's reply. "I'm gonna sit here and kick the back of your seat as you drive, just like you've been doing to me all these years."

The Secret to a Long Life

A tough old cowboy once counseled his grandson that if he wanted to live a long life, the secret was to sprinkle a little gunpowder on his oatmeal every morning. The grandson did this religiously and he lived to the age of 93. When he died, he left 14 children, 28 grandchildren, 35 great grandchildren, and a fifteen foot hold in the wall of the crematorium.

The Magnet Lesson

Miss Jones had just given her second-grade students a science lesson. She had explained about magnets, and showed how they would pick up nails and other bits of iron. Now it was questions time. Miss Jones said, "My name begins with the letter 'M' and I pick up things. What am I?"

A little boy in the front row proudly said, "You're a mother!"

Hand on Your Heart

Little Johnny was at his first day of school. The teacher told the class they always started the day with the pledge of allegiance. He instructed them to put their right hands over their hearts and repeat after him. He looked around the room as they received… "I pledge allegiance to the flag…" When his eyes fell on Johnny, he noticed Johnny's hand was over the right cheek of his buttocks. "Johnny, we will not continue till you put your hand over your heart."

Johnny replied, "It is over my heart."

After several attempts to get Johnny to put his hand over his heart, the teacher asked, "Why do you think that is your heart?"

"Because every time my Grandma comes to visit, she picks me up, pats me here, and says, 'Bless your little heart,' and my Grandma wouldn't lie."

Daddy's Busy

The head of a big company needed to call one of his employees about an urgent problem. He dialed the employee's home and was greet with a child's whispered "Hello?"

Perturbed he had to talk to a youngster, the boss asked, "Is your Daddy home?"

"Yes," whispered the small voice.

"May I talk with him?" the man asked.

To the surprise of the boss, the small voice whispered, "No."

Wanting to talk with an adult, the boss asked, "Is your Mommy there?"

"Yes," came the answer.

"May I talk with her?"

Again the small voice whispered, "No."

"Is there another adult there?" the boss asked the child.

"Yes," whispered the child, "a policeman."

Wondering what a copy would be doing at his employee's home, the boss asked, "May I speak with the policeman?"

"No, he's busy," whispered the child.

"Busy doing what?" asked the boss.

"Talking to Daddy and Mommy and the firemen," came the whispered answer.

The boss, who is now becoming very concerned, thought he heard what sounded like a helicopter in the background. He asked the child, "What is that noise?"

"A hello-copper," answered the whispering voice.

"What is going on there?" asked the boss, now alarmed.

Still whispering, the child answered, "The search team just landed the hello-copper."

Now very frustrated and close to panic, the boss asked, "Why are they there?"

Still whispering, the young voice replied with a muffled giggle, "They're looking for me."

The Doggy Dictionary

LEASH: Strap which attaches to your collar, enabling you to lead your person where you want him/her to go.

DOG BED: Any soft, clean surface, such as the white bedspread in the guest room or the newly upholstered couch in the living room.

DROOL: What to do when your persons have food and you don't. To do this properly you must sit as close as you can and look sad and let the drool fall to the floor or, better yet, on their laps.

SNIFF: A social custom to use when you greet other dogs until your person makes you stop.

GARBAGE CAN: A container which your neighbors put out once a week to test your ingenuity. You must stand on your hind legs and try to push the lid off with your nose. If you do it right you are rewarded with margarine wrappers to shred, beef bones to consume and moldy crusts of bread.

BICYCLES: Two-wheeled exercise machines, invented for dogs to control body fat. To get maximum aerobic benefit, you must hind behind a bush and dash out, bark loudly and run alongside for a few yards; the person then swerves and falls into the bushes, and you complete the exercise by prancing away.

DEAFNESS: A malady which affects a dog when its person wants it in and the dog wants to stay out. Symptoms include staring blankly at the person, then running in the opposite direction, or lying down.

THUNDER: A signal that the world is coming to an end. Humans remain amazingly calm during thunderstorms, so it is necessary to warn them of the danger by trembling uncontrollably, panting, peeing on the rug, rolling your eyes wildly and following at their heels.

WASTEBASKET: A dog toy filled with paper, envelopes, and old candy wrappers. When you get bored, turn over the basket and strew the papers all over the house for your person to play with by putting back in the wastebasket when they come home.

SOFAS: Are to dogs like napkins are to people. After eating it is polite to run up and down the front of the sofa and wipe your whiskers clean.

LEAN: Every good dog's response to the command "sit!" – especially if your person is dressed for an evening out. Incredibly effective before black-tie events.

BUMP: The best way to get your human's attention when they are drinking a fresh cup of coffee or tea.

GOOSE BUMP: A last-resort maneuver used when the Regular Bump doesn't get the attention you require. Especially effective when combined with The Sniff (see above).

LOVE: A feeling intense affection, given freely and without restriction. To show your love, wag your tail and gaze adoringly. If you're lucky, a human will love you in return.

DON'T BELIEVE ATOMS! They make up everything!

Poker Playing Dog

A guy walks into a bar and sees a dog playing poker. The guy is amazed that the dog is playing poker. "Bartender, is that a real dog playing poker?" the guy asks.

"Yep, real as can be." the bartender replies.

"That's amazing!" the customer exclaims.

"Not really," says the bartender. "Every time he gets a good hand he gives it away by wagging his tail."

Man's Best Friend

Bob, an experienced sky diver, was getting ready for a jump one day when he spotted another man outfitted to sky dive wearing dark glasses, carrying a white cane and holding a seeing-eye dog by an extremely long leash. Shocked that the blind man was also going to jump, Bob struck up a conversation, expressing his admiration for the man's courage. Then, curious, he asked, "How do you know when the ground is getting close?"

"Easy," replied the blind man. "The leash goes slack."

Helpful Cow

A man was driving down a country road in the middle of the diary farm country when his car stalled. He got out and raised the hood. A brown and white cow slowly lumbered from the pasture over to the car and stuck her head under the hood beside the man. After a moment the cow looked at the man and said, "Looks like a bad carburetor to me." Then she walked back into the field and resumed her grazing.

Amazed, the man walked back to the farmhouse he had just passed, where he met a farmer. "Hey, mister, is that your cow in the field?" he asked.

The farmer replied, "The brown and white one? Yep, that's old Bessie."

The man then said, "Well my car's broken down, and she just said, 'Looks like a bad carburetor to me.'"

The farmer shook his head and said, "Don't mind old Bessie, son. She don't know a thing about cars."

The Captain's Parrot

A magician was working on a cruise ship in the Caribbean. He has a different audience each week, so he allowed himself to perform the same act over and over again. There was only one problem: The captain's parrot saw the shows each week and began to understand how the magician did every trick.

Once he understood, he started shouting in the middle of every show, "Look, that's not the same hat! Now he's hiding the flowers under the table! Hey, why are all the cards the Ace of Spades?"

The magician was furious but couldn't do anything about it. After all, it was the captain's parrot.

One day the unthinkable happened: The ship had an accident and sank! The magician found himself on a piece of wood in the middle of the ocean with the parrot, of course! They glared at each other, but did not utter a single word for days.

After a week the parrot finally broke the silence and said, "OK, I give up. Where'd you hid the boat?"

Actual Label Instructions on Consumer Goods

- On a Sears hairdryer: Do not use while sleeping.

- On a bag of Fritos: You could be a winner! No purchase necessary. Details inside.

- On a bar of Dial soap: Directions: Use like regular soap.
- On some Swann frozen dinners: Serving suggestions: Defrost.
- On a hotel provided shower cap in a box: Fits one head.
- On the bottom of a Tesco's Tiramisu dessert box: Do not turn upside down.
- On Marks & Spencer Bread Putting: Product will be hot after heating.
- On packaging for a Rowenta iron: Do not iron clothes on body.
- On Boot's Children's cough medicine: Do not drive car or operate heavy machinery.
- On Nytol sleep aid: Warning: may cause drowsiness.
- On a string of Chinese-made Christmas lights: For indoor or outdoor use only.
- On a Japanese food processor: Not to be used for the other use.
- On Sainsbury's peanuts: Warning: contains nuts.
- On an American Airlines packet of nuts: Instructions: open package, eat nuts.
- On a child's Superman costume: Wearing of this garment does not enable you to fly.

Diagnosis

While making the rounds, Dr. Owens points out an X-Ray to a group of medical students. "As you can see," he says, "the patient limps because his left fibula and tibia are radically arched. Aman Preet, what would you do in a case like this?"

Preet pondered for a second and answered, "I guess I'd limp, too."

Ailments

The two young boys were discussing their ailments together in the children's ward. "Are you medical or surgical?" asked the first, who had been in the ward for a week.

"I don't know what you mean," replied the second.

"It's simple," replied the first. "Were you sick when you came in here, or did they make you sick when you got here?"

Advice from Kids

- Never smart off to a teach whose eyes and ears are twitching – Andrew, age 9
- Wear a hat when feeding seagulls. – Rock, age 9
- Sleep in your clothes so you'll be dressed in the morning – Stephanie, age 8
- Don't flush the john when your dad's in the shower. – Lamar, age 10
- Never ask for anything that costs more than $5 when your parents are doing taxes. – Carrol, age 9
- Never bug a pregnant mom. – Nicholas, age 11
- Don't ever be too full for dessert. – Kelly, age 10

- When your dad is mad and asks you, "Do I look stupid?" don't answer him. – Heather, age 16
- Never tell your mom her diet's not working. – Michael, age 14
- Don't pick on your sister when she's holding a baseball bat. – Joel, age 12
- When you get a bad grade in school, show it to your mom when she's on the phone. – Alyesha – age 13
- Never try to baptize a cat. – Laura, age 13
- Never spit when on a roller coaster. – Scott, age 11
- Never do pranks at a police station. – Sam, age 10
- Never tell your little brother that you're not going to do what your mum told you to do. – Hank, age 12
- Remember you're never too old to hold your father's hand. – Molly, age 11
- Listen to your brain. It has lots of information. – Chelsey, age 7
- Never dare your little brother to paint the family car. – Phillip, age 13
- Remember the two places you are always welcome – church and Grandma's house. – Joanne, age 11
- When you want something expensive ask your grandparents. – Matthew, age 12

The wages of sin is death, but by the time taxes are taken out, it's just sort of a tired feeling.

Never Be Afraid To Try Something New.
Remember, Amateurs Built the Ark – Professionals Built the Titanic, and other words of wisdom...
* Experience is something you don't get until just after you need it.
* A conclusion is the place where you got tired of thinking.
* Depression is anger without enthusiasm.
* Remember that half the people you know are below average.
* I wonder how much deeper the ocean would be without sponges?
* Love is grand – divorce is a hundred grand.
* To steal ideas from one person is plagiarism; to steal from many is research.
* Don't be irreplaceable. If you can't be replaced, you can't be promoted.
* Never test the depth of the water with both feet.
* It is far more impressive when others discover your good qualities without your help.
* If you think nobody cares if you're alive, try missing a couple of car payments.
* Good judgment comes from bad experience, and a lot of that comes of bad judgment.

* The quickest way to double your money is to fold it in half and put it back in your pocket.
* A closed mouth gathers no foot.
* If you tell the truth, you don't have to remember anything.
* Never miss a good chance to shut up.
* Generally speaking, you aren't learning much when your mouth is moving.
* Always remember, you're unique, just like everyone else.
* Duct tape is like the force. It has a light side and a dark side, and it holds the universe together.
* Before I criticize a man, I walk a mile in his shoes. That way, if he gets angry, he's a mile away and barefoot.
* It at first you don't succeed, skydiving is not for you.
* The trouble with doing something right the first time is that nobody appreciates how difficult it was.
* What we see depends on mainly what we look for.
* Children have more need of models than of critics.
* If Jimmy cracks corn and no one cares, why is there a song about him?

...And, Nobody cares if you can't dance well. Just get up and dance!

Short Riddles
What goes farther the slower it goes? (Money)
What is always coming but never arrives? (Tomorrow)
What always remains down even when it flies up in the air? (A feather)
What is it that you cannot hold ten minutes, even though it is lighter than a feather? (Your breath)
What is it from which you may take away the whole and still have some life, or take away some and have the whole left? (the word Wholesome)

Don't Force It
One Sunday morning a little girl in her Sunday best was running so she wouldn't be late for church. As she ran she kept praying, "Dear God, please don't let me be late to church. Please don't let me be late to church..."

As she was running she tripped and fell. When she got back up she began praying again, "Please, God don't let me be late to church – ***but don't shove me either!***"

Open Door
An exasperated mother, whose son was always getting into mischief, finally asked him, "How do you expect to get into Heaven?"

The boy thought it over and said, "Well, I'll run in and out and in and out and keep slamming the door until St. Peter says, 'For Heaven's sake, Dylan, come in or stay out!'"

Bad Time to Call
A woman was trying hard to get the catsup to come out of the bottle. During her struggle the phone rang so she asked her four-year old daughter to answer it.

"It's the minister, Mommy," the child said to her mother. Then she said into the phone, "Mommy can't come to the phone to talk to you right now. She's hitting the bottle."

Parenting Abilities Test
MESS TEST – Smear peanut butter on the sofa and curtains. Place a fish stick behind the couch and leave it there all summer.
TOY TEST – Obtain a 55 gallon box of Lego (or you may substitute roofing tacks). Have a friend spread them all over the house. Put on a blindfold. Try to walk to the bathroom or kitchen. Do not scream because this would wake a child at night.
GROCERY STORE TEST – Borrow one or two small animals (goats are best) and take them with you as you shop. Always keep them in sight and pay for anything they eat or damage.
DRESSING TEST – Obtain one large, unhappy, live octopus. Stuff into a small net bag making sure that all the arms stay inside.
FEEDING TEST – Obtain a large plastic milk jug. Fill halfway with water. Suspend from the ceiling with a cord. Start the jug swinging. Try to insert spoonfuls of soggy cereal into the mouth of the jug, while pretending to be an airplane. Now, dump the contents of the jug on the floor.
NIGHT TEST – Prepare by obtaining a small cloth bag and fill it with 8-12 pounds of sand. Soak it thoroughly in water. At 3:00 pm, begin to waltz and hum with the bag until 9:00 pm. Lay down your bag and set your alarm for 10:00 pm. Get up, pick up your bag, and sing every song you have ever heard. Make up about a dozen more and sing these too until 4:00 am. Set alarm for 5:00 am. Get up and make breakfast. Keep this up for 5 years. Look cheerful.
INGENUITY TEST – Take an egg carton. Using a pair of scissors and pot of paint, turn it into an alligator. Now take a toilet paper tube and turn it into an attractive Christmas candle. Use only scotch tape and a piece of foil. Last, take a milk carton, a ping-pong ball, and an empty box of Cocoa Puffs. Make an exact replica of the Eiffel Tower.
AUTOMOBILE TEST – Forget the BMW and buy a station wagon. Buy a chocolate ice cream cone and put it in the glove compartment. Leave it there. Get a dime. Stick it into the cassette player. Take a family size package of

chocolate chip cookies. Mash them into the back seat. Run a garden rake along both sides of the car. There! Perfect.

PHYSICAL TEST (Women) – Obtain a large bean bag chair and attach it to the front of your clothes. Leave it there for 9 months. Now remove 10 of the beans.

PHYSICAL TEST (Men) – Go to the nearest drug store. Set your wallet on the counter. Ask the clerk to help himself. Now proceed to the nearest food store. Go to the head office and arrange for your paycheck to be directly deposited to the store. Purchase a newspaper. Go home and read it quietly for the last time.

FINAL ASSIGNMENT – Find a couple who already have a small child. Lecture them on how they can improve their discipline, patience, tolerance, toilet training and child's table manners. Suggest many ways they can improve. Emphasize to them that they should never allow their children to run wild. Enjoy this experience. It will be the last time you will have all the answers!

Terms from the Parent's Dictionary

FAMILY PLANNING: The art of spacing your children the proper distance apart to keep you on the edge of financial disaster.

FEEDBACK: The inevitable result when your baby doesn't fully appreciate the strained carrots.

FULL NAME: What you call your child when you're mad at him.

GRANDPARENTS: The people who think your children are wonderful even though they're sure you're not raising them right.

HEARSAY: What toddlers do when anyone mutters a dirty word.

INDEPENDENT: What we want out children to be as long as they do everything we say.

OW: The first word spoken by children with older siblings.

PUDDLE: A small body of water that draws other small bodies wearing dry shoes into it.

SHOW OFF: A child who is more talented than yours.

STERILIZE: What you do to your first baby's pacifier by blowing on it.

TOP BUNK: Where you should never put a child wearing Superman pajamas.

Washing the Dog

A young boy about eight years old walks into the local grocery store and picks out a huge box of laundry detergent. The grocer walked over, and trying to be friendly, asked the boy if he had a lot of laundry to do.

"Oh, no laundry," the boy said, "I'm going to wash my dog!"

"But you shouldn't use this to wash your dog. It's very powerful and if you wash your dog in this, he'll get sick. It might even kill him."

But the boy was not to be stopped and carried the detergent to the counter and paid for it, even as the grocer still tried to talk him out of washing his dog.

About a week later the boy was back in the store to buy some candy. The grocer asked the boy how his dog was going.

"Oh, he died," the boy said sadly.

The grocer, trying not to be an I-told-you-so, said he was sorry the dog dies but added, "I tried to tell you not to use that detergent on your dog!"

"Well," the boy replied, "I don't think it was the detergent that killed him."

"Oh? What was it then?"

"I think it was the spin cycle!"

Team Effort

Two guys on a double bike were pedaling up a hill. It took forever to get to the top. When they finally go to the top the first guy said in a pant, "Whew, that was so hard."

The second replied, "Yes, I know! That was a steep hill! If I hadn't been pushing the brakes the whole time we would have rolled down backwards."

Good Fishing!

A game warden noticed how a particular fellow named Sam consistently caught more fish than anyone else. When the other guys would only catch three or four a day, Sam would come in off the lake with a boat full. The warden asked Sam his secret. The successful fisherman invited the game warden to accompany him and observe.

So, the next morning the two men met at the boat dock and took off in Sam's boat. When they got to the middle of the lake, Sam stopped the boat, and the warden sat back to see how it was done.

Sam's approach was simple. He took out a stick of dynamite, lit it, and threw it in the air. The explosion rocked the lake with such a force that dead fish immediately began to surface. Sam took out a net and started scooping them up. Well, you can imagine the reaction of the game warden.

"When he recovered from the shock of it all, he began yelling at Sam, "You can't do this! I'll put you in jail, buddy! You will be paying each fine there is in the book!

Meanwhile, Sam set his net down and took out another stick of dynamite. He lit it and tossed it in the lap of the warden with these words, "Are ya gonna sit there all day complaining, or are ya going to fish?"

You Sure You Know Where We're Going???

A hunting party is hopelessly lost. "I thought you said you were the best guide in Washington!" one of the hunters angrily said to their confused leader.

"I am," replied the guide. "But I think we're in Canada now."

LETTER FROM MAW

Dear Son,

Your Pa has a new job. The first in 48 years. We are a little better off now, getting $17.96 every Thursday. So, we up and thought we'd do a little fixin' up. We sent to Rosemont and Seasbuck for one of them there bathrooms you hear so much about and it took a plumber to put it in shape.

On one side of the room is a great big long thing, something like the hogs drink out of, only you get in it and wash all over. Over on the other side is a little white thing called a sink for light washing like face and hands, but over in the other we really got something.

There you put one foot in, wash it clean, pull a chain and get fresh water for the other foot. Two lids come with the dark thing and we ain't had any use for them in the bathroom, so I'm using one for a bread board and the other we framed grandmother's picture in. They were awful nice people to deal with and they sent us a roll of writing paper with it. Take care of yourself son.

Your Maw

The Trouble With Labeling...

When the mother returned from the grocery store, her small son pulled out the box of animal crackers he had begged for. Then he spread the animal-shaped crackers all over the kitchen counter.

"What are you doing?" his mom asked.

"The box says you can't eat them if the seal is broken," the boy explained, "I'm looking for the seal."

Perspective

Okay, so a Texan rancher comes upon a farmer from Maine. The Texan looks at the Mainer and asks, "Say, how much land you think you got here?"

Mainer: "Bout 10 acres I'd say."

Texan (boasting): "Well, on my lot, it takes me all day to drive completely around my property!"

Mainer: "Yep, I got one of them trucks too."

Hey, God, What's the Deal?

Little Jimmy's mother was serving prunes for dessert, but little Jimmy didn't like prunes one little bit! He grumbled and complained and absolutely refused to eat them.

Mother was very cross and told Jimmy that God would be very angry if he didn't eat his prunes. Still he wouldn't eat them, so in desperation, mother sent him to his room.

Later in the evening a fierce thunderstorm blew up. There was much thunder and lightning. Feeling somewhat sorry for little Jimmy and thinking that he might be afraid of the storm, mother went up to his room.

When she opened the door, Jimmy was kneeling looking out the window.

Mother heard him say, "Gee whiz, God, all this just for two measly prunes?"

What's So Complicated About It?

A Sunday school teacher was discussing the Ten Commandments with her five and six year olds. After explaining the commandment to "honor thy father and mother," she asked, "Is there a commandment that teaches us how to treat our brothers and sisters?"

Without missing a beat one little boy answered: "Thou shalt not kill!"

It <u>Can</u> Get Complicated!

A certain little girl, when asked her name, would reply, "I'm Mr. Sugarbrown's daughter." Her mother told her this was wrong, she must just say, "I'm Jane Sugarbrown."

The minister spoke to her in Sunday School and said, "Aren't you Mr. Sugarbrown's daughter?"

She replied, "Well, I thought I was, but mother says I'm not."

WWJD??

A mother was preparing pancakes for her sons, Kevin, 5, and Ryan 3. The boys began to argue over who would get the first pancake. Their mother saw the opportunity for a moral lesson. "If Jesus were sitting here, He would say, 'Let my brother have the first pancake, I can wait.'"

Kevin turned to his younger brother and said, "Ryan, you be Jesus!"

Instructions

On the first day of school, the kindergarten teacher said, "If anyone has to go to the bathroom, hold up two fingers." A little voice from the back of the classroom asked, "How will that help?"

A wife's definition of retirement: Twice as much husband on half as much pay.

From a guy: "My wife thinks I put football before marriage, even though we just celebrated our third season together."

Try to remember: With the exception of your parents and your children, most people will consider you an adult.

Mark Twain's contention was that the most interesting information comes from children, for they tell all they know…and then stop.

Signs that don't quite give the intended message
On the menu of a New Orleans restaurant: "Blackened bluefish."
In a Maine restaurant: "Open seven days a week and weekends."
In a New York restaurant: "Customers who find our waitresses rude ought to see the manager."

Real Consideration

Mother had just finished waxing the floors when she heard her young son opening the front door. She shouted, "Be careful on that floor, Jimmy; it's just been waxed."

Jimmy, walking right in, replied, "Don't worry, Mom, I'm wearing my cleats."

Gifts for Mama

Four brothers left home for college. They became successful doctors and lawyers and prospered. Some years later, they chatted after having dinner together. They discussed the gifts that they were able to give to their elderly mother who lived far away in another city.

The first said, "I had a big house built for Mama."

The second said, "I had a hundred thousand dollar theater built in the house."

The third said, "I had my Mercedes dealer deliver her an SL600 with chauffeur."

The fourth said, "Listen to this. You know how Mama loved reading the Scriptures. And you know, too, she can't read anymore because she can't see very well. I met this Priest who told me about a parrot that can recite the entire Bible. It took twenty priests twelve years to teach him. I had to pledge to contribute $100,000 a year for twenty years to the church. Let me tell you…it was worth it. All Mama has to do is name a chapter and verse and the parrot will recite it."

The other brothers were impressed. After the holidays Mama sent out her Thank You notes.

She wrote:

"Milton, The house you built is so huge. I live in only one room, but I have to clean the whole house.

Thanks anyway, Marvin, I am too old to travel. I stay home, I have my groceries delivered, so I never use the Mercedes...and the drive you hired is a Democrat. The thought was good.

Thanks, Manny, you gave me an expensive theater with Dolby sound, it could hold 50 people, but all my friends are dead, I've lost my hearing and I'm nearly blind. I'll never use it. Thank you for the gesture just the same.

Dearest Melvin, You were the only son to have the good sense to give a little thought to your gift. The chicken was delicious.

Thank you, Mama."

How much is the dolly?

A little girl walked proudly into a dry goods store to buy material for dress for her doll. When she came to the cash register she asked, "What does this cost?"

"For a sweet little girl like you," replied the man, feeling generous, "I'll charge only one little kiss."

"Thanks," replied the tot. "Grandma said whatever it is, to charge it and she'll be by tomorrow to pay for it."

Bad Baby!

An old country doctor went way out to the boondocks to deliver a baby. It was so far out that there was no electricity. When the doctor arrived, no one was home except for the laboring mother and her 5-year-old child. The doctor instructed the child to hold a lantern high so he could see while he helped the woman deliver the baby. The child did so, the mother purchased, and after a little while, the doctor lifted the new born baby by the feet and spanked him on the bottom to get him to take his first breath.

"Hit him again," the child said. "He shouldn't have crawled up there in the first place!!"

Puzzlement

A young girl was very much interested in the progress of her mother's pregnancy. Finally the day of birth drew near and the girl overheard arrangements being made for her mother to go to the hospital.

She looked at her mother with great puzzlement and said, "Mom, I don't understand. If they're going to deliver the baby, why do you have to the hospital?"

It All Makes Sense Now

A boy had reached four without giving up the habit of sucking his thumb, though his mother had tried everything from bribery to reasoning to painting it with lemon juice to discourage the habit. Finally she tried threats, warning her son that, "If you don't stop sucking your thumb, your stomach is going to blow up like a balloon."

Later that day, walking in the park, mother and son saw a pregnant woman sitting on a bench.

The four-year-old considered her gravely for a minute, then spoke to her saying, "Uh-oh...I know what you've been doing."

Now You Know!
Q: What is a programmer?
A: Someone who solves a problem you didn't know you had in a way you do not understand.

Remember When...an application was for employment; a program was a TV show; a cursor used profanity; a keyboard was a piano? Memory was something you lost with age; a CD was a bank account; a hard drive was a long road trip, a web was a spider's home, and a virus was the flu!

More Signs
- On an established New Mexico dry cleaning store "Thirty-eight years on the same spot."

- In a Tacoma, Washington men's clothing store "15 men's wood suits - $100 – They won't last an hour!"

- On a Tennessee highway "Take notice: when this sign is under water, this road is impassable."

Computer Terms – Country Translation
- LOG ON: Making a wood stove hotter.
- LOG OFF: Don't add no more wood.
- MONITOR: Keeping an eye on the wood stove.
- DOWNLOAD: Getting' the farwood off the truck.
- MEGA HERTZ: When yer not keerful getting' the farwood.
- FLOPPY DISC: Whatcha git from tryin' to carry too much farwood.
- RAM: That thing that splits the farwood.
- HARD DRIVE: Getting' home in the winter time.
- PROMPT: What the mail ain't in the winter time.
- WINDOWS: What to shut when it's cold outside.
- SCREEN: What to shut when it's black fly season.
- BYTE: What them dang flies do.

- CHIP: Munchies fer the TV.
- MICRO CHIP: What's in the bottom of the munchie bag.
- MODEM: Whatcha did to the hay fields.
- DOT MATRIX: Old Dan Matrix's wife.
- LAP TOP: Where the kitty sleeps.
- KEYBOARD: Where ya hang the dang truck keys.
- SOFTWARE: Them dang plastic forks and knives.
- MOUSE: What eats the grain in the barn.
- MOUSE PAD: That's hippie talk fer the mouse hole.
- MAIN FRAME: Holds up the barn roof.
- ENER: Yankee talk fer "c'mon in, y'all"
- RANDOM ACCESS MEMORY: When ya can't 'member what ya paid fer the rifle.

On Aging

Eventually you will reach a point when you stop lying about your age and start bragging about it.

More on Aging

Some people try to turn back their odometers. Not me, I want people to know "why" I look this way. I've traveled a long way and some of the roads weren't paved.

ANAGRAMS

An "anagram" is a word or phrase formed by rearranging the letters of another word or phrase. Have fun with these anagrams. See if you can come up with some of your own.
- GEORGE BUSH…HE BUGS GORE
- DORMITORY…DIRTY ROOM
- DESPERATION…A ROPE ENDS IT
- THE MORSE CODE…HERE COME DOTS
- SLOT MACHINES…CASH LOST IN ME
- ANIMOSITY…IS NOT AMITY
- MOTHER-IN-LAW…WOMAN HITLER
- SNOOZE ALARMS…ALAS NO MORE Z'S
- A DECIMAL POINT…I'M A DOT IN PLACE
- ELEVEN PLUS TWO…TWELVE PLUS ONE

Good Advice

Never frown even when you are sad, because you never know who is falling in love with your smile.

Senior Moment

While on a road trip, an elderly couple stopped at a roadside restaurant for lunch. After finishing their meal, they left the restaurant and resumed their trip.

When leaving, the elderly woman unknowingly left her glasses on the table. She didn't miss them until after they had been driving about twenty minutes. By then, to add to the aggravation, they had to travel quite a distance before they could find a place to turn around in order to return to the restaurant to retrieve her glasses.

All the way back, the elderly husband became the classic grouchy old man. He fussed and complained and scolded his wife relentlessly during the entire return drive. The more he chided her, the more agitated he became. He just wouldn't let up one minute.

To her relief, they finally arrived at the restaurant and as the woman got out of the car and hurried inside to retrieve her glasses, her husband yelled to her, "While you're in there, you might as well get my hat."

"You must first be who you really are, then do what you need to do, in order to have what you want." ~ Margaret Young

Appropriately Enough

The National Football League recently announced a new era. From now on, no offensive team names will be permitted. While the owners of the team rush to change uniforms and such, the National Football League announced, yesterday, its name changes and schedules for the '04 season.

The Washington Native Americans will host the New York Very Tall People on opening day. Other key games include the Dallas Western-Style Laborers hosting the St. Louis Wild Endangered Species, and the Minnesota Plundering Norsemen taking on the Green Bay meat Industry Workers.

In Week 2, there are several key matchups, highlighted by a showdown between the San Francisco Precious Metal Enthusiasts and the New Orleans Pretty Good People. The Atlanta Birds of Prey will play host to the Philadelphia Birds of Prey.

The Monday night game will pit the Miami Pelagic Percoid Food Fishes against the Denver Untamed Beasts of Burden. The Cincinnati Large Bangladeshi Carnivorous Mammals will travel to Tampa Bay for a clash with the West Indies Free Booters later in Week 9. And the Detroit Large Carnivorous Cats will play the Chicago Large Mountain Mammals.

Week 9 also features the Indianapolis Young Male Horses at the New England Zealous Lovers of Country.

Life Insurance

An older gentleman was on the operating table awaiting surgery and he insisted that his son, a renowned surgeon, perform the operation. As he was about to get the anesthesia he asked to speak to his son.

"Yes, Dad, what is it?"

"Don't be nervous, son; do your best and just remember, if it doesn't go well, if something happens to me, your mother is going to come and live with you and your wife!"

"Did you know my wife went to a self-help group for compulsive takers? It's called On and On Anon."

Question: What has four legs, is big, green, fuzzy, and if it fell out of a tree would kill you?
Answer: A pool table.

Experience Speaks Out

"The older we get, the fewer things seem worth waiting in line for."

"How old would you be if you didn't know how old you are?"

"When you are dissatisfied and would like to go back to youth, think of Algebra."

"I don't know how I got over the hill without getting to the top."

Daddy's Work

One day, two little friends were walking home from school and kid #1 said, "I noticed, in the morning while looking out my window that your father goes to work earlier than my dad, yet they work together…why is that?"

Then kid #2 not having a clear answer, relied, "Well, he goes early to swing on the gate."

Divine Game

Preacher decides to skip Sunday services and go to the golf course to hit a few…

When he gets there, he discovers there isn't anybody else around, and he has the entire course to himself..

But he does have witnesses…Seems God and Jesus are keeping an eye on him, and they don't approve of his church hooky-playing..

"Look at that guy," Jesus says, "He should be in church instead of out there. C'mon, Dad, let me hit him with a lightning bolt or something."

"No," God says, "I've something else in mind for him. Watch what happens when he makes his next shot."

Guy sets up a ball, drives it off the tee. It sails 200 yards and lands squarely in the hole.

"What kind of punishment is that, Dad?!" Jesus yells, "That has to be one of the greatest golf shots in history!!"

"That's right, son, indeed it is…and because he's alone and supposed to be in church, he can't tell anyone about it."

The Wise Woman's Stone

A wise woman who was traveling in the mountains found a precious stone in a stream.

The next day she met another traveler who was hungry, and the wise woman opened her bag to share her food.

The hungry traveler saw the precious stone and asked the woman to give it to him. She did so without hesitation.

The traveler left, rejoicing in his good fortune. He knew the stone was worth enough to give him security for a lifetime.

But a few days later he came back to return the stone to the wise woman.

"I've been thinking," He said, "I know how valuable the stone is, but I give it back in the hope that you can give me something even more precious. Give me what you have within you that enabled you to give me the stone. ~ Author Unknown

Totally Useless Facts
* Gilligan of Gilligan's Island had a first name that was only used once, on the never-aired pilot show. His first name was Willy.
* Dr. Seuss and Kurt Vonnegut went to college together. They were even in the same fraternity, where Seuss decorated the fraternity house walls with drawings of his strange characters.
* The Les Nessman character on the TV series WKRP in Cincinnati wore a band-aid in every episode. Either on himself, his glasses, or his clothing.
* John Larroquette of "night Court" and "The John Larroquette Show" was the narrator of "The Texas Chainsaw Massacre."
* Beelzebub, another name for the devil, is Hebrew for "Lord of the Flies," and this is where the book's title comes from.
* The term "devil's advocate" comes from the Roman Catholic church. When deciding if someone should be sainted, a devil's advocate is always appointed to give an alternative view.
* Before Prohibition, Schlitz Brewery owned more property in Chicago than anyone else, except The Catholic Church.

* When the University of Nebraska Cornhuskers play football at home to a sellout crowd, the full stadium becomes the state's third largest city.
* Kermit the Frog is left-handed.
* Non-dairy creamer is flammable.
* The dial tone of a normal telephone is in the key of "F."
* If you put a raisin in a glass of champagne, it will keep floating to the top and sinking to the bottom.

Blind Date

After being with his blind date all evening, the man couldn't take another minute with her. Earlier, he had secretly arranged to have a friend call him to the phone so he would have an excuse to leave if something like this happened. When he returned to the table, he lowered his eyes, put on a grim expression and said, "I have some bad news. My grandfather just died."

"Thank heavens," his date replied, "If yours hadn't, mine would have had to!"

One-Liners:

Q: What do prisoners use to call each other?
A: Cell phones

Q: What do you call four bull fighters in quicksand?
A: Quatro sinko

Q: What do you get when you cross a snowman with a vampire?
A: Frostbite

Q: What lies at the bottom of the ocean and twitches?
A: A nervous wreck.

Q: How do crazy people go through the forest?
A: They take the psycho path.

Q: Why do bagpipers walk when they play?
A: They're trying to get away from the noise.

Q: What do you get when you cross an elephant and a skin doctor?
A: A pachydermatologist.

Q: Did you hear about the guy that lost his left arm and leg in a car crash?
A: He's all right now

Testing

Two young engineers applied for a single position at a computer company. They both had the same qualifications. In order to determine which individual to hire, the applicants were asked to take a test by the Department manager. Upon completion of the test, both men missed only one of the questions. The manager went to the first applicant and said, "Thank you for your interest, but we've decided to give the job to the other applicant."

"Buy why? We both got 9 questions correct," asked the rejected applicant.

"We have based our decision not on the correct answers, but on the question you missed," said the manager. "Your fellow applicant put down for question #5, 'I don't know the answer.' And you put down, 'Neither do I.'"

Friendly Pig

A man was on a walking holiday in a foreign country. He became thirsty so decided to ask at a stranger's home for something to drink. The lady of the house invited him in and served him a bowl of soup by the fire. There was a wee pig running around the kitchen – running up to the visitor and giving him a great deal of attention. The visitor commented that he had never seen a pig this friendly.

The housewife replied: "Ummm, he's not that friendly. That his bowl you're using."

Check Out

The school where the new Principal has been the previous year had used a checkout system only slightly less elaborate than that at Fort Knox.

Cautiously, he asked the school's long time Custodian, "Do you think it's wise to keep the stock room unlocked and to let the teachers take things without requisitions?"

The Custodian looked at him gravely, "We trust them with the children, don't we?"

Wife's Cat

A man hated his wife's cat and he decided to get rid of it. He drove 20 blocks away from home and dropped the cat there. The cat was already walking up the driveway when he approached his home.

The next day, he decided to drop the cat 40 blocks away but the same thing happened.

He kept on increasing the number of blocks but the cat kept on coming home before him. At last he decided to drive a few miles away, turn right, then left, past the bridge, then right again and another right and so on until he reached what he thought was a perfect spot and dropped the cat there.

Hours later, the man calls his wife at home and asked her, "Jen, is the cat there?"

"Yes, why do you ask?" answered the wife.

Frustrated, the man said, "Put that cat on the phone, I am lost and I need directions."

More Shorties But Cuties

Q: What do you get from a pampered cow?
A: Spoiled mil.

Q: What do you call cheese that isn't yours?
A: Nacho Cheese.

Question: How does a spoiled rich girl change a lightbulb?
Answer: She says, "Daddy, I want a new apartment."

Points to Ponder

* A bus station is where a bus stops. A train station is where a train stops. On my desk I have a work station…is that where the work stops?
* Does fuzzy logic tickle?
* If they arrested the Energizer Bunny, would they charge it with battery?
* I believe five out of four people have trouble with fractions.
* How come you never hear about gruntled employees?
* I don't have a solution, but I admire your problem.
* If a tin whistle is made out of tine (and it is), then what, exactly, is a fog horn made out of?
* If quitters never win, and winners never quit, what fool came up with, "Quit while you're ahead?"
* Okay, who stopped the payment on my reality check?
* Do Lipton employees take coffee breaks
* What hair color do they put on the driver's licenses of bald men?
* What WAS the best thing before sliced bread?

Threatening Letters

The fellow stormed into the postmaster's office in a fury. "I've been getting threatening letters in the mail for months and I want them stopped."

"Of course," said the postmaster. "Sending threatening letters through the mail is a federal offense. Do you know who's sending them?"

"Yes," shouted the man. "It's those idiots down at the Internal Revenue Service."

Clear Thinking In A Crisis Situation

Question: You are sitting behind the wheel in a car keeping a constant speed. On your left side there is an abyss. On your right side you have a fire engine and it keeps the same speed as you. In front of you runs a pig, larger than your car. A helicopter is following you, at ground level. Both the helicopter and the pig are keeping the same speed as you. What will you need to do to be able to stop?

Answer: Get out of the car, step down from the merry-go-round, and leave your seat to someone younger.

Polite Dinner

There are two polite people having dinner together. On the table there is a dish with one big piece of fish and one small piece of fish. They politely say to each other, "You may choose first." "No, you may choose first." And this goes on for a while.

Then the first person says, "OK, I'll take first," and he takes the BIG piece of fish.

The second person, "Why did you take the big piece? That's not polite"

The first person says, "Which piece would *you* have taken?"

The second person replies, "Why, I would have taken the SMALL piece, of course."

To which the first person replies, "Well, that's what you have now!"

The Visitor

As a trucker stops for a red light, a visitor from Seattle catches up. She jumps out of her car, runs up to his truck, and knock son the door. The trucker lowers the window, and the girl says, "Hi, my name is Suzie. You are losing some of your load."

The trucker ignores her and proceeds down the street. When the truck stops for another red light, the girl catches up again. She jumps out of her car, runs up and knocks on the door. Again, the trucker lowers the window. As if they've never spoken, the girl says brightly, "Hi, my name is Suzie and you are losing some of your load.

Shaking his head, the trucker ignores her again and continues down the street. At the third red light, the same thing happens again. All out of breath, the girl gets out of her car, runs up, and knocks on the truck door. The trucker lowers the window. Again she says, "Hi, my name is Suzie and you are losing some of your load!!"

When the light turns green the trucker revs up and races to the next light. When he stops this time, he hurriedly gets out of the truck, and runs back to the girl. He knocks on her window, and as she lowers it, he says... "Hi, my name is Kevin, it's winter in Colville, and I'm driving the SAND TRUCK!"

Sound Familiar?

Three men are in a hot-air balloon. Soon, they find themselves lost in a canyon somewhere. One of the three men says, "I have an idea. We can call for help in this canyon and the echo will carry our voices far enough for someone to hear us." So he leans over the basket and yells out, "Helllllooooooooo! Whare are we?" They hear the echo several times.

Much later, the men in the balloon hear an echoing voice, "Helllloooooooooo! You're lost!!"

One of the mean says, "That must be a Microsoft service tech!"

Puzzled, one of the other men asks, "Why do you say that?"

The man replies: "For three reasons: 1. he took a long time to answer, 2. he was absolutely correct, and 3. his answer was absolutely useless.

Crime & Punishment

A woman was found guilty in traffic court and when asked for her occupation she said she was a schoolteacher.

The judge rose from the bench. "Madam, I have waited years for a school teacher to appear before this court." He smiled with delight. "Now sit down at that table and write, 'I will not run a red light' five hundred times."

Shorties

A family was having dinner and the little boy said, "Dad, I don't like the holes in the cheese!"
Well son, eat the cheese and leave the holes on the side of the plate.

"Have you got any kittens going cheap?" asked a customer in a pet shop.
"No, ma'am," replied the owner. "All our kittens go 'Meow.'"

Exasperated dragon on the field of battle: "Mother said there would be knights like this."

"Look over there!" said the frightened skunk to his pal, "There's a human with a gun, and he's getting closer and closer! What are we going to do?" To which the second skunk calmly replied, "Let us spray..."

Questions and Answers
Q: What do you call a blind deer? A: A no-eyed deer (say it out loud)
Q: What do you call a blind deer with no legs? A: A still no-eyed deer

Q: What do you call 13 bunnies in a row, hopping backwards? A: A receding hairline
Q: What do you get if you put 20 ducks in a box? A: A box of Quackers
Q: Why does a chicken coup only have two doors? A: If it had four doors, it would be a chicken sedan

A Heavy Matter

A man takes his dog to the vet. "My dog is crossed eyed, is there anything you can do for him?"

"Well," says the vet, "let's take a look at him. "So he picks the dog up and examines his eyes, then checks his teeth. Finally, he says, "I'm going to have to put him down."

"What? Because he is cross-eyed?"

"No, because he's really heavy."

A Short ~~Narrative Tale~~ Tail!

A very intelligent boy was fortunate enough to be receiving a far better education than his parents had enjoyed, and his vocabulary far outstripped theirs. One day he came home from school and said, "Mommy, may I relate to you a narrative?"

"What's a narrative, Gerald?" she asked.

"A narrative, Mommy, is a tale."

"Oh, I see," said his mother nodding, and Gerald told her his story.

At bedtime as he was about to go upstairs he said, "Shall I extinguish the light Mommy?"

"What's extinguish?" she asked.

"Extinguish means to put out, Mommy," said brainy Gerald.

"Oh, I see. Yes, certainly."

The next day the clergyman came to tea and the family dog began to make a nuisance of himself, as a dog will, by begging for goodies from the table.

"Gerald," said his mother, trying to impress, "take that dog by the narrative and extinguish him!"

Go Ask Your Mother

A little boy was doing his geography homework one evening and turned to his father and said, "Dad, where would I find the Andes?"

"Don't ask me," said the father, "Ask your mother. She puts everything away in this house."

Phone Number Trick
1. Punch the first three digits of your home phone number into your calculator (without the area code).
2. Multiply by 80.
3. Add 1.
4. Multiply by 250.
5. Add the last four digits of your home phone number.
6. Add the last four digits of your home phone number again.
7. Subtract 250.
8. Divide by 2.

RECOGNIZE THE NUMBER?

In the Navy
  A friend of mine joined the Navy and soon after had to attend a wedding. He asked an officer for a pass and was told he had to be back by 7 p.m. Sunday.
  "You don't understand, sir," my friend said. "I'm in the wedding."
  "No, you don't understand," the officer relied. "You're in the Navy."

Laundry
  One day my housework-challenged husband decided to wash his sweatshirt. Seconds after he stepped into the laundry room, he shouted to me, "What setting do I use on the washing machine?"
  "It depends," I replied. "What does it say on your shirt?"
  He yelled back, "University of Washington."

Trip to the Zoo
  A police officer sees a man driving around with a pickup truck full of penguins. He pulls the guy over and says, "You can't drive around with penguins in this town! Take them to the zoo immediately."
  The guy says 'okay,' and drives away.
  The next day, the officer sees the guy still driving around with the truck full of penguins – and they're all wearing sunglasses. He pulls the guy over and angrily states, "I thought I told you to take these penguins to the zoo yesterday!"
  The guy replies, "I did. Today I'm taking them to the beach!"

It's Always Easier When Someone Else is Doing It
  An elephant was walking in a park. With each step he took, he squished many little ants. Upset, the ants began to crawl up on the elephant – first his legs and then up all over his body. When the elephant started feeling all the little ants on him, he shook hard, making all the little ants, except for one, fall to the ground.

As the only ant on the elephant hung on close to the elephant's neck, the ones on the ground began to yell, "Strangle him!!! Strangle him!!!"

Investigation

The investigation of Martha Stewart continues. Her recipe for chicken casserole is quite efficient. First you boil the chicken in water. And then you dump the stock.

Two Reasons Why It's So Hard to Solve a Redneck Murder:
1. All the DNA is the same, and
2. There are no dental records.

The Racehorse

A man has a racehorse that has never won a race. The man, in disgust says, "Horse, you win today or you pull a milk wagon tomorrow morning."

The starting gate opens, the horses take-off, they move the gate away and there lays his horse asleep on the track.

He kicks the horse and asks, "WHY ARE YOU SLEEPING?"

The horse, half asleep says, "I have to get up at three in the morning."

A Real Challenge

A customer comes into a computer store and says, "I'm looking for a mystery adventure game with lots of graphics. You know, something really challenging."

After a while the clerk replied, "Have you tried Windows 2000?"

Ruh, Roh!

"Do you believe in life after death?" the boss asked one of his employees.

"Yes, sir," the clerk replied.

"That's good," the boss said. "After you left early yesterday to go to your grandmother's funeral, she stopped in to see you."

Reportedly, this was an actual classified ad that ran in a New York newspaper: SINGLE FEMALE seeks male companionship, ethnicity unimportant. I'm a very good looking girl who LOVES to play. I love long walks in the woods, riding in your pickup truck, hunting, camping and fishing trips, cozy winter nights lying by the fire. Candlelight dinners will have me eating out of your hand. Rub me the right way and watch me respond. I'll be at the front door waiting for you each day when you get home from work. Call (555-1234) and ask for Daisy.

An estimated 15,000 men found themselves talking to the owner of an 8-week old black Labrador retriever.

Small Business Tip

Two women were comparing notes on the difficulties of running a small business.

"I started a new practice last year," the first one said. "I insist that each of my employees take at least a week off every three months."

"Why in the world would you do that?" The other asked.

She responded, "It's the best way I can learn which ones I can do without."

"No one can offend you without your consent."
~ Eleanor Roosevelt

Dead Donkey

A Cajun named, Jean Paul, moved to Texas and bought a donkey from an old farmer named Ben for $100. The farmer agreed to deliver the donkey the next day. The next day, Ben drove up and said, "Sorry, but I have some bad news. The donkey died."

"Well, then, just give me the money back," said Jean Paul.

"Can't do that. I went and spent it already," replied Ben.

"OK, then. Just unload the donkey," said Jean Paul.

"What ya going to do with him?" asked Ben.

"I'm going to raffle him off," said Jean Paul.

"You can't raffle off a dead donkey!" uttered Ben.

"Sure can. Watch me. I just won't tell that he's dead." Said Jean Paul.

A month later Ben met up with the Cajun and asked, "What happened with that dead donkey?"

"I raffled him off, I did. I sold 500-hundred tickets at two dollars a piece and made a profit of $998," said Jean Paul.

"Didn't anyone complain?" inquired Ben.

"Just the guy who won. So I gave him his two dollars back," said Jean Paul.

Beep! Beep!

Grandpa was driving with his 9 year old granddaughter and beeped the horn by mistake. She turned and looked at him for an explanation. He said, "I did that by accident."

She replied, "I know that, Grandpa."

He replied, "How did you know?"

She said, "Because you didn't say 'idiot!' afterwards."

If love is blind, then marriage is an eye-opener!

**Marketing May Be Everything,
But Don't Underestimate the Power of Customer Feedback**

You see a gorgeous girl at a party.
You go up to her and say, "I am very rich. Marry me!"
That's Direct Marketing.

You're at a party with a bunch of friends and see a gorgeous girl.
One of your friends goes up to her and pointing at you he says, "He's very rich. Marry him."
That's Advertising.

You see a gorgeous girl at a party.
You go up to her and get her telephone number.
The next day you call and say, "Hi, I'm very rich. Marry me."
That's Telemarketing.

You're at a party and see a gorgeous girl.
You get up and straighten your tie; you walk up to her and pour her a drink. You open the door for her; pick up her bag after she drops it, offer her a ride, and then say, "By the way, I'm very rich. Will you marry me?"
That's Public Relations.

You're at a party and see a gorgeous girl.
She walks up to you and says, "You are very rich."
That's Brand Recognition.

You see a gorgeous girl at a party.
You go up to her and say, "I'm rich. Marry me."
She gives you a nice hard slap on your face.
That's Customer Feedback.

The Truth About Huckleberries

Huckleberries are wrapped in secrecy and hidden in the wilderness, and only come out every other year. Or, huckleberries are everywhere in abundance always, and anyone can find them whenever they please.

Huckleberries are sweet. Huckleberries are sour. Huckleberries are woman's work; or a job for a man. Huckleberries are bigger in the shade, or sometimes bigger in the sun; huckleberries are easier to pick with rakes, but should only be picked by hand.

Huckleberries are really blueberries...no! Nothing like blueberries. Huckleberries are worth risking your life for – or one good reason for living.

Wooden You Know ...
Question: What would happen if you have a wooden car, with wooden wheels, a wooden chair, and a wooden engine?
Answer: It wooden start!

It Figures
A man sitting at a bar claiming to be the world's strongest man, squeezed every drop of juice from a lemon.

Then said, "Whoever can squeeze another drop from this lemon will be the world's strongest and will have earned $100."

Just about every man at the bar tried without luck. Then a skinny, wimpy looking guy walks up and squeezes three more drops from the lemon.

The strong man asked, "How did you do that?"

The little man replied, "I am an IRS agent," as he walked out.

I just checked a height/weight chart and found out that I am 4 inches too short.

Remember, free advice is usually worth what it cost.

Lady, Please!
A lady walks into a shop one day. She asks if she could try on a dress in the window.
The manager suggested it might be better to use the changing room.

"Success consists of going from failure to failure without loss of enthusiasm."
~ Sir Winston Churchill

The Pweor of the Hmuan Mnid.
Aoccdrnig to rscheearch codnutced at Cmabridge Uinervtisy, it deosn't mttaer in what order the ltteers in a word are tpyed, the only iprmoetnt thing is that the frist and lsat ltteer be in the rghit oedrer. The rset can be a total mses and you can still raed it wouthit porbelm. Tish is bcuseae the human mind deos not raed ervey lteter by istlef, but the word as a wlohe.

Amzanig huh?

The Tale of Two Brooms
Two brooms falls in love and decide to get married. At the reception, the bride groom wants to dance with the groom broom.

While dancing, the bride broom tells the groom broom,

"I want us to have a little whisk-broom."

The groom broom replies to the bride broom, "We can't, we haven't swept together yet."

Hiccups

A man goes into a drug store and asks the pharmacist if he can give him something for the hiccups.

The pharmacist promptly reaches out and slaps the man's face.

"What did you do that for?" the man asks.

"Well, you don't have the hiccups anymore do you?"

The man says, "No, but my wife out in the car still does!"

Right Man for the Job

The CIA had an opening for an assassin. After all of the background checks, interviews, and testing were done there were three finalists…Two men and a woman.

For the final test, the CIA agents took one of the men to a large metal door and handed him a gun.

"We must know that you will follow your instructions, no matter what the circumstances. Inside of this room, you will find your wife sitting in a chair. Kill Her!!!"

The man said, "You can't be serious. I could never shoot my wife."

The agent said, "Then you're not the right man for this job."

The second man was given the same instructions. He took the gun and went into the room. All was quiet for about five minutes. Then the man came out with tears in his eyes. "I tried, but I can't kill my wife."

The agent said, "You don't have what it takes. Take your wife and go home."

Finally, it was the woman's turn. She was given the same instructions to kill her husband. She took the gun and went into the room. Shots were heard, one shot after another. They heard screaming, crashing, banging on the walls.

After a few minutes, all was quiet. The door opened slowly and there stood the woman. She wiped the sweat from her brow, and said, "This gun is loaded with blanks. I had to beat him to death with the chair."

A Hunting Story

Having shot a moose, two Antartians began dragging it by the tail to their pick-up. On the way they were stopped by a game warden. "Let me see your hunting licenses boys," he said. When he saw that everything was in order he asked if he could give them some advice.

"Sure!" the hunters agreed.

"Well boys, I think that you would find it a lot easier to drag that moose by the horns and not the tail."

"Aye, O.K. and thanks," said the lads.

After about five minutes one said to the other, "Boy, dragging by the horns is sure a lot easier, eh?"

"Aye, you're right," said the friend, "but have you noticed that we are getting further away from the truck?"

Wishful Thinking

Three guys, a Canadian, Osama Bin Laden, and President Bush were walking together one day.

They came across a lantern and a genie popped out, "I will give you each one wish, that's three wishes total."

The Canadian said, "I want the land to be forever fertile in Canada. I'm a farmer, my dad was a farmer, and my son will someday be a farmer." So, with a blink of the genie's eye, "POOF," the land was forever fertile.

Osama Bin Laden says, "I want a wall completely surround Afghanistan so that no Infidels, Jews, or Americans can get in." Again with a blink of the genie's eye *POOF, there was a wall around Afghanistan.

President Bush asks, "I'm curious about this wall, please tell me more."

"Well," says the genie, "the wall is about 15,000 feet high and 500 feet thick, it is practically impenetrable."

So President Bush says, "Fill it with water."

(One question: What is Bush doing going for a walk with Osama Bin Laden?)

All in a Day's Work

A career military man, who had retired as a corporal, was telling the younger men how he handled officers during his years of service...

"It didn't matter a hoot if he was a Major General, an admiral, or the Commander-in-Chief. I met these guys every single day and always told them exactly where to get off!"

"Wow, you musta been something," the admiring young solders remarked. "What was your job in the service?"

He replied, "Elevator operator in the Pentagon..."

Wife: Do you want dinner?
Husband: Yes. What are my choices?
Wife: Yes and No.

I haven't spoken to my wife in 18 months. I don't like to interrupt her!

It's All Relative

An old man lived alone in Idaho. He wanted to spade his potato garden, but it was very hard work. His only son, Bubba, who used to help him, was in prison. The old man wrote a letter to his son and described his predicament.

Dear Bubba:

I am feeling pretty bad because it looks like I won't be able to plant my potato garden this year. I'm just getting too old to be digging up a garden plot. If you were here, all my troubles would be over. I know you would dig the plot for me.
Love, Dad

A few days later, he received a letter from his son.

Dear Dad:

For heaven's sake, Dad, don't dig up that garden. That's where I buried the BODIES.
Love, Bubba

At 4 a.m. the next morning, FBI agents and local police showed up and dug up the entire area without finding any bodies. They apologized to the old man and left.

That same day, the old man received another letter from his son.

Dear Dad:

Go ahead and plant the potatoes now. It's the best I could do under the circumstances.
Love, Bubba

Read the Label

To tag birds migrating, the U.S. Department of the Interior used metal bands that bear the address of the Washington Biological Survey, abbreviated: Wash. Biol. Surv., until the agency received the following letter from a camper:

Dear Sirs, While camping last week I shot one of your birds. I think it was a crow. I following the cooking instructions on the leg tag and I want to tell you it was horrible.

Army of the Lord

A friend was in front of me coming out of church one day, and as always the preacher was standing at the door shaking hands as the congregation departed.

He grabbed my friend by the hand and pulled him aside. The preacher said to him, "You need to join the Army of the Lord!"

My friend replied, "I'm already in the Army of the Lord, Preacher."

The preacher questioned, "How come I don't see you except for Christmas and Easter?"

He whispered back, "I'm in the secret service."

A Fishing Story

One cold winter day on Lake Erie, two guys were fishing about 20 feet apart through the ice. One guy wasn't having any luck. The other guy was pulling out fish every time he put his line in the water.

This made the other guy curious. "Hey," he yelled to the other, "what are you using for bait?"

The other guy yelled back, "Mfff Mfff Ogghh Mfft Offt Berr Wttt!"

The one guy was very puzzled and said, "WHAT?"

And again the other guy yelled back, "Mfff Mfff Ogghh Mfft Offt Berr Wttt!"

Finally, the guy had to know what the other guy was saying to he got up and walked over to him and said, "What the heck did you say?"

And then the guy spit something into his hands and said, "You have to keep your bait warm!"

She'll Get the Message

Hoss rode into town to buy a bull. Unfortunately, when he bought it, he was left with one dollar. Hoss needed to tell his wife to come with the tuck and get the bull, but telegrams cost one dollar per word. Hoss said to the telegram man, "OK. I have my one word – 'comfortable'."

"Why do you want to tell her that?" asked the telegram man.

"Oh, she's not the best reader," Hoss said. "She'll read it really slowly, COM-FOR-TA-BLE."

Texas-Size Story

A Texan is visiting Australia for the first time. He sees a sheep and starts laughing. He says to his Australian guide, "Oh, at home in Texas, sheep are twice as big!" He then sees a cow and bursts, "Puff, in Texas, our cows are much, much bigger!" And suddenly, he sees a kangaroo and asks, "What's that?"

The guide answers, "Oh, that's just a grasshopper."

Train Wreck

A brilliant young boy was applying for a job with railways. The interviewer asked him, "Do you know how to use the equipment?"

"Yes," the boy replied.

"Then what would you do if you realized that 2 trains, one from this station and one from the next were going to crash because they were on the same track?"

The young applicant thought and replied, "I'd press the button to change the point without hesitation."

"What if the button was frozen and wouldn't work?"

"I'd run outside and pull the lever to change the points manually."

"And if the lever was broken?"

"I'd get on the phone to the next station and tell them to change the points," he replied.

"And if the phone was broken and needed an electrician to fix it?"

The boy thought about that one, "I'd run into town and get my uncle."

"Is your uncle an electrician?"

"No, but he's never seen a train crash before?"

Try This At Home

You don't have to be at a desk but you must be sitting. While sitting at your desk, make clockwise circles with your right foot. While doing this, draw the number "6" in the air with your right hand. Your foot will change direction.

Final Instructions

A businessman, on his deathbed, called his friend and said, "Bill, I want you to promise me that when I die, you will have my remains cremated."

"And what," his friend asked, "do you want me to do with your ashes?"

The businessman said, "Just put them in an envelope and mail them to the Internal Revenue Service. Write on the envelope, "Now, you have everything.""

Clarification of the Corporate Structure

Chairman of the Board – Leaps tall buildings in a single bound, is more powerful than a locomotive, faster than a speeding bullet, walks on water, talks with God.

President – Leaps short buildings in a single bound, is more powerful than a switch engine, is faster than a speeding BB, walks on water if the sea is calm, talks with God if special request is approved.

Executive Vice President – Leaps short buildings with a running start and favorable winds, is almost as powerful as a switch engine, can fire a speeding bullet, walks on water in an indoor swimming pool, is occasionally addressed by God.

Vice President – Barely clears a Quonset hut, loses tug-of-war with a locomotive, can sometimes handle a gun without inflicting self injury, swims well, talks to animals.

Manager – Makes high marks on the wall when trying to leap building, is run over by a locomotive, is not issued ammunition, dog paddles, talks to walls.

Supervisor – Runs into buildings, recognizes a locomotive two out of three times, wets himself with a water pistol, can't stay afloat without a life preserver, mumbles to himself.

Secretary – Lifts buildings and walks under them, kicks locomotives off the tracks, catches speeding bullets in her teeth and eats them, freezes water with a single gland, She is God.

"Old age ain't for sissies." ~ Bette Davis

"The hardest years in life are those between 10 and 70." ~ Helen Hayes

What Would We Do Without Secretaries?

A young executive was leaving the office late one evening when he found the CEO standing in front of a shredder with a piece of paper in his hand.

"Listen," said the CEO, "this is a very sensitive and important document here, and my secretary has gone for the night. Can you make this thing work for me?"

"Certainly," said the young executive. He turned the machine one, inserted the paper, and pressed the start button.

"Excellent, excellent!" said the CEO, as his paper disappeared inside the machine. "I just need one copy…"

Have it Your Way

A guy walks in to the Barbershop.

Barber says, "What will it be today?"

Guy says, "Well I want it going with my waves on top, faded on one side, plug the other, and just make it all out of shape and messed up."

Barber says, "Now why in the world do you want your hair cut like that?"

Guy says, "That's how you cut it last time."

Overworked

For a couple years I've been blaming it on lack of sleep and too much pressure from my job, but now I found out the real reason: I'm tired because I'm overworked. The population of this country is 237 million. 104 million are retired. That leaves 133 million to do the work. There are 85 million in school, which leaves 48 million to do the work. Of this, there are 29 million employed by the federal government, leaving 19 million to do the work. 2.8 million are in the Armed Forces, which leaves 16.2 million to do the work. Take from the total the 14,800,000 people who work for State and City Governments and that leaves 1.4

million to do the work. At any given time there are 188,000 people in hospitals, leaving 1,212,000 to do the work. Now, there are 1,211,998 people in prisons. That leaves just two people to do the work. You and me. And you're sitting there reading jokes.

Call In The Marines!
The young army doctor was stationed at a remote dispensary in the South Pacific. One day he was puzzled about treatment for one of his patients.
He radioed a base hospital: 'Have case of beriberi. What shall I do?"
A prankster got hold of the message. This was the reply: 'Give it to the Marines. They'll drink anything."

In the Beginning
In the beginning God covered the earth with broccoli and cauliflower and spinach, green and yellow and red vegetables of all kinds, so Man and Woman would live long and healthy lives.
Then using God's bountiful gifts, Satan created ice cream and doughnuts. And Satan said, "You want hot fudge with that?" And Man said "Yes!" and Woman said, "I'll have another with sprinkles." And lo, they gained 10 pounds.
So God said, "Try my fresh green salad."
And Satan presented crumbled Bleu Cheese dressing and garlic toast on the side. And Man and Woman unfastened their belts following the repast.
God then said, "I have sent you heart healthy vegetable and olive oil in which to lightly sauté the wholesome vegetables."
And Satan brought forth deep fried coconut shrimp, chicken-fried steak so big it needed its own platter, and chocolate cheesecake for dessert. And Man's glucose levels spiked through the roof.
God then brought forth running shoes so that His children might lose those extra pounds.
And Satan came forth with a cable TV with remote control so Man would not have to toil changing the channels. And Man and Woman laughed and cried before the flickering light and started wearing stretch jogging suits.
Then God brought forth lean meat so that Man might consume fewer calories and still satisfy his appetite.
And Satan created the 99-cent double cheeseburger, and said, "You want fries with that?" And Man replied, "Yes! And supersize 'em!" And Man went into cardiac arrest.
God sighed and created quadruple bypass surgery.
And Satan created HMOs.

Only in America
- Can a pizza get to your house faster than an ambulance.
- Do drugstores make the sick walk all the way to the back of the store to get their prescription while healthy people can buy cigarettes at the front.
- Do banks leave both doors open and then chain the pens to the counters.
- Do we leave cars worth thousands of dollars in the driveway and put our useless junk in the garage.
- Do we use answering machines to screen calls and then have call waiting so we won't miss a call from someone we didn't want to talk to in the first place.
- Do we buy hot dogs in packages of ten and buns in packages of eight.
- Do we use the word 'politics' to describe the process so well: 'Poli' in Latin meaning 'many' and 'tics' meaning bloodsucking creatures.'
- Do they have drive-up ATM machines with Braille lettering.

That's Cold!
It was sooooo cold last winter (How Cold Was It?) that I saw a lawyer with his hands in his OWN pockets!

Short Ones
A chicken crossing the road is poultry in motion.

The man who fell into an upholstery machine is fully recovered.

A lot of money is tainted – It taint ours and it taint mine.

True Story: A woman called the Canon help desk with a problem with her printer. The tech asked her if she was running it under "Windows." The woman responded, "No, my desk is next to the door. But that is a good point. The man sitting in the cubicle next to me is under a window and his printer is working fine."

Mafia Bookeeper
A Mafia Boss finds out that his bookkeeper has embezzled ten million bucks from him. The bookkeeper is deaf. It was considered an occupational benefit and the reason he got the job in the first place. It was assumed that since a deaf bookkeeper would not be able to hear anything, he'd never have to testify in court. When the boss went to shake down the bookkeeper about his missing $10 million bucks, he brings along his attorney, who knows sign language.

The Boss asks the bookkeeper: "Where is the 10 million bucks you embezzled from me?"

The attorney, using sign language, asks the bookkeeper where the 10 million dollars is hidden.

The bookkeeper signs back: "I don't know what you're talking about."

The attorney tells the Boss: "He says he doesn't know what you're talking about."

That's when the Boss pulls out a 9mm pistol, puts it to the bookkeeper's temple, and says: "Ask him again!"

The attorney signs to the underling: "He'll kill you for sure if you don't tell him!"

The bookkeeper signs back: "OK! You win! The money is in a brown briefcase, buried behind the shed in my cousin Enzo's backyard in Queens!"

The Boss asks the attorney: "Well, what'd he say?"

The attorney replied: "He says you don't have it in you to pull the trigger."

Bungee Prototype

The two inventors of the bungee rope went to Spain to test their invention. They climbed a 50-foot tower. At the top, one of the guys stood on the edge of the platform and dove into the air with the rope tied to his feet. The other guy, standing up on the platform, waited until his friend returned up so that he could grab him. The first time his friend sprung up, he tried to grab him but missed and noticed that his head was swollen. The next time, he missed again and again there was a bruise on his head and face. This time, with much concern, he dove forward to get his partner, pulled him in and asked, "What happened? Is the cord too long?"

His partner replied with his face all bloody, "What is 'piñata?'"

You Gotta Stand For Something

"I hear the boys are gonna strike," one worker told another.

"What for?" asked the friend.

"Shorter hours."

"Good for them, I always did think 60 minutes was too long for an hour."

Driving Safety

This morning on the Interstate, I looked over to my left and there was a woman in a brand new Cadillac doing 65 mph with her face up next to her rear view mirror putting on her eyeliner. I looked away for a couple seconds and when I looked back she was halfway over in my lane, still working on that makeup. As a man, I don't scare easily. But she scared me so much, I dropped my electric shaver, which knocked the donut out of my other hand. In all the confusion of trying to straighten out the car using my knees against the steering wheel, it knocked my cell phone away from my ear which fell into the coffee between my legs, splashed, and burned my legs, ruined the phone, soaked my trousers, and disconnected an important call. Them dang women drivers!

It's Tax Time – Have You Taken Every Allowable Deduction?

Answering the phone, the priest was surprised to hear the caller introduce herself as an IRS auditor.

"But we do not pay taxes," the priest said.

"It isn't you, Father, it's one of your parishioners, Sean McCullough. He indicates on his tax return that he gave a donation of $15,000 to the church last year. Is this, in fact, the truth?"

The priest smiled broadly. "The check hasn't arrived yet, but I'm sure I'll have it when I remind dear Sean."

Women Think of the Most Clever Things

After 17 years of marriage, a man dumped his wife for a younger woman. He wanted to continue living in their downtown luxury apartment with his new lover so he asked his wife to move out and get another place. His wife agreed to this, provided that he would give her 3 days alone at the apartment to pack up her things. She spent the first day packing her belongings into boxes, crates and suitcases. On the second day, she had the movers come and collect her things. On the third day, she sat down for the last time at their beautiful dining table by candlelight, put on some soft background music, and feasted on a pound of shrimp and a bottle of Chardonnay. When she had finished, she went into each room and deposited a few of the half-eaten shrimp shells into the hollow of the curtain rods. She then cleaned up the kitchen and left. When the husband returned with his new girlfriend, all was bliss for the first few days. Then slowly the apartment began to smell. They tried everything; cleaning and mopping and airing the place out. Vents were checked for dead rodents, carpets were steam cleaned. Air fresheners were hung everywhere. Exterminators were brought in to set off gas canisters, during which they had to move out for a few days, and in the end they even paid to replace the expensive carpet. Finally, they could not take it any longer and decided to move. They could not find a buyer for their stinky apartment so they had to get a loan from the bank to purchase a new place. The moving company arrived and did a very professional packing job, taking everything to their new home ... including the curtain rods.

A THREE YEAR OLD put his shoes on by himself. His mother noticed the left shoe was on the right foot. She said, "Son, your shoes are on the wrong feet." He looked up with a puzzled look and said, "Mom, stop joking. I know they're my feet!"

REMEMBER...Growing Older is Mandatory. Growing Up is Optional ... and, We make a Living by what we get, we make a Life by what we give.

Sunday School

"If I sold my house and my car, had a big garage sale, and gave all my money to the church, would that get me into heaven?" the teacher asked the children in her Sunday school class.

"NO!" the children all answered.

"If I cleaned the church every day, mowed the yard, and kept everything neat and tidy, would that get me into heaven?"

Again the answer was, "NO!"

"Well, then, if I was kind to animals and gave candy to all the children and loved my husband, would that get me into heaven?" she asked them again.

Once more they all answered, "NO!"

"Well," she continued, thinking they were a good bit more theologically sophisticated than she had given them credit for, "then how can I get into heaven?"

A five-year-old boy shouted out, "YOU GOTTA BE DEAD!"

Call for Help

An exasperated caller to Dell Computer Tech Support couldn't get her new Dell Computer to turn on. After ensuring the computer was plugged in, the technician asked her was happened when she pushed the power button. Her response, "I pushed and pushed on this foot pedal and nothing happens." The "foot pedal" turned out to be the computer's mouse.

And Then, Some Need More Help Than Others...

Another customer called Compaq tech support to say her brand-new computer couldn't work. She said she unpacked the unit, plugged it in and sat there for 20 minutes waiting for something to happen. When asked what happened when she pressed the power switch, she asked, "What power switch?"

An IBM customer had trouble installing software and rang for support. "I put in the first disk, and that was OK. It said to put in the second disk, and I had some problems with the disk. What it said to put in the third disk, I couldn't even fit it in..." The user hadn't realized that "Insert Disk 2" meant to remove Disk 1 first.

"Computers are like air conditioners. They work fine until you start opening windows."

The Trouble Tree
Contributed by Jocelyn Eddy

I hired a plumber to help me restore an old farmhouse, and after he had just finished a rough first day on the job, (a flat tire made him lose an hour of work and his electric drill quit), his ancient one-ton truck refused to start. While I drove him home, he sat in stoney silence. Upon arriving he invited me in to meet his family. As we walked toward the front door, he paused briefly at a small tree, touching the tips of the branches with both hands. When opening the door he underwent an amazing transformation. His tanned face was wreathed in smiles and he hugged his two small children and gave his wife a kiss. Afterwards he walked me to the car. We passed the tree and my curiosity got the better of me.

I asked him about what I had seen him do earlier.

"Oh that's my trouble tree," he replied. "I know I can't help having troubles on the job, but one thing's for sure, those troubles don't belong in the house with my wife and children. So I just hang them up on the tree every night when I come home and ask God to take care of them. Then in the morning I pick them up again. Funny thing is," he smiled, "when I come out in the morning to pick them up, there aren't nearly as many as I remembered hanging up the night before.

"Rolex and Timex"

A girl was visiting her friend in Seattle who had acquired two new dogs, and asked her friend what the names of the new dogs were.

The friend responded by saying that one was named "Rolex" and one was named "Timex."

Her friend said, "Whoever heard of someone naming dogs like that?"

"HELLOOOOOooo," answered the friend from Seattle, "They're watch dogs!"

Excuse for Speeding

There was a middle aged guy who bought a brand new Mercedes convertible. He took off down the road, flooring it up to 80 mph and enjoying the wind blowing through what little hair he had left on his head. "This is great," he thought and floored it some more. Then he looked in his rear view mirror and there was a highway patrol trooper behind him, blue lights flashing and siren blaring. "I can get away from him with no problem," thought the man, as he floored it some more and flew down the road at over 100 mph. Then he though, "What am I doing? I'm too old for this kind of thing," and pulled over to the side of the road and waited for the state trooper to catch up with him.

The trooper pulled in behind the Mercedes and walked up to the man. "Sir," he said, looking at his watch. "My shift ends in 30 minutes and today is Friday the 13th. If you can give me a reason why you were speeding that I've never heard before, I'll let you go."

The man looked back at the trooper and said, "Last week my wife ran off with a state trooper and I thought you were bringing her back."

The state trooper replied, "Have a nice day."

(Heh, Heh, Heh)...

There was a group of scientists sitting around discussing which one of them was going to go to God and tell Him that they didn't need him anymore. One of the scientists volunteered and went to go tell God he was no longer needed. The scientist says to God, "God, you know, a bunch of us have been thinking and I've come to tell you that we really don't need you anymore. I mean, we've been coming up with great theories and ideas, we've cloned sheep, and we're on the verge of cloning humans. So as you can see, we really don't need you."

God nods understandingly and says, "I see. Well, no hard feelings. But before you go, let's have a contest. What do you think?

The scientist says, "Sure, What kind of contest?"

God: "A man-making contest."

The scientist: "Sure! No problem."

The scientist bends down and picks up a handful of dirt and says, "Okay, I'm ready!"

God replies, "No, no, no...You go get your own dirt."

4-Letter Words

A young couple had just married and went on their honeymoon. When they got back, the bride immediately called her mother, "Well," said her mother, "so how was the honeymoon?"

"Oh, mama," replied, "the honeymoon was wonderful! So romantic..." Suddenly she burst out crying. "But, mama, as soon as we returned, Sam started using the most horrible language – things I'd never heard before! I mean, all these awful 4-letter words! You've got to take me home..., PLEASE MAMA!"

"Sarah, Sarah," her mother said, "calm down! You need to stay with your husband and work this out. Now, tell me, what could be so awful? WHAT 4-letter words?"

"Please don't make me tell you, Mama," wept the daughter. "I'm so embarrassed, they're just too awful! COME GET ME, PLEASE!!"

"Darling, baby, you must tell me what has you so upset. Tell your mother these horrible 4-letter words!"

Sobbing, the bride said, "Oh, Mama..., he used words like: dust, wash, iron, cook..."

"I'll pick you up in twenty minutes," said the mother.

One kids asks the other:
Q: "How old is your grandfather?"
A: "I don't know but we've had him for a long time."

Ever Wonder Why They Really Put a Moratorium on New Construction Permits in King County?

Some men from Seattle in a pickup truck drove to a lumber yard. One of the men walked into the office and said, "We need some four-by-twos." The clerk asked, "You mean two-by-fours, don't you?" The man said, "I'll go check," and went back to the truck. He returned shortly and said, "Yeah, I meant two-by-four."

"All right. How long do you need them?" asked the clerk.

The customer paused for a moment and said, "I'd better go check." After a while, he returned to the office and said, "A long time. We're gonna build a house…"

Some Special 'Southernisms'

* Well…Bless my grits and fry my tomatoes!
* Only a true Southerner knows the different between a hissie fit and a conniption fit, and that you don't "HAVE" them—You pitch a hissie fit, and throw a conniption fit.
* Only a true Southerner knows how many fish are in "a mess."
* Only a true Southerner can show or point out to you the general direction of "younder."
* Only a true Southerner knows exactly how long "directly" is – as in: "Going to town, be back directly."
* All true Southerners know exactly when "by and by" is.
* Only a true Southerner knows and understands the difference between a redneck, a good ol' boy, and po' white trash.
* A true Southerner knows that "fixing" can be used as a noun, a verb, or an adverb.
* Only a true Southerner knows that the term "booger" can be a resident of the nose, or a descriptive, as in "that ol' booger," or a first name or something that jumps out at you in the dark and scares you senseless.
* Only true Southerners make friends while standing in lines. They don't do "queues," they stand in "lines," and when they're "in line," they talk to everybody!
* Only true Southerners say "sweet milk." "Sweet milk" means you don't want buttermilk.

* And a true Southerner knows you don't scream obscenities at little old ladies who drive 30 mph on the freeway. You just say, "Bless her little heart...!" and go on your way.

The best way to make a long story short is to stop listening.

No Room for Argument ... Really
An elderly couple had an ice cream craving, having none in the freezer. She agreed to take a trip to the store to pick some up.

The old guy rudely said to her, "You'd better write it down because you know how your memory is bad and you're forgetting things all the time."

She said, "No, I won't forget, I will remember."

About 45 minutes later she walked up to him with a serving of scrambled eggs and the old man looking angrily at her, said, "I told you to write it down! You forgot the bacon!"

Be Careful What You Wish For
A man and his wife, now in their 60s, were celebrating their 40th wedding anniversary. On their special day a good fairy came to them and said that because they had been such a devoted couple she would grant each of them a very special wish. The wife wished for a trip around the world with her husband. Whoosh! Immediately she had airline/cruise tickets in her hands. The man wished for a female companion 30 years youngers...Whoosh...immediately he turned ninety.

Life Really is Like Sports
Examining his new will, the old man said to his attorney, "I guess this makes my son and I sort of like football players."

"How's that?" the lawyer asked.

"Well, until I kick off, he doesn't receive."

SIGNS
- On a New York convalescent home, "For the sick and tired of the Episcopal Church."
- A sign seen on a restroom dryer at O'Hare Field in Chicago, "Do not activate with wet hands."
- In the offices of a New Jersey loan company, "Ask about our plans for owning your home."
- In the window of an Oregon general store, "Why go elsewhere to be cheated, when you can come here?"
- On a poster on a telephone pole in Oregon, "Are you an adult that cannot read? If so, we can help."

- On the grounds of a private school in Connecticut, "No trespassing without permission."
- In a New York medical building, "Mental Health Prevention Center."
- At a number of US military bases, "Restricted to unauthorized personnel."
- In a Florida maternity ward, "No children allowed."
- In front of a New Hampshire car wash, "If you can't read this, it's time to wash your car."
- In a Los Angeles clothing store, "Wonderful bargains for men with 16 and 17 necks."
- In a Texas funeral parlor, "Ask about our layaway plan."

The Land of the Free

Can you imagine working for an organization that has a little more than 500 employees and has the following statistics:

* 29 have been accused of spousal abuse
* 7 have been arrested for fraud
* 19 have been accused of writing bad checks
* 117 have directly or indirectly bankrupt at least 2 businesses
* 3 have done time for assault
* 71 cannot get a credit card due to bad credit
* 14 have been arrested on drug-related charges
* 21 are currently defendants in lawsuits
* 84 have been arrested for drunk driving in the last year

Can you guess which organization this is? Give up yet? It's the 535 members of the United States Congress.

I Ran Over the Rooster

A man was driving down a quiet country lane when out into the road strayed a rooster. Whack! The rooster disappeared under the car. A cloud of feathers billowed in the air.

Shaken, the man pulled over at the farmhouse and rang the doorbell.

A farmer appeared at the door. The man, somewhat nervously said, "I think I killed your rooster. Please allow me to replace him."

"Suit yourself," the farmer replied, "you can go join the other chickens that are around the back."

Oxymoron: Removing the Ten Commandments from the courthouse while asking people in court to swear to tell the truth, the whole truth and nothing but the truth, so help you God ... while your hand in on a Bible.

"Whoever named it necking is a poor judge of anatomy." Groucho Marx

Proper Diagnosis

A man walks into a doctor's office with a stick of celery in one year, a carrot in the other and grape in his nose. Confused, the man asks, "Doctor what's wrong with me?"

The doctor looks at the man and replies, "You're not eating properly!"

Ruh, Roh!

Jim and Mary were both patients in a Mental Hospital. One day while they were walking past the hospital swimming pool, Jim suddenly jumped into the deep end. He sank to the bottom and stayed there. Mary promptly jumped in to save him. She swam to the bottom and pulled Jim out.

When the medical director became aware of Mary's heroic act he immediately ordered her to be discharged from the hospital as he now considered her to be mentally stable.

When he went to tell Mary the news, he said, "Mary, I have good news and bad news. The good news is you're being discharged because since you were able to jump in and save the life of another patient, I think you've regained your senses. The bad news is Jim, the patient you saved, hung himself with his bathrobe belt in the bathroom. I am so sorry, but he's dead."

Mary replied, "He didn't hang himself, I put him there to dry."

Visit to the Doctor

"What's wrong, Doctor? You look puzzled," asked the patient.

"I can't figure out exactly what's wrong with you. I think it's the result of heavy drinking."

"Well then, I'll just come back when you're sober."

What is this Place?

A man and his wife were driving their RV across the country and were nearing a town spelled "Kissimee." They noted the strange spelling and tried to figure how to pronounce it: KISS-a-me; kis-A-me; kiss-a-ME. They grew more perplexed as they drove into the town.

Since they were hungry, they pulled into a place to get something to eat. At the counter, the man said to the waitress, "My wife and I can't seem to be able to figure out how to pronounce this place. Will you tell me where we are and say it very slowly so that I can understand."

The waitress looked at him and said, "Buuuuurrrrgerrrr Kiiiiinnnnng."

Q: Why does a man twist his wedding ring on his finger?
A: He's trying to figure out the combination.

Your Wife Just Fell Out

On a rural road a state trooper pulled this farmer over and said, "Sir, do you realize your wife fell out of the car several miles back?"

The farmer replied, "Thank God, I thought I had gone deaf!"

Bad Day

Two men got out of their cars after they collided at an intersection. One took a flask from his pocket and said to the other, "Here, maybe you'd like a nip to calm your nerves."

"Thanks," he said, and took a long pull from the container. "Here, you have one, too," he added, handing back the whiskey.

Reprimand

After putting her children to bed, a mother changed into old slacks and a droopy blouse and proceeded to wash her hair. She then carefully applied cold cream all over her face except her eyes, which she outlined with a different cream. She then proceeded to put her hair in high rollers. As she heard the children getting more and more rambunctious, her patience grew thin. At last she threw a towel around her head and stormed into their room, putting them back to bed with stern warnings. As she left the room, she heard her three-year-old sayd with a trmebling voice, "Who was that?"

Two Workers in a Factory

Two Seattle factory workers were talking.

"I think I'll take some time off from work," said the man.

"How do you think you'll do that?" said the co-worker.

He proceeded to show her, by climbing up to the rafters, and hanging upside down. The boss walked in, saw the worker hanging from the ceiling, and asked him what on earth he was doing?

"I'm a light bulb," answered the guy.

"I think you need some time off," said the boss.

So, the man jumped down and walked out of the factory. The co-worker began walking out too. The boss asked her where did she think she was going?

"Home." The co-worker answered, "I can't work in the dark."

Food Choices

The children were lined up in the cafeteria of a Catholic elementary school for lunch. At the head of the table was a large pile of apples. The nun made a note, and posted on the apple tray: "Take only ONE. God is watching."

Moving further along the lunch line, at the other end of the table was a large pile of chocolate chip cookies. A child had written a note, "Take all you want. God is watching the apples."

More Food Choices

Two little boys were visiting their grandfather. The grandfather took the boys to a restaurant for lunch. The boys couldn't make up their minds about what they wanted to eat. Finally, the grandfather grinned at the server and said, "Just bring them bread and water."

One of the little boys looked up and quavered, "Can I have ketchup on it?"

What Club?

The duffer muffed his tee shot into the woods, then hit into a few trees, then proceeded to hit across the fairway into another woods. Finally, after banging away several more times, he proceeded to hit into a sand trap. All the while, he'd noticed that the club professional had been watching.

"What club should I use now?" he asked the pro.

"I don't know," the pro replied. "What game are you playing?

Taking Care of What Needs to be Done

Little Lucy was in the garden filling in a hole when her neighbor peered over the fence. Interested in what the cheeky-faced youngster was doing, he politely asked, "What are you up to there, Lucy?"

"My goldfish died," replied Lucy tearfully, without looking up, "and I've just buried him."

The neighbor was concerned. "That's an awfully big hole for a goldfish, isn't it?"

Lucy patted down the last heap of earth, then replied, "That's because he's inside your darn cat!"

Surgery

Before going in for surgery I thought it would be funny if I posted a note on myself telling the surgeon to be careful. After the surgery I found another note on myself which read: "Anyone know where my cell phone is????????"

Ready For Heaven

A man died and went to The Judgment, they told him, "Before you meet with God, I should tell you — we've looked over your life, and to be honest you really didn't do anything particularly good or bad. We're not really sure what to do with you. Can you tell us anything you did that can help us make a decision?"

The newly arrived soul thought for a moment and replied, "Yeah, once I was driving along and came upon a person who was being harassed by a group of thugs. So I pulled over, got out a bat, and went up to the leader of the thugs. He was a big, muscular guy with a ring pierced through his lip. Well, I tore the ring out of his lip, and told him he and his gang had better stop bothering this guy or they would have to deal with me!"

"Wow that's impressive! When did this happen?"

"About three minutes ago," came the reply.

Clean Restaurant

So, these two roaches, Tom and Oscar, are hanging out next to a dumpster enjoying a snack.

"Hey Tom," said Oscar to his friend, "You know that restaurant down the block? I went there yesterday to pick up some scraps, and I couldn't believe how clean it was, I could practically see my reflection through the shiny waxed floor."

"Oscar" hollered Tom, spitting the food out of his mouth, "please not while I am eating!"

Lawyer's Daughter

QUESTION: What did the lawyer name his daughter?   **ANSWER**: Sue.

Can You Hear Me Now?

An old man went to the Doctor complaining that his wife could barely hear.

The Doctor suggested a test to find out the extent of the problem. "Stand far behind her and ask her a question, and then slowly move up and see how far away you are when she first responds."

The old man excited to finally be working on a solution for the problem, runs home and sees his wife preparing supper. "Honey," the man asks standing around 20 feet away, "whats for supper?"

After receiving no response he tried it again 15 feet away, and again no response.

Then again at 10 feet away and again no response.

Finally, he was 5 feet away, "Honey, what's for supper?"

She replies "FOR THE FOURTH TIME, IT'S LASAGNA!"

Whoops, Sorry About That

Marvin, was in the hospital on his death bed. The family called Marvin's Preacher to be with him in his final moments.

As the Preacher stood by the bed, Marvin's condition seemed to deteriorate, and Marvin motioned for someone to quickly pass him a pen and paper.

The Preacher quickly got a pen and paper and lovingly handed it to Marvin. But, before he had a chance to read the note, Marvin died.

The Preacher, feeling that now wasn't the right time to read it, put the note in his jacket pocket.

It was at the funeral while speaking that the Preacher suddenly remembered the note. Reaching deep into his pocket the Preacher said, "And, you know what, I suddenly remembered that right before Marvin died he handed me a note, and knowing Marvin, I'm sure it was something inspiring that we can all gain from."

With that introduction the Preacher ripped out the note and opened it. The note said "HEY, YOU ARE STANDING ON MY OXYGEN TUBE!"

The "Bottom"
Q. What has a bottom at its top?
A. A leg.

Going To a Psychic After Husband Dies
Suzie was all alone. It was two months since her dear Herbie had passed, and she just couldn't seem to move on.

"Listen here Suzie," said her good friend Barbara, "maybe you should go see a psychic. One of my friends did it after her husband died and it made her feel so much better knowing that her dearest was happy."

So, that's how, on the next Tuesday, Suzie found herself in a dim room with a crystal ball and a psychic talking in a calm voice.

"Is he here?" Suzie asked.

"Yes, I sense him," was her reply.

"Can you ask him if he's happy?" Suzie hesitantly asked.

"He's putting his hand to his mouth like he wants to smoke," said the psychic.

"Oh, of course," said Suzie, "he needs a cigar. Herbie can never last more then a few hours without a cigar. I guess they don't have cigars up there. Did he say where he is or how I could get one to him?" Questioned Suzie urgently.

"Hmm," said the psychic. "I can't seem to get that question across to him. But, then again," said the psychic after a brief pause, "he didn't say anything about needing a lighter!"

Loss For Words
Adam woke up suddenly, sweating all over. "What's the problem," asked his wife. "Are you OK?"

"I just dreamed that I died!" responded a shaken Adam.

"And, it was so bad up there, and that's why you're sweating all over?" asked his wife.

"You bet!" exclaimed Adam. "I got up there, and was right in front of God himself, when he suddenly sneezed... and I didn't know what to say to him! Whoa was that traumatic!"

At a Dance
Boy: Would you like to dance?
Girl: Yes!
Boy: So I can take this chair?

Bad Employee Reviews
- "This employee has reached rock bottom and has started to dig."
- "I would not allow this employee to breed."
- "Works well when under constant supervision and cornered like a rat in a trap."
- "He would be out of his depth in a parking lot puddle."
- "This employee is depriving a village somewhere of an idiot."
- "This employee should go far, and the sooner he starts, the better."
- "I would like to go hunting with him sometime."
- "He brings a lot of joy whenever he leaves the room."
- "When his I.Q. reaches 50, he should sell."
- "If you see two people talking and one looks bored, he's the other one."
- "Donated his brain to science before he was done using it."
- "If he were any more stupid, he'd have to be watered twice a week."
- "If you gave him a penny for his thoughts, you'd get change."
- "If you stand close enough to him, you can hear the ocean."
- "Takes him two hours to watch 60 Minutes."
- "The wheel is turning, but the hamster is dead."

Paycheck Error
An employee approached his boss regarding a dispute on his pay-check...
EMPLOYEE: Sir, this is $100 less than my salary.
BOSS: I know. But last month, when you were overpaid $100, by mistake, you didn't complain!
EMPLOYEE: Well, I don't mind an occasional mistake, sir, but it seems to be becoming a habit, now!

Homework
PUPIL: "Would you punish me for something I didn't do?"
TEACHER: "Of course not."
PUPIL: "Good, because I haven`t done my homework."

Item on Craigslist: Antique Sewing table $30. If my wife is home, price is $100.

WOMAN TO MAN IN BAR: I would probably find you more interesting had I studied psychology.

It's All Relative
WIFE: You hate my relatives!
HUSBAND: No, I don't! In fact, I like your mother-in-law more than I like mine.

I'm Busy
"I'm busy now. Can I ignore you some other time?"

Got 'R Fixed!
PATIENT: So, Doc, what's the diagnosis?
DOC: Your X-Ray showed a broken rib, but we fixed it with Photoshop.

Pregnant
Brian's stress level was at unsurpassed levels. His wife, Maggie, was in labor and Brian was sure it was time to head to the hospital.

Breathing heavily, Brian grabbed the phone and called the doctor. "MY WIFE, SHE'S READY, SHOULD WE COME?"

The doctor tried to relax the poor fellow, "Just try to relax. Now tell me how much time elapses between the contractions?"

"SHIRLEY!" Brian screamed on the top of his lungs, "HOW MUCH TIME IN BETWEEN THE CONTRACTIONS? TEN MINUTES? OK, TEN MINUTES IN BETWEEN!"

"And is this her first child?" Questioned the doctor.
"NO YOU NITWIT, THIS IS HER HUSBAND!"

Quarantine
"I hate to have to tell you this," said the Doctor in a sad compassionate voice, "but, unfortunately, you have been diagnosed with a highly contagious disease. We will have to quarantine you and you'll only be fed cheese and bologna."

"That's terrible!" Said the distraught young man, quickly sitting down before he could faint. "I don't know if I could handle being in quarantine...and the cheese and bologna diet... What's with the cheese and bologna diet anyway? I've never of such a diet before?!"

"It's not exactly a diet," responded the Doctor matter of factly, "it's just the only food that will fit under the door!"

High Fever
My four-year-old daughter had a terrible case of the flu. She was achy, had a high fever, and was terribly hoarse.

After sitting in the waiting room at the doctor's office for over an hour we were finally admitted to see the Doctor.

After the usual routine of listening to her breathing and checking her ears, the Doctor looked my daughter in the eye and said, "so what would you say is bothering you the most?"

Without skipping a beat my daughter promptly answered, "Billy, he always breaks my toys!"

Just Being Practical

A man wasn't feeling well so his wife took him to the doctor.

After examining him the doctor took his wife aside, and said, "Your husband has a very sensitive heart. I am afraid he's not going to make it, unless you treat him like a king, which means you are at his every beckoned call, 24 hours a day and that he doesn't have to do anything himself."

On the way home the husband asked with a note of concern, "What did he say?"

The wife responded, "He said it looks like you probably won't make it."

Medical History

Due to a job transfer, Brian moved from his hometown to New York City.

Being that he had a very comprehensive health history, he brought along all of his medical paperwork, when it came time for his first check up with his new Doctor.

After browsing through the extensive medical history, the Doctor stared at Brian for a few moments and said, "Well there's one thing I can say for certain, you sure look better in person than you do on paper!"

Injury

JOE: Did you hear about the guy who lost his whole left side?
SAM: No, I sure didn't. What happened to him?
JOE: He's all right now!

The Mommies

PAM: Johnny's running a fever today.
MARY: Oh! Did you try giving him some Tylenol?
PAM: Yeah, but I thought I'd wait a little while before I gave him some. You know how good they are when they're not feeling well.

Nervous Dad

"Just relax," the hospital staff kept telling Jim, but it was to no avail. Jim's wife was in labor and Jim was a nervous wreck.

After what seemed like a week to both Jim and the hospital staff, a nurse came out with the happy news, "It's a girl!" she cried.

"Thank God, a girl," said Jim, "at least she won't have to go through what I just went through!"

Worried Mom

MOTHER: I need to speak to the doctor, it's an emergency. My infant has a temperature of 101.
DOCTOR TO SECRETARY: Find out how she's taking the temperature.
SECRETARY: How are you taking it?
MOTHER: Oh, I'm holding up OK.

Can't Be Old Age!

An old man went to the doctor complaining of a terrible pain in his leg.

"I am afraid it's just old age;" replied the doctor, "there is nothing we can do about it."

"That can't be!" fumed the old man, "You don't know what you are doing."

"How can you possibly know I am wrong?" countered the doctor.

"Well it's quite obvious," the old man replied, "my other leg is fine, and it's the exact same age!"

Polite Child

I work as a pediatric nurse, and often have the painful job of giving shots to the children. One day upon entering the examining room to give a shot the little girl starting screaming "NO! NO! NO!"

"Jessica," her mother scolded, "that is not polite behavior!"

At that the girl continued to scream, "NO THANK YOU! NO THANK YOU! NO THANK YOU!"

Hospital Gown

Helping her husband change into his hospital gown, the wife stood behind him to tie the strings closed. Looking at how it revealed the backside of her husband, the wife commented, "Now I see why they call it I.C.U."

High Blood Pressure

A doctor remarked on his patient's ruddy complexion.

"I know" the patient said "It's high blood pressure. It's from my family."

"Your mother's side, or father's side?" questioned the doctor.

"Neither. My wife's."

The doc said, "That can't be. How can you get it from your wife's family?"

"Oh yeah," the patient responded, "You should meet them sometime!"

OOPS?

Jerry was in the hospital recovering from surgery when a nurse asks him how he is feeling.

"I'm OK; but, I didn't like the four-letter-word the doctor used in surgery," he answered.

"What did he say," asked the nurse.

"OOPS!"

Pregnant?

A lady went to a doctor's office where she was seen by a Doctor.

A few minutes into the examination, screeching could be heard from the room, and then the lady burst out of the room as if running for her life.

After much effort a nurse finally managed to calm her down enough to tell her story.

The nurse barged into the office of the Doctor and screamed, "Shame on you! Mrs. Smith is 82-years-old and you told her she's pregnant?"

The Doctor continued writing calmly and barely looking up said, "Does she still have the hiccups?"

Memory Problem

PATIENT: Doctor! I have a serious problem. I can never remember what I just said.

DOCTOR: When did you first notice this problem?

PATIENT: What problem?

The Revenge On The Doctor

A colleague and I were fitting clothes for a fashion show benefit. All the models were residents of our small town, including the local doctor. He tried on one outfit and then asked, "What should I do next?"

Gleefully seizing the opportunity my friend replied, "Go to the dressing room remove your clothes put on a paper robe and wait."

Round Is A Shape:
"They tell me to get into shape. Round is a shape."

Uh, Yeah, Right, Dad.

DAD TO DAUGHTER: Honey, when you grow up I want you to be assertive, independent, and strong-willed. But, while you're a kid I want you to be passive, pliable, and obedient.

Last Word
BOB: You need to show your wife you have the final word!
JOE: Bob, my wife may be the boss, but I always get the final word. It's "yes, ma'am."

Good News and Bad News
WIFE: Honey, I have some good news and some bad news!
HUSBAND: Give me the good news first.
WIFE: The airbags work.

No Body Riddle
Q: What has a face and 2 hands but no body?
A: A clock.

Riddle
Q. What word becomes shorter when you add two letters to it?
A. Short

Marriage Spat:
HUSBAND: I was a fool when I married you!
WIFE: I know, Dear, but I was in love and I didn't notice.

The Not-So-Helpful-Husband
WIFE: (Looking into mirror) I'm only 40 years old, but I look like I'm over 55. My face is all wrinkly, my back is bent over, and my hair is starting to thin.
HUSBAND: At least your eyesight seems to be working fine.

KISS!
WIFE: Our neighbor, Mr. Smith, kisses his wife each morning at the door before he goes to work. How come you never do?
HUSBAND: Honey! How could I?! I don't even know her!

A Thinking Joke (See If You Can Follow It)
   Two men at a bus stop struck up a conversation. One kept complaining of family problems. Finally, the other man said: "You think you have family problems? A few years ago I met a young widow with a grown-up daughter. We got married and I got myself a stepdaughter. Later, my father married my stepdaughter. That made my stepdaughter, my step-mother. And my father became my stepson. Also, my wife became mother-in-law of her father-in-law. Much later, the daughter of my wife, my stepmother, had a son. This boy was my half-brother because he was my father's son. But he was also the son of my wife's

daughter which made him my wife's grandson. That made me the grandfather of my half-brother. This was nothing until my wife and I had a son. Now the half-sister of my son, my stepmother, is also the grandmother. This makes my father, the brother-in-law of my child, whose stepsister is my father's wife, I am my stepmother's brother-in-law, my wife is her own child's aunt, my son is my father's nephew and I am my OWN GRANDFATHER!"

Experience
BOSS: This is a citrus grove. Do you have any experience picking lemons?
LADY: Well, I've been divorced 3 times!?

Spelling Test
TEACHER: Billy, let me hear you use the word T-O-A-D in a sentence.
BILLY: Well, I toad my mother to get me a turtle.

Cough Remedy
Doctor to Nurse: We were out of cough medicine, so I gave him a laxative. It really worked! See how he's afraid to cough?

Old Lady
NEWS REPORTER TO OLD LADY: So, what's the best thing about being 104 years old?
OLD LADY: No peer pressure!

Doctor, Doctor!
DOCTOR: You only two weeks to live.
PATIENT: If I've only got two weeks to live, I'll take the last one in July and the first one in August.

The Two Snowmen
1st SNOWMAN: Do you smell that?
2nd SNOWMAN: That's funny, I smell carrots, too!

Just Like You But Different
Q. What's bigger than you, but doesn't weigh anything?
A. Your shadow.

Kidnapping!
Q: Did you hear about the kidnapping at school?
A: It's okay, he woke up.

Chicken Crossing
1st CHICKEN: How do I get to the other side?
2nd CHICKEN: You ARE on the other side, bird brain.

The Low Down
MIDGET: I was minding my own business when someone picked my pocket.
SHERIFF: I can't believe someone would stoop so low.

Cat Talk
Q: What did the cat say after eating two robins lying in the sun?
A. I just love baskin' robins.

Don't Exaggerate!
MOM TO KID: If I've told you once I've told you a million times, DON'T EXAGGERATE!

I've Been Thinking About This One
I thought a thought. But the thought I thought wasn't the thought I thought I thought. If the thought I thought I thought had been the thought I thought, I wouldn't have thought so much. I think.

Clever Riddle
Joe was once again caught lying to his teacher, and his teacher, Mr. Rogers, had enough.

"Come here, Joe," he said. "Here is your punishment: I want you to make a statement; if it's true you get detention, if it's false you get suspended."

Q. What did the Joe say that caused him not to get punished at all?

A. I will be suspended.

Life! Life is just a phase you're going through... you'll get over it.

Ever laugh so hard no sound is coming out, so you sit there, clapping like a retarded seal.

Sometimes I forget how to spell a word; so, I change the whole sentence to avoid using it.

Riddles *(Answers are posted at end of riddle list)*
1. Johnny 's mother had three children. The first child was named April The second child was named May. What was the third child 's name?

2. There is a clerk at the butcher shop, he is five feet ten inches tall, and he wears size 13 sneakers. What does he weigh?

3. Before Mt. Everest was discovered, what was the highest mountain in the world?

4. How much dirt is there in a hole that measures two feet by three feet by four feet?

5. What word in the English Language is always spelled incorrectly?

6. Billy was born on December 28th, yet his birthday is always in the summer. How is this possible?

7. In California, you cannot take a picture of a man with a wooden leg. Why not?

8. What was the President's Name in 1975?

9. If you were running a race, and you passed the person in 2nd place, what place would you be in now?

10. Which is correct to say, "The yolk of the egg are white" or "The yolk of the egg is white"?

11. If a farmer has 5 haystacks in one field and 4 haystacks in the other field, how many haystacks would he have if he combined them all in another field?

ANSWERS: 1. Johnny of course. 2. Meat 3. Mt. Everest. It just hadn't been discovered, yet. 4. There is no dirt in a hole. 5. Incorrectly. 6. Billy lives in the Southern Hemisphere. 7. You can't take pictures with a wooden leg. You need a camera to take pictures. 8. The same as it is now; he's just older now. 9. You would be in 2nd. You passed the person in second place, not first. 10. Neither, the yolk of the egg is yellow [Duh]. 11. One. If he combines all of his haystacks, they all become one big one.

Fisherman Tongue Twister
There was a fisherman named Fisher
Who fished for some fish in a fissure.
Till a fish with a grin,
pulled the fisherman in.
Now they're fishing the fissure for Fisher.

Saw That One Coming!
Q. What goes black and white, black and white, black and white?
A. A penguin rolling down a hill.

Q. What's black, and white, and laughing?
A. The penguin that pushed him.

Riddle Me Up
Q. What goes up but never goes down?
A. Your age.

Hmmmm... What Is It?
Q. What has four wheels and flies?
A. A garbage truck.

Riddle Me Down
Q. What grows down, when it grows up?
A. A goose.

Dry Up, Sweetheart!
Q. What gets wetter the more it dries?
A. A towel.

Success Question
Ever Wonder? If you try to fail, and succeed, which have you done?

Parenting In A Nutshell
We spend the first twelve months of our children's lives teaching them to walk and talk and the next twelve telling them to sit down and be quiet.

Being Unique
Always remember you're unique, just like everyone else.

Music
Remember: If the music's too loud you're too old.

Workout
I get enough exercise just pushing my luck!

Meaning Of Life
Every time I find the meaning of life, they change it.

Half Full or Half Empty?
The pessimist may be right in the long run, but the optimist has a better time during the trip.

Thought On Atheism
Atheism is a non-prophet organization.

Manly Men
Behind even the manliest men is a little boy, who's thinking, "what do I do next?"

Who's Really Happy?
I don't suffer from insanity. I enjoy every minute of it.

The Final Solution
When everything else fails – try the directions.

Marriage
Married men should forget their mistakes. There is no need for two people, to remember the same thing.

God's Name
Despite what people think @#!*% is not God's last name.

The Secret of a Happy Marriage
The secret of a happy marriage remains a secret.

A cop pulled me over and said, "Papers?" So, I said "Scissors! I win!" Then, I drove off!

Of course I need expert advice! That's why I talk to myself!

All my life I thought air was free, until I bought a bag of chips.

Life is not a fairytale. If you lose your shoe at midnight, you're drunk!

Raisin cookies that look like chocolate chip cookies are the main reason I have trust issues.

Marriage is a Workshop... where the husband works and the wife shops.

Old people at weddings poke me and say, "You're next!" So, I started doing the same thing to them at funerals.

When I feel down and someone tells me to "Suck it up," I get the urge to break their legs with a baseball bat and tell them to "Walk it off."

Hey, I'll be back in 5 minutes; but, in case I'm not, just read this message again.

New York, New York!
The whole world should be worried that North Korea has a missile that can hit New York; because, if it can make it there, it can make it anywhere.

It's The Little Things
For her birthday, I bought my wife new beads for her abacus.
It's the little things that count.

Origami Developments
Vandals have attacked the National Origami Museum in Tokyo.
We'll keep you updated as the story unfolds.

Please, Hurry!
When people go underwater in movies, I like to hold my breath to see if I would've survived in that situation. I almost died during Finding Nemo.

Pass The Word
Set your WiFi password to fourwordsalluppercase. When someone asks you what it is, then you can tell them, "One word all lower case, four words all upper case."

I asked my North Korean friend how it was there, he said he couldn't complain.

Knock, knock.
Who's there?
Yourself.
Yourself who?
Your cell phone's ringing you better answer it.

Knock, knock.
Who's there?
Tank.
Tank who?
You're welcome!

Knock, knock.
Who's there?
Owls say.
Owls say who?
Yep.

Knock, knock.
Who's there?
Cows say.
Cows say who?
No silly, cows say moo!

Knock, knock.
Who's there?
Boo.
Boo who?
Please don't cry. There are plenty more Chuckleberries in the next volume!

"Angels fly because they take themselves lightly."
~ GK Chesterton

QUICK! NOTIFY GREENPEACE!

Recently the DEA had filled up a warehouse and had to dispose of tons of marijuana. They took the weed to a field and started a bonfire. While burning the chronic, they noticed terns flying overhead in circles and became concerned for their health and safety due to the rising column of primo smoke. They immediately called the Audubon Society to notify them of the problem. The Audubon Society arrived and confirmed the DEA's worst fears. There was no tern left unstoned.

IT'S A MIRACLE!

A young Nun who worked for a local home health care agency was out making her rounds when she ran out of gas. As luck would have it there was a gas station just one block away. She walked to the station to borrow a can with enough gas to start the car and drive to the station for a fill up.
The attendant regretfully told her that the only gas can he owned had just been loaned out, but if she would care to wait he was sure it would be back shortly. Since the nun was on the way to see a patient she decided not to wait and walked back to her car.
After looking through her car for something to carry to the station to fill

with gas, she spotted a bedpan she was taking to the patient. Always resourceful, she carried it to the station, filled it with gasoline, and carried it back to her car. As she was pouring the gas into the tank of her car two men watched her from across the street. One of them turned to the other and said: "I know that it is said that Jesus turned Water into Wine, but if that car starts, I'll become a Catholic for the rest of my life!"

JOHNNY IS A MAN of very few words. One Sunday he went to church, but his wife, Mary, was sick and stayed home. When he returned, she asked, "Was the sermon good?"
"Yup," was Johnny's brief reply.
"What was it about?" Mary asked.
"Sin."
"And what did the Pastor say?"
"He's against it."

GRANDMA ISN'T STUPID

The doctor who had been seeing an 80-year-old woman for most of her adult life finally retired. At her next checkup, the new doctor told her to bring a list of all the medicines that had been prescribed for her. As the young doctor was looking through these, his eyes grew wide as he realized she had a prescription for birth control pills.

"Mrs. Smith, do you realize these are BIRTH CONTROL pills?!?"
"Yes, they help me sleep at night."
"Mrs. Smith, I assure you there is absolutely NOTHING in these that could possibly help you sleep."

She reached out and patted the young doctor's knee. "Yes, dear, I know that. But every morning, I grind one up and mix it in the glass of orange juice that my 16-year-old granddaughter drinks.
Believe me, it helps me sleep at night!"

HOSPITAL BILL

A man was brought to Mercy Hospital, and taken quickly in for coronary surgery. The operation went well and, as the groggy man regained consciousness, he was reassured by a Sister of Mercy, who was waiting by his bed. "Mr. Smith, you're going to be just fine," said the nun, gently patting his hand. "We do need to know, however, how you intend to pay for your stay here. Are you covered by insurance?"

"No, I'm not," the man whispered hoarsely.
"Can you pay in cash?" persisted the nun.
"I'm afraid I cannot, Sister."
"Well, do you have any close relatives?" the nun essayed.

"Just my sister in New Mexico," he volunteered. "But she's a humble spinster nun."

"Oh, I must correct you, Mr. Smith. Nuns are not 'spinsters;' they are married to God."

"Wonderful," said Smith. "In that case, please send the bill to my brother-in-law."

DATSUN 280Z WATER PUMP

A woman calls an import parts warehouse and asks for a 28- ounce water pump.

"A what?" says the confused parts guy.

"My husband says he needs a 28-ounce water pump."

"A 28-ounce water pump? What kind of car does it fit?"

"A Datsun."

As the parts guy writes down "Datsun, 28 oz. water pump" the light in his head goes on. "Oh yes ma'am. We've got 28-ounce water pumps. We have 24-ounce and 26-ounce water pumps too."

"Finally," she says. "You're the first place I've called that knew what I was talking about."

"Yes ma'am. That's because we're a full-service parts warehouse; it's our job to have the parts you need, like a 28-ounce water pump," he says, smiling, as he jots down customer pick-up, Datsun 280Z water pump, part number..."

IF PRACTICE MAKES PERFECT, and no one is perfect, why practice?

DINNER WITH THE BABY SITTER

Kyle and Justin were about to eat with the baby sitter when 6 year old Kyle said, "You can't sit in Daddy's seat!"

"Daddy's not home," the baby sitter replied. "Since I'm responsible for you while he's gone, I can sit here. Today I'm the boss."

Justin, the 4 year old, quickly piped up, "If you're the boss, you sit over there in Mommy's chair!"

THE FOLLOWING ARE MEDICAL RECORDS [SUPPOSEDLY] TAKEN FROM PATIENTS' ACTUAL MEDICAL CHARTS.

* The baby was delivered, the cord clamped and cut and handed to the pediatrician, who breathed and cried immediately.

* She stated that she had been constipated for most of her life until 1989 when she got a divorce.

* The patient was in his usual state of good health until his airplane ran out of gas and crashed.

* I saw your patient today, who is still under our car for physical therapy.
* The patient lives at home with his mother, father, and pet turtle, who is presently enrolled in day care three times a week.
* She is numb from her toes down.
* While in the emergency room, she was examined, X-rated and sent home.
* The patient was to have a bowel resection. However he took a job as a stockbroker instead.
* Occasional, constant, infrequent headaches.
* Patient was alert and unresponsive.
* When she fainted, her eyes rolled around the room.

QUESTIONS TO PONDER
- Why do we put suits in garment bags and garments in a suitcase?
- If I melt dry ice, can I take a bath without getting wet?
- Why is it that bullets ricochet off of Superman's chest, but he ducks when the empty gun is thrown at him?
- When your pet bird sees you reading the newspaper, does he wonder why you're just sitting there, staring at carpeting?
- Why do tourists go to the tops of tall buildings and then put money into telescopes so they can see things on the ground close-up?
- After eating, do amphibians have to wait one hour before getting out of the water?
- Why do we press harder on a remote control when we know the batteries are getting weak?
- Why do banks charge a fee on "insufficient funds" when they know there is not enough?
- Why does someone believe you when you say there are four billion stars, but check when you say the paint is wet?
- Why doesn't glue stick to the bottle?
- Why doesn't Tarzan have a beard?
- Why do Kamikaze pilots wear helmets?
- Whose idea was it to put an "S" in the word "lisp?"
- If people evolved from apes, why are there still apes?
- Why is it that no matter what color bubble bath you use the bubbles are always white?
- Is there ever a day that mattresses are not on sale?
- Why do people constantly return to the refrigerator with hopes that something new to eat will have materialized?
- Why do people keep running over a string a dozen times with their vacuum cleaner, then reach down, pick it up, examine it, then put it down to give the vacuum one more chance?

• Why is it that no plastic bag will open from the end you first try?
• Why is it that whenever you attempt to catch something that's falling off the table you always manage to knock something else over?
• In winter why do we try to keep the house as warm as it was in summer when we complained about the heat?

ABOUT 2 YEARS AGO Diana and I were on a cruise through the Western Mediterranean aboard a Princess liner. At dinner we noticed an elderly lady sitting alone along the rail of the grand stairway in the main dining room. I also noticed that all the staff, ships officers, waiters, busboys, etc., all seemed very familiar with this lady. I asked our waiter who the lady was, expecting to be told she owned the line, but he said he only knew that she had been on board for the last four cruises, back to back.

As we left the dining room one evening I caught her eye and stopped to say hello. We chatted and I said, "I understand you've been on this ship for the last four cruises."

She replied, "Yes, that's true."

I stated, "I don't understand," to which she replied without a pause, "It's cheaper than a nursing home!"

ATTITUDE
* Accept that some days you're the pigeon, and some days you're the statue.
* Always keep your words soft and sweet, just in case you have to eat them.
* Always read stuff that will make you look good if you die in the middle of it.
* Drive carefully. It's not only cars that can be recalled by their maker.
* If you can't be kind, at least have the decency to be vague.
* If you lend someone $20 and never see that person again, it was probably worth it.
* It may be that your sole purpose in life is simply to serve as a warning to others.
* Never buy a car you can't push.
* Never put both feet in your mouth at the same time, because then you won't have a leg to stand on.
* Nobody cares if you can't dance well. Just get up and dance.
* Since it's the early worm that gets eaten by the bird, sleep late.
* The second mouse gets the cheese.
* When everything's coming your way, you're in the wrong lane.
* Birthdays are good for you. The more you have, the longer you live.
* You may be only one person in the world, but you may also be the world to one person.
* Some mistakes are too much fun to only make once.

* We could learn a lot from crayons. Some are sharp, some are pretty and some are dull. Some have weird names, and all are different colors, but they all have to live in the same box.
* A truly happy person is one who can enjoy the scenery on a detour.

AN ELEPHANT AND A CROCODILE were swimming in the jungle, when the elephant spots a turtle sunning himself on a rock. The elephant walks over to the turtle, picks him up in his trunk and hurls him far into the jungle.

"What did you do that for?" asked the crocodile.

The elephant answered, "That turtle was the one that bit me almost fifty years ago."

The crocodile said, "And you remembered him after all these years? Boy, you sure do have a good memory."

"Yep," says the elephant. "Turtle recall."

DID YOU KNOW ...
- The State with the highest percentage of people who walk to work: Alaska
- The percentage of Africa that is wilderness: 28%
- The percentage of North America that is wilderness: 38%

Knock, Knock!
Who's there?
Irish!
Irish who?
Irish you a happy St. Patrick's Day!

Q: What is out on the lawn all summer and is Irish?
A: Paddy O'Furniture

Q: What do you call a fake stone in Ireland?
A: A Sham Rock

Q: Why do frogs like St. Patrick's Day?
A: Because they're always wearing green!

Q: When is an Irish Potato not an Irish Potato?
A: When it's a French fry!

Q: What does it mean when you find a horseshoe?
A: Some poor horse is going barefoot!

Q: Why did the elephant wear his red sneakers on St. Patrick's Day instead of his green ones?
A: The green ones were in the wash!

Q: What does a leprechaun call a happy man wearing green?
A: A Jolly Green Giant!

Q: Why did St. Patrick drive all the snakes out of Ireland?
A: He couldn't afford plane fare!

Q: What happens when a leprechaun falls into a river?
A: He gets wet! What did you think?

Q: What do you call a diseased Irish criminal?
A: A leper con!

A MAN GOES TO HIS DOCTOR and says, "I've got a problem, Doc. Sometimes I dream that I'm a teepee and sometimes I dream that I'm a wigwam. Teepee, wigwam, teepee, wigwam, teepee... I need help!"

"I know what your problem is," said the doctor. "You need to relax...you're two tents!"

PET PEEVE

I was in a bank when a man entered with a rather large dog on a leash. When he asked if it was okay to bring his pet into the building, a bank official answered, "Yes, provided he doesn't make a deposit."

Volume 2

What about those Huckleberries!

    One man was about to buy a gallon of huckleberries when he heard the price. He stopped short, snorted, "At that rate, I'll go pick them myself!"
    And off he went.
    He returned that very afternoon, looking a little worse for the wear, and handed over the money. "You're not charging enough," he said.

    The mountains of the northwest are home to huckleberries. Seasonal and oh so particular, huckleberries come in season in late July and early August. They can be found in elevations above 3500 feet. They are a favorite food of bears and bees. Weather, precipitation, and a variety of other factors determine the outcome of each year's crop. Logging roads and old mountain paths are the gateway to the best huckleberry picking areas. Usually quite a rigorous walk is in store for the picker, quite often on steep hillsides. Huckleberries cannot be cultivated for commercial growth, so we are at the mercy of nature for our take of the crop. Huckleberries are similar to the blueberry, smaller in size, a little more tart, and more purple in color. Once you have tasted a huckleberry, there is no comparison to any other berry.

GOLF TEAM

Taking advantage of a balmy day in New York, a priest and three other men of the cloth swapped their clerical garb for polos and khakis and time out on the golf course.

After several really horrible shots, their caddy asked, "You guys wouldn't be priests by any chance?"

"Actually, yes, we are," one cleric replied. "How did you know?"

"Easy," said the caddy, "I've never seen such bad golf and such clean language!"

RELIGIOUS HOLIDAYS

An atheist complained to a friend, "Christians have their special holidays, such as Christmas and Easter; and Jews celebrate their holidays, such as Passover and Yom Kippur; Muslims have their holidays. EVERY religion has its holidays. But we atheists," he said, "have no recognized national holidays. It's an unfair discrimination."

His friend replied, "Well, why don't you celebrate April first?"

MIDDLE AGE PILLOW TALK

A wife and husband both talked in their sleep. She loved auctions while his hobby was golf.

The other night, during a deep sleep, the man yelled, 'Fore!'

His wife, also in a deep sleep and not missing a beat, yelled back, 'Four Fifty!'

BURGLAR

A man went to the police station wishing to speak with the burglar who had broken into his house the night before.

"You'll get your chance in court," the desk sergeant told him.

"No, no, no!" replied the man. "I want to know how he got into the house without waking my wife. I've been trying to do that for years!"

A VERY ELDERLY GENTLEMAN, mid-nineties, very well dressed, hair well groomed, great looking suit, flower in his lapel, smelling slightly of a good after shave, presenting a well looked after image, walks into an upscale cocktail lounge.

Seated at the bar is an elderly looking lady, (mid eighties). The gentleman walks over, sits alongside of her, orders a drink, takes a sip, turns to her and says, "So, tell me, do I come here often?"

BABY BOOMERS' TEST

How many can you answer or finish?
1. "Brylcream: ..." (6 words)
2. Bob Dylan advised us never to trust anyone .... (2 words)
3. "I wonder, wonder, wonder, wonder who ..." (6 words)
4. "War, uh-huh, huh, yeah, what is it good for? ..." (2 words)
5. Where have all the flowers gone?
6. Superman, "disguised as Clark Kent, mild mannered reporter for a great metropolitan newspaper, fights a never ending battle for truth, justice, and ..." (3 words)
7. Who came from the University of Alabama to become one of the greatest QB's in NFL history and appeared in a TV commercial wearing women's pantyhose? Extra credit if you know his nickname!
8. "I'm Popeye the sailor man! I'm Popeye the sailor man! I'm strong to the finish ..." (5 words)
9. Who played Peter Pan before all these other imitators?
10. In "The Graduate," Benjamin Braddock (Dustin Hoffman) was advised about his future and told to consider one thing. What?
11. In 1962, a dejected politician, having lost a race for governor, announced his retirement and chastised the press saying, "Just think, you don't have ... to kick around any more." (2 words)
12. "Every morning at the mine you could see him arrive. He stood six feet six, weighed 245 pounds, kinda broad at the shoulder and narrow at the hip, and everybody knew you didn't give no lip to ..." (2 words)
13. Where did Fats Domino find his thrill? (3 words)
14. "Good night, Mrs. Calabash, ..." (3 words)
15. "Good night, Chet. ..." (3 words)
16. "Liar, liar, ..." (3 words) And it's not a Jim Carrey movie!
17. "When it's least expected, you're elected. You're the star today! Smile! ..." (4 words)

ANSWERS:
1)"a little dab will do ya." 2)over 30! 3)"...who wrote the book of love." 4)"absolutely nothing!" 5)"long time passing." 6)"the American way." 7)"Joe Nameth," aka "Broadway Joe," aka "Joe Willie." 8)"...'cause I eats me spinach." 9)Mary Martin. 10)"Plastic." 11)Dick Nixon. 12)"Big John." 13)on blueberry hill. 14)"...wherever you are." 15)"Good night, David." 16)"...pants on fire." 17)"You're on Candid Camera."

ON YOUR NERVES

Seven months pregnant, my hand on my aching back, I stood in line at the post office for what seemed an eternity.

"Honey," said a woman behind me, "I had back pain during my pregnancy. I was bedridden for four months because my baby was sitting on a nerve."

The man in front of me piped up... "You'd better get used to it now. Once those young ones get on your nerves, they can stay there till they're 18."

HUH? CAN YOU RUN THAT BY ME AGAIN?

Jill complained to Nina, "Rosey told me that you told her the secret I told you not to tell her."

"Well," replied Nina in a hurt tone, "I told her not to tell you I told her."

"Oh dear!" sighed Jill. "Well, don't tell her I told you that she told me."

FOR ALL YOU BRILLIANT WOMEN AND MEN

Three women and three men are traveling by train to the Super Bowl. At the station, the three men each buy a ticket and watch as the three women buy just one ticket.

"How are the three of you going to travel on only one ticket?" asks one of the men.

"Watch and learn," answers one of the women.

They all board the train. The three men take their respective seats but all three women cram into a toilet together and close the door. Shortly after the train has departed, the conductor comes around collecting tickets. He knocks on the toilet door and says, "Ticket, please."

The door opens just a crack, and a single arm emerges with a ticket in hand. The conductor takes it and moves on. The men see this happen and agree it was quite a clever idea. After the game, they decide to do the same thing on the return trip and save some money. When they get to the station they buy a single ticket for the return trip but see, to their astonishment, that the three women don't buy any ticket at all!!

"How are you going to travel without a ticket?" says one perplexed man.

"Watch and learn," answer the women.

When they board the train, the three men cram themselves into a toilet, and the three women cram into another toilet just down the way. Shortly after the train is on its way, one of the women leaves her toilet and walks over to the toilet in which the men are hiding. The woman knocks on their door and says, "Ticket, please."

HOW TO CLEAN THE HOUSE USING YOUR COMPUTER:
1. Open a new file in your PC.
2. Name it "Housework."
3. Send it to the RECYCLE BIN
4. Empty the RECYCLE BIN
5. Your PC will ask you, "Are you sure you want to delete housework permanently?"
6. Answer calmly, "Yes," and press the mouse button firmly....
7. All done. Feel better.

I JOINED A GYM over the holidays and I am working on my abs, like I am ABSolutely too tired to work out, and I ABSolutely would like a pizza.

DO YOU KNOW if you give a man a twenty dollar bill you will feed him for a day. But if you teach him how to make a twenty dollar bill he will be fed for three to five years.

I NEVER CRITICIZE ANYONE until I've walked a mile in their shoes. This way if they get mad at me they will be a mile away and barefooted.

DRIVING INSTRUCTIONS
My teen-aged niece, Elizabeth, was nervous as she took the wheel for her first driving lesson. As she was pulling out of the parking lot, the instructor said, "Turn left here, and don't forget to let the people behind you know what you're doing."

Elizabeth turned to the students sitting in the backseat and announced, "I'm going left."

QUESTION: What is the only food that doesn't spoil?
ANSWER: Honey.

DID YOU KNOW ... The first couple to be shown in bed together on prime time TV were Fred and Wilma Flintstone.

WHAT A RIDE!
On my four-year-old daughter's first trip to Disneyland, she couldn't wait to get on Mr. Toad's Wild Ride. As the car zoomed through the crazy rooms, into the path of a speeding train, and through walls that fell away at the last second, she clutched the little steering wheel in front of her.

When the ride was over, she said to me a little shakily, "Next time, you drive. I didn't know where I was going."

A LESSON TO BE LEARNED HERE

Mr. Combs had a furniture store specializing in ornate antiques in the baroque style. He had walking pneumonia last month but was at the store anyway. He was in one of the baroque style chairs rubbing Vicks Vaporub on his aching chest when he serendipitously discovered that the soothing ointment gave the furniture a wonderful, deep, rich shine.

He immediately told the other furniture store owners since their furniture was more modern in style and they were not competitors. Soon he got reports that the Vicks treatment not only failed to work on the modern furniture, but ruined some of it.

Mr. Combs is very unpopular now, and his only consolation is that he learned one important rule: If it's not baroque, don't Vicks it.

DID YOU KNOW ...

Only two people signed the Declaration of Independence on July 4th, John Hancock and Charles Thomson. Most of the rest signed on August 2, but the last signature wasn't added until 5 years later.

YOU KNOW YOU'RE LIVING IN 2005 WHEN...

1. You accidentally enter your password on the microwave.
2. You haven't played solitaire with real cards in years.
3. You have a list of 15 phone numbers to reach your family of 3.
4. You e-mail the person who works at the desk next to you.
5. Your reason for not staying in touch with friends and family is that they don't have e-mail addresses.
6. You go home after a long day at work you still answer the phone in a business manner.
7. Your boss doesn't have the ability to do your job.
8. You pull up in your own driveway and use your cell phone to see if anyone is home.
10. Every commercial on television has a web site at the bottom of the screen.
11. Leaving the house without your cell phone, which you didn't have the first 20 or 30 years of your life, is now a cause for panic and you turn around to go and get it.
12. You get up in the morning and go online before getting your coffee.
13. You start tilting your head sideways to smile. :)
14. You are too busy to notice there was no #9 on this list.
15. You actually looked back up to check that there wasn't a #9 on this list.

IT'S A RECORD

A woman meant to call a record store, but dialed the wrong number and got a private home instead. "Do you have 'Eyes of Blue' and 'A Love Supreme?'" she asked.

"Well, no," answered the puzzled homeowner. "But I have a wife and eleven children."

"Is that a record?" she inquired, puzzled in her turn.

"I don't think so," replied the man, "but it's as close as I want to get."

OLD HAROLD'S IN THE HOSPITAL

Harold was an old man. He was sick and in the hospital. There was one young nurse that just drove him crazy. Every time she came in, she would talk to him like he was a little child.

She would say in a patronizing tone of voice, "And how are we doing this morning, or are we ready for a bath, or are we hungry?"

Old Harold had had enough of this particular nurse. One day, Old Harold had breakfast, pulled the juice off the tray, and put it on his bed side stand. He had been given a urine bottle to fill for testing. The juice was apple juice. So, you know where the juice went!

The nurse came in a little later, picked up the urine bottle and looked at it. "My, but it seems we are a little cloudy today."

At this, Old Harold snatched the bottle out of her hand, popped off the top, and drank it down, saying, "Well, I'll run it through again. Maybe I can filter it better this time."

The nurse fainted! Old Harold just smiled!
DON'T MESS WITH OLD PEOPLE!

A LITTLE CONFUSING

A five year old boy went for a weekend trip with his grandparents. On the way home, they stopped at a country restaurant for lunch. The little boy left the table to use the restroom by himself. A moment later he returned with a confused look on his face. He says, "Grandpa, am I a rooster or a hen?"

OLD NAVAJO WOMAN'S WISDOM

All women can benefit from the wisdom of the Navajo. A woman was driving toward home in Northern Arizona when she came upon a Navajo woman hitchhiking. Because the trip had been long and quiet, she stopped the car and invited the Navajo woman climb in, which she does silently. During their eventual small talk, the Navajo woman glanced surreptitiously at a brown bag on the front seat between them.

"If you're wondering what's in the bag," offered the woman, "it's a bottle of wine; I got it for my husband."

The Navajo woman is silent for a while, nodded understandingly several times and said solemnly, "Good trade."

REDEMPTION

A man appeared before St. Peter at the pearly gates. "Have you ever done anything of particular merit?" St. Peter asked.

"Well, I can think of one thing," the man offered. "Once, on a trip to the Black Hills out in South Dakota, I came upon a gang of high-testosterone bikers, who were threatening a young woman. I directed them to leave her alone, but they wouldn't listen. So, I approached the largest and most heavily tattooed biker and smacked him on the head, kicked his bike over, ripped out his nose ring, and threw it on the ground." I yelled, "Now, back off!! Or you'll answer to me!"

St. Peter was impressed: "When did this happen?"

"Just a couple minutes ago."

Well, There Ya Go!

Most of us have a bad habit we are constantly trying to break. For me, it's biting my fingernails. One day I told my husband about my latest solution: press-on nails.

"Great idea, Honey," he smiled. "You can eat them straight out of the box."

BREAKFAST SPECIAL

An older friend and I went to eat breakfast at a restaurant where the "Seniors' Special" was two eggs, bacon, hash browns and toast for $1.99.

"Sounds good" my friend said; "But I don't want the eggs."

"Then I'll have to charge you two dollars and forty-nine cents because you're ordering a la carte" the waitress warned her.

"You mean I'd have to pay for not taking the eggs?" My friend asked incredulously. "Then, I'll take the special."

"How do you want your eggs?" asked the waitress.

She replied, "Raw and in the shell."

She took the two eggs home.

"Someone has said that there are only two kinds of people in the world:
Those who wake up in the morning and say, "Good Morning, Lord," and those who wake up in the morning and say, "Good Lord, it's morning."

Did you hear about the semi-colon who broke the law? He was given two consecutive sentences.

Was It Something I Said? The Polish Divorce

A Polish man married a Canadian girl after he had been in Canada a year or so and, although his English was far from perfect, they got on very well. Until one day he rushed into a lawyer's office and asked him if he could arrange a divorce for him, "very quick."

The lawyer said that the speed of getting a divorce would depend on the circumstances and asked him the following questions:

LAWYER: Have you any grounds?
POLE: JA, JA, an acre and half and a nice little home with 3 bedrooms.
LAWYER No, I mean what is the foundation of this case?
POLE: It is made of concrete, brick and mortar.
LAWYER: Does either of you have a real grudge?
POLE: No, we have a two-car carport and have never really needed one.
LAWYER: I mean, what are your relations like?
POLE: All my relations are in Poland.
LAWYER: Is there any infidelity in your marriage?
POLE: Yes, we have hi fidelity stereo set &DVD player with 6.1 sound. We don't necessarily like the music, but the answer to your questions is yes.
LAWYER: No, I mean does your wife beat you up?
POLE: No, I'm always up before her.
LAWYER: Is your wife a nagger?
POLE: No, she white.
LAWYER: WHY do you want this divorce?
POLE: She going to kill me.
LAWYER: What makes you think that?
POLE: I got proof.
LAWYER: What kind of proof?
POLE: She going to poison me. She buy a bottle at the drug store and put on shelf in bathroom. I can read -- it says, "Polish Remover."

REVIVAL MEETING

After the revival had concluded, the three pastors were discussing the results with one another.

The Methodist minister said, "The revival worked out great for us! We gained four new families."

The Baptist preacher said, "We did better than that! We gained six new families."

The Presbyterian pastor said, "Well, we did even better than that! We got rid of our ten biggest troublemakers!"

EVER WONDER HOW THEY EARN THEIR PAY?

A postal worker picked up a postcard addressed to God from one of the regulars on his route. It read:

Dear God,

I am an 83 year old widow living on a very small pension. Yesterday someone stole my purse. It had $100.00 in it, which was all the money I had until my next pension check. Next Sunday is Christmas, and I had invited two of my friends over for dinner. Without that money, I have nothing to buy food with. I have no family to turn to, and you are my only hope. Can you please help me?"

The postal worker was touched, and went around showing the letter to all the others. Each of them dug into his wallet and came up with a few dollars. By the time he made the rounds, he had collected $96.00, which they put into an envelope and sent over to her.

The rest of the day, all the workers felt the warm glow of the kind thing they had done.

Christmas came and went. A few days later another letter came from the old lady to God. All the workers gathered around while the letter was opened. It read:

Dear God,

How can I ever thank you enough for what you did for me? Because of your gift of love I was able to fix a
glorious dinner for my friends. We had a very nice day and I told my friends of your wonderful gift. By the way, there was $4 missing. I think it must have been those thieving idiots at the Post Office."

SAY SOMETHING NICE, HARVEY

Harvey and Gladys Gold are getting ready for bed. Gladys is standing in front of her full-length mirror, taking a long, hard look at herself.

"You know, Harvey," she comments. "I stare into this mirror and I see an ancient creature. My face is all wrinkled, my breasts sag so much that they dangle to my waist, my arms and legs are as flabby as popped balloons, and...my butt looks like a sad, deflated version of the Hindenberg!"

She turns to face her husband and says, "Dear, please tell me just one positive thing about my body so I can feel better about myself."

Harvey studies Gladys critically for a moment and then says in a soft, thoughtful voice, "Well...there's nothing wrong with your eyesight."

... AT SOME POINT IN LIFE ...

Using a new painting program on my computer, I managed to come up with a very credible still life of fruit. I made a color printout and sent it to my daughter, a graphic designer.

She called when it arrived.

"Isn't it good?" I asked.

She chuckled, and in a tone that echoed mine from years ago, replied, "Mom, it's beautiful. We put it on the refrigerator."

HOW TO PAY YOUR TAX BILL

Dear IRS,

Enclosed is my 2004 Tax Return & payment. Please take note of the attached article from the USA Today newspaper. In the article, you will see that the Pentagon is paying $171.50 for hammers and NASA has paid $600.00 for a toilet seat.

Please find enclosed four toilet seats (value $2,400) and six hammers (value $1,029). This brings my total payment to $3,429.00. Please note the overpayment of $22.00 and apply it to the "Presidential Election Fund," as noted on my return.

Might I suggest that you send the above mentioned fund a "1.5 inch screw." (See attached article...HUD paid $22.00 for a 1.5 inch Phillips Head Screw).

It has been a pleasure to pay my tax bill this year, and I look forward to paying it again next year. I just saw an article about the Pentagon and "screwdrivers."

OUCH!

Two little kids are in a hospital, lying on stretchers next to each other, outside the operating room.

The first kid leans over and asks, "What are you in here for?"

The second kid says, "I'm in here to get my tonsils out and I'm a little nervous."

The first kid says, "You've got nothing to worry about. I had that done when I was four. They put you to sleep, and when you wake up they give you lots of Jell-O and ice cream. It's a breeze."

The second kid then asks, "What are you here for? The first kid says, "A circumcision."

The second kid replies, "Whoa, Good luck buddy! I had that done when I was born ... couldn't walk for a year."

CUCKOO

The other night I was invited out for a night with "the boys." I told my wife that I would be home by midnight... promise!

Well, the hours passed and the beer was going down way too easy. At around 2:30 a.m., drunk as a skunk, I headed for home. Just as I got in the door, the cuckoo clock in the hall started up and cuckooed 3 times.

Quickly, I realized she'd probably wake up, so I cuckooed another 9 times. I was really proud of myself, having a quick-witted solution, even when smashed, to escape a possible conflict.

The next morning my wife asked me what time I got in, and I told her twelve o'clock. She didn't seem disturbed at all. Whew! Got away with that one!

She then told me that we needed a new cuckoo clock. When I asked her why, she said, "Well, last night our clock cuckooed three times, then said "oh crap," cuckooed 4 more times, cleared its throat, cuckooed another 3 times, giggled, cuckooed twice more, and then passed gas."

SHE HAS A POINT ...

My husband had run to the store with our daughters, Sarah (4) and Hannah (2) and on the way home he drove through a neighborhood looking for houses for sale.

After a bit Sarah asked, "Daddy, what are we doing?"

My husband said he was looking at the houses that were for sale.

Sarah asked "Are you gonna buy a new house?"

Dad replied "Maybe."

Then Sarah said with much concern, "But Dad, how will we get it HOME?!"

GOING TO SCHOOL

Mother was having a hard time getting her son to go to school in the morning.

"Nobody in school likes me," he complained. "The teachers don't like me, the kids don't like me, the superintendent wants to transfer me, the bus drivers hate me, the school board wants me to drop out, and the custodians have it in for me. I don't want to go to school."

"But you have to go to school," said his mother sternly. "You're healthy, you have a lot to learn, you have something to offer others, and you are a leader. Besides, you are 45 years old and you are the 'Principal'."

FEAR OF FLYING

A man has an hour before his flight to Los Angeles. He decides to kill some time at an airport bar. He walks in and sits down next to a clearly nervous guy, who has three empty whiskey glasses in front of him. The man introduces himself to the nervous guy, and buys him a drink.

The man asks, "Nervous about flying?"

The nervous guy replies, "N-n-nervous? I'm t-terrified. I j-just know the p-plane is g-going t-to crash and we're g-going to d-die."

"Is this your first time flying?"

"N-no, I fly c-cross-c-country all the t-time. It's m-my job."

"Why don't you just ask your boss if you can drive cross-country?"

"H-he would never l-let me do that"

"Why not?" asks the man.

The nervous guy replies, "B-because, I'm the p-pilot."

CONFERENCE WITH THE TEACHER

Miss Crabtree and Little Johnny's father were having a parent-teacher conference. Miss Crabtree said to Little Johnny's father, "Well, at least there's one thing I can say about your son."

Little Johnny's father asked, "What's that?"

"With grades like these, he couldn't possibly be cheating."

CIGARETTES UNDER THE CARPET

A carpet installer was laying new living room carpeting in a large mansion. After laboriously pulling, stretching, and tacking the carpet, he finally finished, and gratefully sat back to enjoy a cigarette.

Reaching into his shirt pocket, however, he found that his cigarettes were gone, and looking toward the center of the room, he saw a bulge the size of a cigarette pack under the new carpeting. He of course had no intention of pulling up the carpet, so instead he took a large mallet, and he pounded the lump flat, so it could not be seen.

He then hopped in his truck and headed back to the office. On the way, he found his cigarettes in the glove compartment.
Just then his cellular telephone rang. When he answered it, he discovered it was the dispatcher from his office. The dispatcher said that the homeowner had just called them in a terrible panic.
It seems their son's favorite pet hamster was missing. Had the carpet layer seen the hamster while he was in the house?

LOW BRIDGE

A truck driver was driving along on the freeway. He passed a sign that said "low bridge ahead." Before he knew it, the bridge was right ahead of him and he got stuck under the bridge. You could say that he got a rock solid "Trucker's Wedgie."

Cars were backed up for miles.

Finally, a police car pulled up. The cop got out of his car and walked around to the truck driver, put his hands on his hips and said, "Got stuck, huh?"

The truck driver said, "No officer,... I was delivering this bridge and ran out of gas!"

COMPANY POLICY

When the wise company president learned that his employees were tanking up on no-trace vodka martinis during their lunch hours, he issued the following memo:

To all employees; If you must drink during your lunch hour, please drink whiskey. It is better for our customers to know you're drunk than to think you're stupid.

OH, BROTHER ... DON'T RUIN THE SURPRISE!

In an upscale pet-supply store, a customer wanted to buy a red sweater for her dog. The clerk suggested that she bring her dog in for a proper fit.

"Oh, no, I can't do that!" the lady said. "See, the sweater is going to be a surprise!"

NEWLYWED SURPRISE

The newly wed wife said to her husband when he returned from work, "I have great news for you. Pretty soon we're going to be three in this house instead of two."

The husband started glowing with happiness and kissing his wife said, "Oh darling, I'm the happiest man in the world."

Then she said: "I'm glad that you feel this way because tomorrow morning my mother moves in with us."

WEDDING WOES

My Dad and I were talking the other night about love and marriage. He told me that he knew as early as their wedding what marriage to my Mom would be like. It seems the minister asked my Mom, "Do you take this man to be your husband."

And she said, "I do."

Then the minister asked my Dad, "Do you take this woman to be your wife," and my Mom said, "He does."

REVEREND BEECHER'S LETTERS

Reverend Henry Ward Beecher entered Plymouth Church one Sunday and found several letters awaiting him. He opened one and found it contained a single word, "Fool."

Quietly and with becoming seriousness he shared the letter with the congregation and announced: "I have known many an instance of a person writing a letter and forgetting to sign his name, but this is the only instance I have ever known of someone signing his name and forgetting to write the letter."

TRANSLATORS ARE TRAITORS

Computers have been developed which can translate any language into another. Ideally, if the translated passage were then translated by computer back into the first language, the original words ought to be regained. This, however, does not allow for the ambiguity of languages.

Thus, there is the story of the computer that was ordered to translate a common English phrase into Russian and then translate the Russian translation back into English.

What went in was "Out of sight, out of mind."

What came out was "Invisible insanity."

IDENTITY

The new father ran out of the delivery room and announced to the rest of his family who were waiting for the news: "We had twins!"

The family was so excited they immediately asked, "Who do they look like?"

The father paused, smiled, and said, "Each other."

INFANT WEIGHT PROBLEM

At a pharmacy, a woman asked to use the infant scale to weigh the baby she held in her arms.

The clerk explained that the device was out for repairs, but said that she would figure the infant's weight by weighing the woman and baby together on the adult scale, then weighing the mother alone and subtracting the second amount from the first.

"It won't work," countered the woman. "I'm not the mother, I'm the aunt."

ALL ABOUT GROWING UP AS A CAMEL

A mother and baby camel are talking one day when the baby camel asks, "Mom, why have I got these huge three toed feet?"

The mother replies, "Well son, when we trek across the desert your toes will help you to stay on top of the soft sand."

"OK," said the son.

A few minutes later the son asks, "Mom, why have I got these great long eyelashes?"

"They are there to keep the sand out of your eyes on the trips through the desert."

"Thanks Mom," replies the son.

After a short while, the son returns and asks, "Mom, why have I go t these great big humps on my back??"

The mother, now a little impatient with the son replies, "They are there to help us store water for our long treks across the desert, so we can go without drinking for long periods."

"That's great Mom, so we have huge feet to stop us sinking, and long eyelashes to keep the sand from our eyes and these humps to store water, but Mom..."

"Yes, son?"

"Why the heck are we in the San Diego zoo?"

THE SMART PHONE

A young man from Seattle wanted to get his beautiful wife something nice for their first wedding anniversary. So he decides to buy her a cell phone. She is all excited, she loves her phone. He shows and explains all the features on the phone. The next day she goes shopping. Her phone rings and it's her husband, "Hi Hun," he says, "how do you like your new phone?"

She replies, "I just love it, it's so small and your voice is clear as a bell but there's one thing I don't understand though."

"What's that, baby?" asks the husband.

"How did you know I was at Wal-Mart?"

HARD TO SWALLOW

When the wealthy businessman choked on a fish bone at a restaurant, he was fortunate that a doctor was seated at a nearby table. Springing up, the doctor skillfully removed the bone and saved his life.

As soon as the fellow had calmed himself and could talk again, he thanked the surgeon enthusiastically and offered to pay him for his services.

"Just name the fee," he croaked gratefully.

"Okay," replied the doctor. "How about half of what you'd have offered when the bone was still stuck in your throat?"

HONEST MECHANIC

Barbara told her friend, "I was worried that my mechanic might try to rip me off when I took my car in for maintenance."

"Did he try to repair something that wasn't broken?" asked her friend.

"No, he didn't."

"Did he try to overcharge you?"

"No. In fact, all he said I needed was blinker fluid."

GOLF IN HEAVEN

Bart and Art have been a twosome on the links every day since they've been retired. One day, as they're putting on their golf shoes in the clubhouse, they get into a conversation about heaven and whether there are any golf courses there. They make a pact. The first one to die will come back and tell the other one. Bart dies first, and sure enough, comes back to visit Art.

Art says, "Well are there any golf courses in heaven?"

"I have good news and I have bad news," says Bart.

"We have the ultimate golf course in the sky and tournament which starts tomorrow."

"So what's the bad news?"

"You're my partner!"

GOLFER IN HEAVEN

A golfer hit his drive on the first hole 300 yards right down the middle. When it came down, however, it hit a sprinkler and the ball went sideways into the woods. He was angry, but he went into the woods and hit a very hard 2 iron which hit a tree and bounced back straight at him. It hit him in the temple and killed him.

He was at the Pearly Gates and St. Peter looked at the big book and said, "I see you were a golfer, is that correct?"

"Yes, I am," he replied.

St Peter then said, "Do you hit the ball a long way?"

The golfer replied, "You bet. After all, I got here in 2, didn't I?"

ANNIVERSARY DINNER

On their anniversary night in Seattle, the husband sat his wife sat down in the den with her favorite magazine, turned on the soft reading lamp, slipped off her shoes, patted and propped her feet and announced that he was preparing dinner all by himself.

"How romantic!" she thought.

Two-and-a-half hours later, she was still waiting for dinner to be served. She tiptoed to the kitchen and found it a colossal mess.

Her harried husband, removing something indescribable from the smoking oven, saw her in the doorway. "Almost ready!" he vowed. "Sorry it took me so long but I had to refill the pepper shaker."

"Why, honey, how long could that have taken you?"

"More'n an hour, I reckon. Wasn't easy stuffin' it through those dumb little holes."

BIG SWINDLE

A newsboy was standing on the corner with a stack of papers, yelling, "Read all about it. Fifty people swindled! Fifty people swindled!"

Curious, a man walked over, bought a paper, and checked the front page. What he saw was yesterday's paper.

The man said, "Hey, this is an old paper, where's the story about the big swindle?"

The newsboy ignored him and went on calling out, "Read all about it. Fifty-one people swindled!"

THE FORGIVEN AND FORGOTTEN

Once upon a time in their marriage, my Dad did something really stupid. My Mom chewed him out for it. He apologized, they made up.

However, from time to time, my mom mentions what he had done. "Honey," my Dad finally said one day, "why do you keep bringing that up? I thought your policy was 'forgive and forget.'"

"It is," she said. "I just don't want you to forget that I've forgiven and forgotten."

Cooking 101

Every morning during our coffee break, my co-workers and I listened to the culinary disasters of a newlywed colleague. We then tried to share some helpful hints and recipes.

One day she asked us for step-by-step instructions on cooking sweet potatoes, one of her husband's favorites. "I've finally been able to make them sweet," she said, "but how do you make them orange?"

COMPUTER AGE

Working as a computer instructor for an adult-education program at a community college, I am keenly aware of the gap in computer knowledge between my younger and older students.

My observations were confirmed the day a new student walked into our library area and glanced at the encyclopedia volumes stacked on a bookshelf.

"What are all these books?" he asked.

Somewhat surprised, I replied that they were encyclopedias.

"Really?" he said. "Someone printed out the whole thing?"

ANXIOUS

After learning the Lamaze method of natural childbirth, I was admitted to the delivery room with my wife.

It seemed like an eternity before the doctor finally announced, "I've got the head now; just a few more minutes."

"Is it a girl or boy?" I asked excitedly.

The doctor replied, "I don't know. It's hard to tell by the ears."

COULD YOU PLEASE READ THAT AGAIN?

A nearsighted minister glanced at the note that Mrs. Jones had sent to him by an usher. The note read: "Bill Jones having gone to sea, his wife desires the prayers of the congregation for his safety."

Failing to observe the punctuation, he startled his audience by announcing: "Bill Jones, having gone to see his wife, desires the prayers of the congregation for his safety."

ASK A SMART QUESTION, GET A SMART ANSWER

I had given our daughter, who was 15 at the time, a driver's manual. On the way to town one day, I was coaching her as I drove. I told her to be studying her book so as to be ready when it came time to get her driver's permit.

"Oh," she said, "I already know everything in the book."

"You do?" I returned.

"Yep", she said, very smugly.

I thought, "OK, we'll just see about that. I'll give her a hard one."

So I asked her, "How many feet does it take to stop the car if you are driving 60 miles an hour and have to slam on the brakes real hard?"

"One," she replied.

"What?" I asked. "One?!"

She repeated her answer and then because of the confused look on my face, she added...

"Only one, Mom. You always told me never to use my left foot on the brakes, only use my right one."

REAL SIGNS AND ADVERTISEMENTS...
- Signs In a clothing store: "Wonderful bargains for men with 16 and 17 necks."
- In the window of an Oregon general store: "Why go elsewhere to be cheated, when you can come here?"
- In a Pennsylvania cemetery: "Persons are prohibited from picking flowers from any but their own graves."
- On a Tennessee highway: "Take notice: when this sign is under water, this road is impassable."
- From the safety information card in America West Airline seat pocket: "If you are sitting in an exit row and cannot read this card, please tell a crew member."
- On a Maine shop: "Our motto is to give our customers the lowest possible prices and workmanship."
- On a delicatessen wall: "Our best is none too good."

POINTS TO PONDER ...
- If you love something, set it free. If it comes back, it will always be yours. If it doesn't come back, it was never yours to begin with. But, if it just sits in your living room, messes up your stuff, eats your food, uses your telephone, takes your money, and doesn't appear to realize that you had set it free ... you either married it or gave birth to it.
- The nice part about living in a small town: when you don't know what you're doing, someone else always does.
- The best way to forget all your troubles is to wear tight shoes.
- Amazing!! You hang something in your closet for a while and it shrinks two sizes!
- Just when I was getting used to yesterday, along came today.
- Sometimes I think I understand everything ... then, I regain consciousness.

Q. What's the difference between a King's son, a monkey's mother, a bald head, and an orphan?
A. One's an heir apparent, the next is a hairy parent, the next has no hair apparent, and the last has nary a parent.

SCARY AIRLINES

Passengers on a small plane are waiting for the flight to leave. They're getting a little impatient, but the airport staff assures them the pilots will be there soon, and the flight can take off.

The entrance opens, two men dressed in pilots' uniforms walk up the aisle. Both are wearing dark glasses, one is using a guide dog, and the other is tapping his way along the aisle with a cane.

Nervous laughter spreads through the cabin, but the men enter the cockpit, the door closes, and the engines start up. The passengers begin glancing nervously around, searching for some sign that this is just a little practical joke. None is forthcoming.

The plane moves faster and faster down the runway, and the people sitting in the window seats realize they're headed straight for the water at the edge of the airport territory. As it begins to look as though the plane will plow into the water, panicked screams fill the cabin.

At that moment, the plane lifts smoothly into the air. The passengers relax and laugh a little sheepishly, and soon all retreat into their magazines, secure in the knowledge that the plane is in good hands.

In the cockpit, one blind pilot turns to the other and says, "You know, Joe, one of these days, they're gonna scream too late and we're all gonna die."

HERE, TAKE THIS ...

When Peters learned that he was being fired, he went to see the head of human resources. "Since I've been with the firm for so long," he said, "I think I deserve at least a letter of recommendation."

The human resources director agreed and said he'd have the letter that next day. The following morning, Peters found the letter on his desk.

It read, "Jonathan Peters worked for our company for eleven years. When he left us, we were very satisfied."

SOME THINGS ARE BETTER LEFT UNSAID ...

A tour bus driver drives with a bus full of seniors down a highway, when he is tapped on his shoulder by a little old lady. She offers him a handful of peanuts, which he gratefully munches up.

After approx.15 minutes, she taps him on his shoulder again and she hands him another handful of peanuts. She repeats this gesture about eight times. At the ninth time he asks the little old lady why they do not eat the peanuts themselves, whereupon she replies that it is not possible because of their old teeth, they are not able to chew them.

"Why do you buy them then?" he asks puzzled.

Whereupon the old lady answers, "We just love the chocolate around them!"

In Our Small Community, It's Good To Be Reminded That We Are, Indeed, Irreplaceable.

However, It's Always Fun To Take A Look At The More Practical Side:
JUDGE: Is there any reason you could not serve as a juror in this case?
JUROR: I don't want to be away from my job that long.
JUDGE: Can't they do without you at work?
JUROR: Yes, but I don't want them to know it.

YEEOWWW!

Although we were being married in New Hampshire, I wanted to add a touch of my home state, Kansas, to the wedding.

My fiancée, explaining this to a friend, said that we were planning to have wheat rather than rice thrown after the ceremony.

Our friend thought for a moment. Then he said solemnly, "It's a good thing she's not from Idaho."

OIL SHORTAGE

A lot of folks can't understand how we came to have an oil shortage here in America. Well, there's a very simple answer. Nobody bothered to check the oil. We just didn't know we were getting low.

The reason for that is purely geographical. Our OIL is located in ALASKA - CALIFORNIA - MONTANA - OKLAHOMA - TEXAS and WYOMING.

Our DIPSTICKS are located in Washington DC!

GRAVESIDE SERVICE

A young preacher was asked by a funeral director to hold a grave side service for a man who died with no family or friends.

The funeral was held way back in the country and the young preacher got lost on the way.

When he arrived an hour late, he saw a backhoe and crew; but, the hearse was nowhere in sight. The workmen were eating lunch.

The diligent pastor went to the open grave to find the vault lid in place, but still he poured out his heart and preached an impassioned and lengthy service.

Returning to his car, the young preacher felt that he had done his duty and he would leave with a renewed sense of purpose and dedication, in spite of his tardiness. As he got into his car, he overheard one of the workers talking to another worker.

"I've been putting in septic tanks for 20 years, and I ain't never seen anything like that before. Sort of gives new meaning to the term 'holy poop.'"

Woman without her man is nothing

An English professor wrote the words, "Woman without her man is nothing" on the blackboard and directed his students to punctuate it correctly.

The men wrote: "Woman, without her man, is nothing."

The women wrote: "Woman: Without her, man is nothing."

Question and Answer

QUESTION: How many men does it take to change a roll of toilet paper?
ANSWER: We don't know; it has never happened.

MAN OF THE HOUSE

The husband had just finished his book titled: "MAN OF THE HOUSE." He stormed into the house and walked directly up to his wife. Pointing a finger in her face, he said, "Woman, from now on, I want you to know that I am the man of this house, and my word is law! I want you to prepare me a gourmet meal tonight. And, when I'm finished eating my meal, I expect a sumptuous dessert afterward. Then, after dinner, you're going to draw me a nice hot bath so I can relax. And when I'm finished with my bath, guess who's going to dress me and comb my hair?"

His wife replied, "The funeral director."

DOES COLD WATER GET PLATES CLEAN?

John went to visit his 90 year old grandfather in a very secluded rural area of Georgia. After spending a great evening chatting the night away, John's grandfather prepared breakfast of bacon, eggs and toast. However, John noticed a film like substance on his plate, and questioned his grandfather asking, "Are these plates clean?"

His grandfather replied, "They're as clean as cold water can get them. Just you go ahead and finish your meal, Sonny!"

For lunch the old man made hamburgers. Again, John was concerned about the plates as his appeared to have tiny specks around the edge that looked like dried egg and asked, "Are you sure these plates are clean?"

Without looking up the old man said, "I told you before, Sonny, those dishes are as clean as cold water can get them. Now don't you fret, I don't want to hear another word about it!"

Later that afternoon, John was on his way to a nearby town and as he was leaving, his grandfather's dog started to growl, and wouldn't let him pass. John yelled and said, "Grandfather, your dog won't let me get to my car."

Without diverting his attention from the football game he was watching on TV, the old man shouted, "COLDWATER, GO LAY DOWN!!!!"

A HUSBAND WALKS INTO Victoria's Secret to purchase some sheer lingerie for his wife. He is shown several possibilities that range from $250 to $500 in price, the sheerer, the higher the price. He opts for the sheerest item, pays the $500 and takes the lingerie home. He presents it to his wife and asks her to go upstairs, put it on and model it for him.

Upstairs, the wife thinks, "I have an idea. It's so sheer that it might as well be nothing. I won't put it on, but I'll do the modeling naked, return it tomorrow and keep the $500 refund for myself." So, she appears naked on the balcony and strikes a pose.

The husband says, "Good Lord! You'd think that for $500, they'd at least iron it!"

He never heard the shot. Funeral on Friday.

YOU NEED A TIE

This guy wants to go into this hip new nightclub, but the bouncer says, "Sorry, bud, you need a tie to enter this place."

The guy goes back to his car and rummages around, but there's no necktie to be found. Finally, in desperation, he takes his jumper cables, wraps them around his neck, ties a nice knot, and lets the ends dangle free.

Back to the nightclub he goes, where the bouncer takes a long look at him and says, "Well, OK, I guess you can come in. But, don't start anything."

SO, YOU THINK A GALLON OF GAS IS EXPENSIVE?

This makes one think, and also puts things in perspective:
Diet Snapple 16 oz $1.29 ...... $10.32 per gallon
Lipton Ice Tea 16 oz $1.19 .... $9.52 per gallon
Gatorade 20 oz $1.59 ...... $10.17 per gallon
Ocean Spray 16 oz $1.25 ...... $10.00 per gallon
Brake Fluid 12 oz $3.15 ...... $33.60 per gallon
Vick's Nyquil 6 oz $8.35 ...... $178.13 per gallon
Pepto Bismol 4 oz $3.85 ...... $123.20 per gallon
Whiteout 7 oz $1.39 ...... $25.42 per gallon
Scope 1.5 oz $0.99 ...... $84.48 per gallon

THE LETTER

A father passing by his son's bedroom was astonished to see the bed was nicely made and everything was picked up. Then he saw an envelope propped up prominently on the center of the bed. It was addressed, "Dad." With the worst premonition, he opened the envelope and read the letter with trembling hands:

Dear Dad,

It is with great regret and sorrow that I'm writing you. I had to elope with my new girlfriend because I wanted to avoid a scene with mom and you. I've been finding real passion with Joan and she is so nice -- even with all her piercing, tattoos, and her tight motorcycle clothes.

But it's not only the passion Dad, she's pregnant and Joan said that we will be very happy. Even though you don't care for her as she is so much older than I, she already owns a trailer in the woods and has a stack of firewood for the whole winter.

She wants to have many more children with me and that's now one of my dreams too.

Joan taught me that marijuana doesn't really hurt anyone and we'll be growing it for us and trading it with her friends for all the cocaine and ecstasy we want.

In the meantime, we'll pray that science will find a cure for AIDS so Joan can get better; she sure deserves it!!

Don't worry Dad, I'm 15 years old now and I know how to take care of myself. Someday I'm sure we'll be back to visit so you can get to know your grandchildren.

Your son,
John

P.S. Dad, none of the above is true. I'm over at the neighbor's house. I just wanted to remind you that there are worse things in life than the report card that's under my pillow. I really love you Dad, Please call when it is safe for me to come home.

GETTING SHOT FOR PIERCED EARS

The students in a third grade class were bombarding their teacher with questions about her newly pierced ears. "Does the hole go all the way through?"

"Yes."

"Did it hurt?"

"Just a little."

"Did they stick a needle through your ears?"

"No, they used a special gun."

Silence followed, and then one solemn voice called out, "How far away did they stand?"

And this is the REAL KICKER:

Evian water 9 oz $1.49..........$21.19 per gallon?! $21.19 for WATER - and the buyers don't even know the source. (Evian spelled backwards is Naive.)

So, the next time you're at the pump, be glad your car doesn't run on water, Scope, or Whiteout, or God forbid, Pepto Bismol or Nyquil.

(Editor's note: this submission was just a little humor to help ease the pain of your next trip to the pump. If your prices are different, please don't write us).

PREGNANCY QUESTIONS & ANSWERS!

Q: Should I have a baby after 35?
A: No, 35 children is enough.
Q: I'm two months pregnant now. When will my baby move?
A: With any luck, right after he finishes college.
Q: What is the most reliable method to determine a baby's sex?
A: Childbirth.
Q: My wife is five months pregnant and so moody that sometimes she's borderline irrational.
A: So what's your question?
Q: My childbirth instructor says it's not pain I'll feel during labor, but pressure. Is she right?!
A: Yes, in the same way that a tornado might be called an air current.
Q: When is the best time to get an epidermal?
A: Right after you find out you're pregnant.
Q: Is there any reason I have to be in the delivery room while my wife is in labor?
A: Not unless the word "alimony" means anything to you.
Q: Is there anything I should avoid while recovering from childbirth?
A: Yes, pregnancy.
Q: Do I have to have a baby shower?
A: Not if you change the baby's diaper very quickly.
Q: Our baby was born last week. When will my wife begin to feel and act normal! again?
A: When the kids are in college.

10 WAYS TO KNOW IF YOU HAVE "ESTROGEN ISSUES"

1. Everyone around you has an attitude problem.
2. You're adding chocolate chips to your cheese omelet
3 The dryer has shrunk every last pair of your jeans.
4. Your husband is suddenly agreeing to everything you say.
5. You're using your cellular phone to dial up every bumper sticker that says: "How's my driving-call 1- 800-"
6. Everyone's head looks like an invitation to batting practice.
7. Everyone seems to have just landed here from "outer space."
8. You can't believe they don't make feminine protection bigger than Super Plus.

9. You're sure that everyone is scheming to drive you crazy.
10. The ibuprofen bottle is empty and you bought it yesterday.

TOP TEN THINGS ONLY WOMEN UNDERSTAND
10. Cats' facial expressions.
9. The need for the same style of shoes in different colors.
8. Why bean sprouts aren't just weeds.
7. Fat clothes.
6. Taking a car trip without trying to beat your best time.
5. The difference between beige, ecru, cream, off-white, and eggshell.
4. Cutting your hair to make it grow.
3. Eyelash curlers.
2. The inaccuracy of every bathroom scale ever made.
AND, the Number One Number One thing only women understand:
OTHER WOMEN

ASKING GOD FOR A MIRACLE

A man walking along a California beach was deep in prayer. Suddenly the sky clouded above his head and in a booming voice the Lord said, "Because you have TRIED to be faithful to me in all ways, I will grant you one wish."

The man said, "Build a bridge to Hawaii so I can drive over anytime I want."

The Lord said, "Your request is very materialistic. Think of the enormous challenges for that kind of undertaking. The supports required to reach the bottom of the Pacific! The concrete and steel it would take! It will nearly exhaust several natural resources. I can do it, but it is hard for me to justify your desire for worldly things. Take a little more time and think of something that would honor and glorify me."

The man thought about it for a long time. Finally he said, "Lord, I wish that I could understand my wife - I want to know how she feels inside, what she's thinking when she gives me the silent treatment, why she cries, what she means when she says 'nothing's wrong', and how I can make a woman truly happy."

The Lord replied..."You want two lanes or four on that bridge?"

NOT JUST A MEDICAL CONDITION

A man went to visit his doctor. "Doctor, my arm hurts bad. Can you check it out please?" the man pleads.

The doctor rolls up the man's sleeve and suddenly hears the arm talk ... "Hello Doctor, could you lend me twenty bucks please? I'm desperate," the arm says.

The doctor says, "Aha! I see the problem. Your arm is broke!"

THE ALL-IN-ONE

While shopping for vacation clothes, my husband and I passed a display of bathing suits. It had been at least ten years and twenty pounds since I had even considered buying a bathing suit, so I sought my husband's advice.

"What do you think?" I asked. "Should I get a bikini or an all-in-one?"

"Better get a bikini," he replied. "You'd never get it all in one."

HEARING PROBLEM

An elderly gentleman had serious hearing problems for a number of years. He went to the doctor and the doctor was able to have him fitted for a set of hearing aids that allowed the gentleman to hear 100%.

The elderly gentleman went back in a month to the doctor and the doctor said, "Your hearing is perfect. Your family must be really pleased that you can hear again."

The gentleman replied, "Oh, I haven't told my family yet. I just sit around and listen to the conversations. I've changed my will three times!"

NEW HOME

When Little Johnny's family moved into a new double wide trailer one of their former neighbors dropped by. Seeing Johnny out front, he asked, "So, how do you like your new place?"

"It's terrific," Little Johnny answered. "I have my own room, my brother has his own room, and my sister has her own room. But poor Mom still has to share a room with Dad."

CEREMONY

Ken and Meg had finished their breakfast at the retirement home and were relaxing in the library.

"You know," said Meg, "today, in most marriage ceremonies, they don't do them like they used to. For instance, they don't use the word 'obey' anymore."

"Too bad, isn't it?" retorted Ken. "It used to lend a little humor to the occasion."

WHAT DOES LOVE MEAN?

- When my grandma got arthritis, she couldn't bend over and paint her toenails anymore. So my grandpa does it for her now all the time, even when his hands got arthritis too. That's love. - Rebecca - age 8
- When someone loves you, the way they say your name is different. You just know that your name is safe in their mouths. - Billy - age 4
- Love is when a girl puts on perfume and a boy puts on shaving Cologne and

they go out and smell each other. - Kari - age 5
- Love is when you go out to eat and give somebody most of your French Fries without making them give you any of theirs. - Chrissy - age 6
- Love is what makes you smile when you're tired. - Terri - age 4
- Love is when my mommy makes coffee for my daddy and she takes a sip giving it to him, to make sure the taste is OK. - Danny - age 7
- Love is when you kiss all the time. Then when you get tired of kissing, you still want to be together and you talk more. My mommy and daddy are like that.. They look gross when they kiss. - Emily - age 8
- Love is what's in the room with you at Christmas if you stop opening presents and listen. - Bobby - age 7 (wow!)
- If you want to learn to love better, you should start with a friend who you hate. - Nikka - age 6
- Love is when you tell a guy you like his shirt, then he wears it everyday. - Noelle - age 7
- Love is like a little old woman and a little old man who are still friends even after they know each other so well. - Tommy - age 6
- My mommy loves me more than anybody. You don't see anyone else kissing me to sleep at night. Clare - age 6

CHECKING ACCOUNT
Jim's beautiful, blonde wife was having trouble mastering the fine points of balancing the checking account.
"The bank returned the check you wrote to the department store," he said.
"Good," she replied. "Now I can use it to buy something else.

LATE FOR WORK
"How come you're late?" asked the bartender, as the waitress walked into the bar.

"It was awful," she explained. "I was walking down Elm street and there was a terrible accident. A man was thrown from his car and he was lying in the middle of the street. His leg was broken, his skull was fractured, and there was blood everywhere. Thank God I took that first-aid course."

"What did you do?" asked the bartender.

"I sat down and put my head between my knees to keep from fainting!"

NAW, HE "WOODEN" DO THAT!
A man with a nagging secret couldn't keep it any longer. He went to Church and in the confessional he admitted that for years he had been stealing building supplies from the lumberyard where he worked.

"How much material did you take?" his priest asked.

"Enough to build my own house, and enough for my son's house, and houses for our two daughters and our cottage at the lake."

"This is very serious," the priest said. "I shall have to think of a far-reaching penance. Have you ever done a retreat?"

"No, Father, I haven't," the man replied. "But if you can get the plans, I can get the lumber."

"I FEEL LIKE..."

Two elderly gentlemen from a retirement center were sitting on a bench under a tree when one turns to the other and says . . . "Jim, I'm 83 years old now and I'm just full of aches and pains. I know you're about my age. How do you feel?"

Jim says, "I feel just like a newborn baby."

"Really!? Like a new-born baby!?"

"Yep. No hair, no teeth, and I think I just wet my pants."

BOSS AND EMPLOYEE

The boss called one of his employees into the office. "Rob," he said, "you've been with the company for a year. You started off in the post room, one week later you were promoted to a sales position, and one month after that you were promoted to district manager of the sales department. Just four short months later, you were promoted to vice-chairman. Now it's time for me to retire, and I want you to take over the company. What do you say to that?"

"Thanks," said the employee.

"Thanks?" the boss replied. "Is that all you can say?"

"I suppose not," the employee said. "Thanks, Dad."

THE OBEDIENT WIFE

There was a man who had worked all of his life, had saved all of his money, and was a real miser when it came to his money. Just before he died, he said to his wife, "When I die, I want you to take all my money and put it in the casket with me. I want to take my money to the afterlife with me."

And so he got his wife to promise him with all of her heart that when he died, she would put all of the money in the casket with him. Well, he died. He was stretched out in the casket, his wife was sitting there in black, and her friend was sitting next to her. When they finished the ceremony, just before the undertakers got ready to close the casket, the wife said, "Wait just a minute!"

She had a box with her; she came over with the box and put it in the casket. Then the undertakers locked the casket down, and they rolled it away.

So her friend said, "Girl, I know you weren't foolish enough to put all that money in there with your husband."

The loyal wife replied, "Listen, I'm a Christian; I can't go back on my word. I promised him that I was going to put that money in that casket with him."

"You mean to tell me you put that money in the casket with him!!!!?"

"I sure did," said the wife. "I got it all together, put it into my account and wrote him a check. If he can cash it, he can spend it."

FRUIT CASE

I was examining cantaloupes at the grocery store and turned to the produce clerk, who was refilling the bins. "Choosing a cantaloupe is like picking a mate for marriage," I observed casually. "A person has no idea what he's getting until it's too late."

"I know," the clerk replied. "I've had three cantaloupes."

AUNT EMMA

A couple's happily married life almost went on the rocks because of the presence in their household of old Aunt Emma. For seventeen long years she lived with them, always crotchety, always demanding. Eventually, the old girl passed away.

On the way back from the cemetery, the husband confesses to his wife, "Darling, if I didn't love you so much, I don't think I would have put up with having your Aunt Emma in our house all those years!"

His wife looked at him aghast. "Huh? My Aunt Emma!?" she cried. "I thought she was *your* Aunt Emma!"

BALANCING CHECKBOOK

My accountant father and my artist mother have very different views on balancing a checkbook. Mom usually kept the checkbook, but when Dad retired, he took over all the financial duties. He was really taken aback when he looked over the checkbook and found only dollar amounts recorded. It seems Mom hadn't wanted to deal with any more math than she had to, so she'd eliminated the cents from every check. She'd round up if the partial dollar amounts were 50 cents or more and drop those under 50 cents. Dad feverishly went through stacks of canceled checks and registers, trying to correct her method. The difference in seven years of dollars only? ... Sixteen cents...

JUST RELAX!

A fellow computer programmer for a consulting group had designed some software for one of our largest accounts. He asked my help in putting it into operation. At first, he handled most of the work. Eventually, though, he asked me to help with the last phase of the training. When I sat down with one woman and told her I would be showing her how to make changes to the files, she sighed with relief. "I'm so glad you're teaching me instead of him."

Surprised, I said that my colleague was far more experienced than I was.

"Yes," she said, "but I feel much more comfortable with you. I get nervous around really smart people."

THE COST OF VANITY
In George Washington's days, there were no cameras. One's image was either sculpted or painted. Some paintings of George Washington showed him standing behind a desk with one arm behind his back, while others showed both legs and both arms. Prices charged by painters were not based on how many people were to be painted, but by how many limbs were to be painted. Arms and legs are "limbs" therefore, painting them would cost the buyer more. Hence the expression . . . "Okay, but it'll cost you an arm and a leg."

THAT'S HOW IT GOES ...
The Postal Service honored legendary Secretariat with his own stamp. That shows you how strange life is for race-horses. You win the race, you wind up on the front of a stamp. Lose a race, you wind up on the back.

"MEOW! WOOF!"
I was at a yard sale one day and saw a box marked "Electronic cat and dog caller-- guaranteed to work." I looked inside and was amused to see... ...an electric can opener!

A PUSH
A man and his wife are awakened at 3 o'clock in the morning by a loud pounding on the door. The man gets up and goes to the door where a drunken stranger, standing in the pouring rain, is asking for a push.

"Not a chance," says the husband, "it is 3 o'clock in the morning! He slams the door and returns to bed.

"Who was that?" asked his wife.

"Just some drunk guy asking for a push," he answers.

"Did you help him?" she asks.

"No, I did not, it is 3 o'clock in the morning and it is pouring out there!"

"Well, you have a short memory," says his wife. "Can't you remember about three months ago when we broke down, and those two guys helped us? I think you should help him, and you should be ashamed of yourself!"

The man does as he is told, gets dressed, and goes out into the pounding rain. He calls out into the dark, "Hello, are you still there?"

"Yes" comes back the answer.

"Do you still need a push?" calls out the husband.

"Yes, please!" comes the reply from the dark.

"Where are you?" asks the husband.

"Over here on the swing!" replies the drunk.

TWO THINGS NAVY SEALS ARE ALWAYS TAUGHT:
1. Keep your priorities in order
2. Know when to act without hesitation

A college professor, an avowed atheist and active in the ACLU, was teaching his class. He shocked several of his students when he flatly stated that for once and for all he was going to prove there was no God.

Addressing the ceiling he shouted, "GOD, if you are real, then I want you to knock me off this platform. I'll give you exactly 15 minutes!"

The lecture room fell silent. You could hear a pin drop. Ten minutes went by.

"I'm waiting God, if you're real, knock me off this platform!"

Again after a few more minutes, the professor taunted God saying, "Here I am, God! I'm still waiting!"

His count down got down to the last couple of minutes when a NAVY SEAL, just released from the Navy after serving in Afghanistan and Iraq and newly registered in the class, walked up to the Professor.

The SEAL hit him full force in the face, and sent the Professor tumbling from his lofty platform. The Professor was out cold! The students were stunned and shocked. They began to babble in confusion. The SEAL nonchalantly took his seat in the front row and sat silent. The class looked at him and fell silent ... waiting. Eventually, the professor came to and was noticeably shaken. He looked at the SEAL in the front row.

When the professor regained his senses and could speak he asked, "What the heck is the matter with you?! Why did you do that?!"

"God was really busy protecting America's soldiers, who are protecting your right to say stupid stuff and act like a fool! So he sent me!"

GET MY CAR STARTED
Jill was out driving her car and while stopped at a red light, the car just died. It was a busy intersection and the traffic behind her starting growing. The guy in the car directly behind her started honking his horn continuously as Jill continued to try getting the car to start up again. Finally Jill gets out of her car and approaches the guy in the car behind her. "I can't seem to get my car started," Jill said, smiling. "Would you be a sweetheart and go and see if you can get it started for me. I'll stay here in your car and lean on your horn for you."

PRESSING THE BELL
Passing an office building late one night, a lady in Tacoma saw a sign that said, "Press bell for night watchman."

She did so, and after several minutes she heard the watchman clomping down the stairs. The uniformed man proceeded to unlock first one gate, then another, shut down the alarm system, and finally made his way through the revolving door.

"Well," he snarled at the lady, "what do you want?"

"I just want to know why you can't ring the bell for yourself?"

ALLIGATOR'S TEETH
A tourist was admiring the necklace worn by a local Indian. "What is it made of?" she asked.

"Alligator's teeth," the Indian replied. "I suppose," she said patronizingly, "that they mean as much to you as pearls do to us."

"Oh no," he objected. "Anybody can open an oyster."

CAMPING
A loaded mini van pulled in to the only remaining campsite. Four children leaped from the vehicle and began feverishly unloading gear and setting up the tent. The boys rushed to gather firewood, while the girls and their mother set up the camp stove and cooking utensils.

A nearby camper marveled to the youngsters' father, "That, sir, is some display of teamwork."

The father replied, "I have a system; no one goes to the bathroom until the camp is set up."

KING OF THE BAR-B-QUE
It's the only type of cooking a "real" man will do. When a man volunteers to do such cooking, the following chain of events is put into motion:
1. The woman goes to the store.
2. The woman "fixes" the salad, vegetables, and dessert.
3. The woman prepares the meat for cooking, places it on a tray along with the necessary cooking utensils, and takes it to the man, lounging beside the grill.
4. The man places the meat on the grill.
5. The woman goes inside to set the table and check the vegetables.
6. The woman comes out to tell the man that the meat is burning.
7. The man takes the meat off the grill and hands it to the woman.
8. The woman prepares the plates and brings them to the table.
9. After eating, the woman clears the table and does the dishes.

10. The man asks the woman how she enjoyed "her night off."
And, upon seeing her annoyed reaction, concludes that there's just no pleasing some women.

HOW TO KEEP YOUR SANITY

Mary Simpson was almost crazy with her three kids. She complained to her best friend, "They're driving me nuts. Such pests, they give me no rest and I'm half-way to the nut hatch."

"What you need is a playpen to separate the kids from yourself," her friend said.

So Mary bought a playpen. A few days later, her friend called to ask how things were going.

"Superb! I can't believe it," Mary said. "I get in that playpen with a good book and the kids don't bother me one bit!"

THE WORKOUT

The Doctor told me I should start an exercise program. I decided to:
- Beat around the bush
- Jump to conclusions
- Climb the walls
- Wade through the morning paper
- Drag my heels
- Push my luck
- Make mountains out of mole hills
- Hit the nail on the head
- Bend over backwards
- Jump on the band wagon
- Run around in circles
- Toot my own horn
- Pull out all the stops
- Add fuel to the fire
- Open a can of worms
- Put my foot in my mouth
- Start the ball rolling
- Go over the edge
- Pick up the pieces
- Kneel in prayer
- Bow my head in thanksgiving
- Uplift my hands in praise
- Hug someone and encourage them
- What a Workout! Rest At Last.

PLEA

After a trial had been going on for three days, Smith, the man accused of committing the crimes, stood up and approached the judge's bench. "Your Honor, I would like to change my plea from 'innocent' to 'guilty' of the charges."

The judge angrily banged his fist on the desk. "If you're guilty, why didn't you say so in the first place and save this court a lot of time and inconvenience?" he demanded.

Smith looked up wide-eyed and stated, "Well, when the trial started I thought I was innocent, but that was before I heard all the evidence against me."

HOW TO EAT STRAWBERRIES

A farmer was driving along the road with a load of fertilizer. A child playing in front of his house saw him and called, "What are you hauling?"

"Fertilizer," the farmer replied.

"What are you going to do with it?" asked the child.

"Put it on strawberries," answered the farmer.

"You ought to live here," the child advised him. "We put sugar and cream on them."

Great Truths About Life That Little Children Have Learned

1. No matter how hard you try, you can't baptize cats.
2. When your mom is mad at your dad, don't let her brush your hair.
3. If your sister hits you, don't hit back. They always catch the second person.
4. Never ask your 3 year-old brother to hold a tomato.
5. You can't trust dogs to watch your food.
6. Reading what people write on desks can teach you a lot.
7. Don't sneeze when someone is cutting your hair.
8. Puppies still have bad breath even after eating a breath mint.
9. Never hold a vacuum and a cat at the same time.
10. School lunches stick to the wall.
11. You can't hide a piece of broccoli in a glass of milk.
12. Don't wear polka-dot underwear under white shorts - no matter how cute the underwear is.

Did you hear about the crook who stole the calendar? He got 12 months.

HANDWRITING

In school one day, a teacher asked my six-year-old son why his handwriting wasn't as neat as it usually was.

"I'm trying out a new font," he explained.

"Remember, once you get over the hill, you'll begin to pick up speed."

DEAR LORD
A visiting minister waxed eloquent during the offertory prayer. "Dear Lord," he began with arms extended and a rapturous look on his upturned face, "without you we are but dust..." He would have continued but at that moment my very obedient daughter (who was listening carefully for a change!) leaned over to me and asked quite audibly in her shrill little girl voice, "Mom, what is butt dust?"

TALK IS CHEAP
A New Yorker was forced to take a day off from work to appear for a minor traffic summons. He grew increasingly restless as he waited hour after endless hour for his case to be heard. When his name was called late in the afternoon, he stood before the judge, only to hear that court would be adjourned for the rest of the afternoon and he would have to return the next day. "What for?!?!?" he snapped at the judge. His honor, equally irked by a tedious day and sharp query, roared out loud: "Twenty dollars contempt of court! That's why!" Then, noticing the man checking his wallet, the judge relented: "That's all right. You don't have to pay now." The young man replied, "I know. But I'm just seeing if I have enough for two more words."

BUYING STAMPS
There she stood in the line at the post office, a line that wound its way almost out the front door.

A fellow customer spoke to the elderly lady waiting to buy some stamps, "Ma'am, you must be very tired. Did you know there's a stamp machine over there in the corner?" He pointed to the machine built into the wall.

"Why yes, thank you," the lady replied, "but I'll just wait here a little while longer. I'm getting close to the window."

The customer became insistent. "But it would be so much easier for you to avoid this long line and buy your stamps from the machine."

The woman patted him on the arm and answered, "Oh, I know. But that old machine would never ask me how my grandchildren are doing."

THE DOG
The delivery man looked over the gate towards the house which was his package's destination, and saw a large and aggressive-looking dog on the lawn, staring at him. There was also a woman looking at him from an open first-floor window. He shouted to the woman, "Is your dog friendly?"

She said, "Yes." So the delivery man opened the gate, and was promptly savaged by the dog. When he had been rescued from the dog, the delivery man angrily said to the woman, "I thought you said your dog was friendly!"

"He is," said the woman, "but that's not my dog."

SENIOR DRIVING

As a senior citizen was driving down the freeway, his car phone rang. Answering, he heard his wife's voice urgently warning him, "Herman, I just heard on the news that there's a car going the wrong way on 280 Interstate. Please be careful!"

"It's not just one car," said Herman. "It's hundreds of them!"

GOLF - SENIOR STYLE

"How was your golf game, dear?" asked Jack's wife, Tracy.

"Well, I was hitting pretty well, but my eyesight's gotten so bad I couldn't see where the ball went."

"But you're seventy-five years old, Jack!" admonished his wife, "Why don't you take my brother Scott along?"

"But he's eighty-five and doesn't even play golf anymore," protested Jack.

"But he's got perfect eyesight. He could watch your ball," Tracy pointed out.

The next day Jack teed off with Scott looking on. Jack swung, and the ball disappeared down the middle of the fairway. "Do you see it?" asked Jack.

"Yup," Scott answered.

"Well, where is it?" yelled Jack, peering off into the distance.

"I forgot."

DISASTER

One afternoon a man came home from work to find total mayhem in his house. His three children were outside, still in their pajamas, playing in the mud, with empty food boxes and wrappers strewn all around the front yard. The door of his wife's car was open, as was the front door to the house. Proceeding into the entry, he found an even bigger mess. A lamp had been knocked over, and the throw rug was wadded against one wall. In the front room the TV was loudly blaring a cartoon channel, and the family room was strewn with toys and various items of clothing. In the kitchen, dishes filled the sink, breakfast food was spilled on the counter, dog food was spilled on the floor, a broken glass lay under the table, and a small pile of sand was spread by the back door.

He quickly headed up the stairs, stepping over toys and more piles of clothes, looking for his wife. He was worried she may be ill, or that something serious had happened. He found her lounging in the bedroom, still curled in the bed in her pajamas, reading a novel.

She looked up at him, smiled, and asked how his day went.

He looked at her bewildered and asked, "What happened here today?"

She again smiled and answered, "You know every day when you come home from work and ask me what in the world did I do today?"

"Yes," was his incredulous reply.

She answered, "Well, today I didn't do it."

TOO MUCH COMPUTER

While getting dressed one morning, I decided I'd been spending too much time on the computer, when I caught myself checking the lower right corner of my makeup mirror to see what time it was.

TREND-SETTER

They say imitation is the sincerest form of flattery. As a plumber, I'm delighted to see all these teenagers wearing low-rider jeans.

NOT WELL READ

There was a history professor and a psychology professor sitting on a deck at a nudist colony. The history professor asked the psychology professor, "Have you read Marx?"

The psychology professor replied, "Yes, I think it's from the wicker chairs."

CROSSING THE RIVER

Three men were hiking through a forest when they came upon a large, raging violent river. Needing to get on the other side, the first man prayed, "Lord, please give me the strength to cross the river."

Poof! Lord gave him big arms and strong legs and he was able to swim across in about 2 hours, having almost drowned twice.

After witnessing that, the second man prayed, "Lord, please give me strength and the tools to cross the river."

Poof! Lord gave him a rowboat and strong arms and strong legs and he was able to row across in about an hour after almost capsizing once.

Seeing what happened to the first two men, the third man prayed, "Lord, please give me the strength, the tools and the intelligence to cross this river."

Poof! He was turned into a woman. She checked the map, hiked one hundred yards up stream and walked across the bridge.

She wanted a puppy. I didn't want a puppy. We compromised and got a puppy.

DO YOU KNOW YOUR JUDGMENT DAY?

Fellow 1 : "Now my grandfather, he knew the exact day of the year that he was going to die. It was the right year too. Not only that, but he knew what time he would die that day, and he was right about that, too."

Fellow 2 : "Wow, that's Incredible. How did he know all of that?"

Fellow 1 : "A judge told him."

REALLY ABSENT!

The local high school has a policy that the parents must call the school if a student is to be absent for the day. Alice decided to skip school and go to the mall with her friends. So she waited until her parents had left for work and called the school herself.

"Hi, I'm calling to report that Alice is unable to make it to school today because she is ill."

Secretary at high school answered, "I'm sorry to hear that. I'll note her absence. Who is this calling please?"

"This is my mother."

LIFE'S A BEACH

A bedouin wandering in the Sahara happened upon an American dressed in a bathing suit, flip-flops, a big, over-sized t-shirt and sunglasses. The Bedouin gazed at him in amazement, "What are you doing all the way out here dressed like that!?"

"I'm going swimming," the tourist explained.

"But the ocean is eight hundred miles away," the Arab informed him.

"Eight hundred miles!" the American exclaimed with a whistle of appreciation. "Boy, what a beach!"

TRUE CRIMES

My wife has not spoken to me in three days. I think it has something to do with what happened on Sunday night when she thought she heard a noise downstairs. She nudged me and whispered, "Wake up, wake up!"

"What's the matter?" I asked.

"There are burglars in the kitchen. I think they're eating the tuna casserole I made tonight."

"That'll teach them!" I replied.

WORSE YET ...

It was a full auditorium. Halfway through the author's talk, she began to feel sick. In a calm voice, she announced that she had left a few pages of her speech offstage, in her bag. She walked off slowly and, as soon as she was out of sight, ran to the bathroom where she immediately threw up. She was just about finished when someone came into the bathroom to tell her that her lapel mike was still on.

- 42.7% OF ALL STATISTICS ... are made up on the spot.

- I'D KILL ... for a Nobel Peace Prize.

- IF YOU WANT THE RAINBOW ... you gotta put up with the rain

The world tongue-twister champion just got arrested. I hear they're going to give him a really tough sentence.

DIET, SCHMIET!

My friend and I joined a weight-loss organization. At one meeting the instructor held up an apple and a candy bar. "What are the attributes of this apple," she asked, "and how do they relate to our diet?"

"Low in calories" and "lots of fiber," were among the answers.

She then detailed what was wrong with eating candy, and concluded, "Apples are not only more healthful but also less expensive. Do you know I paid fifty-five cents for this candy bar?"

We stared as she held aloft the forbidden treat. From in back of the room a small voice spoke up. "I'll give you seventy-five cents for it."

Ole's Obituary

OLE DIED. So Lena went to the local paper to put a notice in the obituaries. The gentleman at the counter, after offering his condolences, asked Lena what she would like to say about Ole.

Lena replied, "You yust put 'Ole died'."

The gentleman, somewhat perplexed, said, "That's it? Just 'Ole died.'? Surely, there must be something more you'd like to say about Ole... If it's money you're concerned about, the first five words are free. We must say something more."

So Lena pondered for a few minutes and finally said, "O.K. You put 'Ole died. Boat for sale.'"

Ole Checks Da Turn Signals

LARS SAY TO OLE: "Ole, stant in front of my car and tell me if da turn signals are vorking."

OLE: "Yes, No, Yes, No, Yes, No, Yes, No..."

Lena Calls Da Airlines

LENA CALLED the airlines information desk and inquired, "How long does it take to fly from Minneapolis to Fargo?"

The clerk, who was busy with another customer answered, "Yust a minute."

"Vell," said Lena, "if it has to go DAT fast, I tink I'll yust take da bus."

Ole and Lars' Take The Train

OLE AND LARS were on their very first train ride. They had brought along bananas for lunch. Just as they began to peel them, the train entered a long, dark tunnel.

"Lars! Haff you eaten your banana yet?" Ole asked excitedly.

"No," replied Lars.

"Vell, don't touch it den," Ole exclaimed."I yust took vun bite and vent blind!"

Ole and Lena

OLE BOUGHT LENA a piano for her birthday. A few weeks later, Lars inquired how she was doing with it.

"Oh," said Ole, "I persuaded her to svitch to da clarinet."

"How come you do dat?" asked Lars.

"Vell," Ole answered, "because vith a clarinet she can't sing!"

Ole and Sven

"HEY, SVEN," said Ole. "How many Swedes does it take to grease a combine?"

After Sven replied, "I don't know."

Ole said, "Only two, if you run dem through real slow."

Ole and Lena at Da Olympics

OLE AND LENA went to the Olympics. While sitting on a bench a lady turned to Ole and said, "Are you a pole vaulter?"
Ole said, "No, I'm Norvegian and my name isn't Valter."

Lars Asks Ole

LARS THE BARTENDER asked Ole, "Do ya know da difference between a Norvegian and a canoe?"

"No, I don't," said Ole. Lars snarled,

"....Even a canoe will sometimes tip!"

Cheap Ole

OLE IS SO CHEAP that after his airplane landed safely he grumbled, "Vell, DERE gose five dollars down da drain for dat flight insurance!"

Lena Divorces Ole

THE JUDGE had just awarded a divorce to Lena, who had charged her husband Ole with non-support.

He said to Ole, "I have decided to give your wife $400 a month for support."

"Vell, dat's fine, Judge," said Ole. "And vunce in a while I'll try to chip in a few bucks, myself."

THREE TOURISTS AT BIG BEN

Three tourists climbed up the tower at London's Big Ben and decided to throw their watches off the top, run down the stairs and try to catch them before they hit the ground.

The first tourist threw his watch but heard it crash before he had taken three steps.

The second threw his watch and made only two steps before hearing his watch shatter.

The third tourist threw his watch off the tower, went down the stairs, bought a snack at a shop up the street and walked slowly back to Big Ben in time to catch the watch."

How did you do that?" asked one of his friends.

"My watch is 30 minutes slow."

HALF OF THE PEOPLE YOU KNOW ... are below average.

99% OF LAWYERS ... give the rest a bad name.

TWO NORWEGIAN HUNTERS

Two Norwegian hunters from Minnesota got a pilot to fly them to Canada to hunt moose. They bagged six good sized bulls, and as they started loading the plane for the return trip, the pilot said the plane could take only four moose.

The two lads objected strongly. "Last year ve shot six of deez and da pilot let us put dem all on board; he had da same plane as yours."

Reluctantly, the pilot gave in and all six were loaded. However, even on full power, the little plane couldn't handle the load and went down in the field beyond the runway a few moments after
take-off.

Climbing out of the wreck, one Norski asked the other, "You got any idea vere ve are?"

"Yaaah.." says the other, "... I tink we's pretty close to where we crashed last year."

Bernie in the Hospital

Bernie was unfortunate enough to be hit by a truck and ended up in the hospital. His best friend Morris came to visit him. Bernie struggles to tell Morris, "My wife Sadie visits me three times a day. She's so good to me. Every day, she reads to me at the bedside."

"What does she read?" asks Morris.

"My life insurance policy."

CAPTAIN

Although this married couple enjoyed their new fishing boat together, it was the husband who was behind the wheel operating the boat. He was concerned about what might happen in an emergency.

So one day out on the lake he said to his wife, "Please take the wheel, dear. Pretend that I am having a heart attack. You must get the boat safely to shore and dock it."

So she drove the boat to shore. Later that evening, the wife walked into the living room where her husband was watching television. She sat down next to him, switched the TV channel, and said to him, "Please go into the kitchen, dear. Pretend I'm having a heart attack and set the table, cook dinner and wash the dishes."

YOU KNOW IT'S TIME TO DIET WHEN . . .

. . . you dance and it makes the band skip.
. . . you are diagnosed with the flesh eating virus, and the doctor
  gives you 22 more years to live.
. . . you put mayonnaise on an aspirin.
. . . you go to the zoo and the elephants throw you peanuts.
. . . your driver's license says, "Picture continued on other side."
. . . you ran away and they had to use all four sides of the milk
  carton for your picture.
. . . you learn you were born with a silver shovel in your mouth.
. . . you could sell shade.
. . . your blood type is Ragu.
. . . you need an appointment to attend an 'open house'.
. . . The buttons on your shirts are declared legal weapons.
. . . You go to Sam's Tent and Awning for custom fit clothing.

PRISON and WORK
Just In Case You Ever Get These Two Environments Mixed Up, This Should Make Things A Little Bit More Clear.

• IN PRISON you spend the majority of your time in an 10X10 cell; AT WORK you spend the majority of your time in an 8X8 cubicle.
• IN PRISON you get three meals a day; AT WORK you get a break for one meal and you have to pay for it.
• IN PRISON you get time off for good behavior; AT WORK you get more work for good behavior.
• IN PRISON the guard locks and unlocks all the doors for you; AT WORK you must often carry a security card and open all the doors for yourself.
• IN PRISON you can watch TV and play games; AT WORK you could get fired for watching TV and playing games.
• IN PRISON you get your own toilet; AT WORK you have to share the toilet with some people who pee on
the seat.
• IN PRISON they allow your family and friends to visit; AT WORK you aren't even supposed to speak to your family.
• IN PRISON all expenses are paid by the taxpayers with no work required; AT WORK you get to pay all your expenses to go to work, and they deduct taxes from your salary to pay for prisoners.
• IN PRISON you spend most of your life inside bars wanting to get out; AT WORK you spend most of your time wanting to get out and go inside bars.
• IN PRISON you must deal with sadistic wardens; AT WORK they are called managers.
(This was just for fun. Please don't write or call to complain).

A TELEPHONE RANG.
"Hello! Is your phone number 444-4444?"
"Yes, it is," came the reply.
"Thank God! Could you call 911 for me? I super-glued my finger to the phone."

SENILITY PRAYER:
God grant me the senility to forget the people I never liked anyway, the good fortune to run into the ones I do, And the eyesight to tell the difference.

GO FOR A RIDE!
At The Boeing Museum of Flight in Seattle, there is a full size mockup of an F/A-18 fighter. A ramp allows visitors to climb into the cockpit and get a sense of what the pilot sees and feels. A guide at the top of the ramp points out the

various controls and gauges in the cockpit and gives information about the aircraft's capabilities to each visitor who gets in.

When my two-year-old son sat down in the plane, he seemed fascinated by all he saw and heard. Then, he looked out at us and said, "Gramma, could I have a quarter?"

THE BIG TEST

Jesus and Satan were having an on-going argument about who was better on the computer. They had been going at it for days, and frankly God was tired of hearing all the bickering.
Finally fed up, God said, "THAT'S IT! I have had enough. I am going to set up a test that will run for two hours, and from those results, I will judge who does the better job."

So Satan and Jesus sat down at the keyboards and typed away. They moused. They faxed. They e-mailed. They e-mailed with attachments. They downloaded. They did spreadsheets! They wrote reports. They created labels and cards. They created charts and graphs. They did some genealogy reports. They did every job known to man.
Jesus worked with heavenly efficiency and Satan was faster than (heck). Then, ten minutes before their time was up, lightning suddenly flashed across the sky, thunder rolled, rain poured, and, of course, the power went off.
Satan stared at his blank screen and screamed every curse word known in the underworld. Jesus just sighed. Finally the electricity came back on, and each of them restarted their computers.
Satan started searching frantically, screaming "It's gone! It's all GONE! I lost everything when the power went out!"
Meanwhile, Jesus quietly started printing out all of his files from the past two hours of work.
Satan observed this and became irate. "Wait!" he screamed. "That's not fair! He cheated! How come he has all his work and I don't have any?"

God just shrugged and said, "JESUS SAVES."

7 AMAZINGLY SIMPLE HOME REMEDIES

1. If you are choking on an ice cube, don't panic. Simply pour a cup of boiling water down your throat and presto! The blockage will be almost instantly removed.
2. Clumsy? Avoid cutting yourself while slicing vegetables by getting someone else to hold them while you chop away.
3. Avoid arguments with the Mrs. about lifting the toilet seat by simply using the sink.

4. For high blood pressure sufferers: simply cut yourself and bleed for a few minutes, thus reducing the pressure in your veins. Important: Remember to use a timer.

5. A mouse trap, placed on top of your alarm clock, will prevent you from rolling over and going back to sleep after you hit the snooze button.

6. If you have a bad cough, take a large dose of laxatives, then you will be afraid to cough.

7. Have a bad toothache? Smash your thumb with a hammer and you will forget about the toothache.

HEAVEN AND THE CLOCKS

Hillary Clinton died and went to Heaven. St. Peter was giving her a tour of Heaven when she noticed that there were dozens of clocks on the wall.

Each clock displayed a different time of day. When she asked St. Peter about the clocks, he replied, "We have a clock for each person on earth and every time they tell a lie the hands move. The clock ticks off one second each time a lie is told."

Special attention was given to two clocks. The clock belonging to Mother Teresa has never moved, indicating that she never told a lie. The clock for Abraham Lincoln has only moved twice. He only told two lies in his life.

Hillary asked, "Where is Bill's clock?" St. Peter replied, "Jesus has it in His office... He is using it as a ceiling fan."

I'M DEAD, I KNOW I'M DEAD

An older couple is lying in bed one morning, having just awakened from a good night's sleep. He takes her hand and she responds, "Don't touch me."

"Why not?" he asks.

She answers back, "Because I'm dead."

The husband says, "What are you talking about? We're both lying here in bed together and talking to one another."

She says, "No, I'm definitely dead."

He insists, "You're not dead. What in the world makes you think you're dead?"

"Because I woke up this morning and nothing hurts."

QUICKIES!

- If it weren't for stress, I'd have no energy at all!
- Everyone has a photographic memory. Some just don't have any film.
- I always know God won't give me more than I can handle but there are times I wish He didn't trust me so much.
- Never be too open minded, your brains could fall out.

- Just going to church doesn't make you a Christian any more than standing in a garage makes you a car.
- If you look like your passport picture, you probably need the trip.
- Some days are a total waste of makeup.
- Middle age is when broadness of the mind and narrowness of the waist change places.
- Opportunities always look bigger going than coming.
- Junk is something you've kept for years and throw away three weeks before you need it.

IMPROVEMENT

The road by my house was in bad condition. Every day I dodged potholes on the way to work, so I was relieved to see a construction crew working on the road one morning.

Later, on my way home, I noticed the men were gone and no improvement in the road.

But where the crew had been working stood a new, bright-yellow sign with the words, "Rough Road."

REAL PATIENCE

Two hillbilly moonshine distillers were discussing their illegal business.

"When I drive to town with a load of likker," said one, "I go real slow."

"Scared of being arrested for speeding?" asked his friend.

Nope," answered the first. "But you gotta let the stuff age a little."

RANCH WIDOW

A successful rancher died and left everything to his devoted wife. She was a very good-looking woman, and determined to keep the ranch, but knew very little about ranching, so she decided to place an ad in the newspaper for a ranch hand. Two men applied for the job. One was gay and the other a drunk. She thought long and hard about it, and when no one else applied, she decided to hire the gay guy, figuring it would be safer to have him around the house than the drunk. He proved to be a hard worker who put in long hours every day and knew a lot about ranching.

For weeks, the two of them worked, and the ranch was doing very well. Then one day, the rancher's widow said to the hired hand, "You have done a really good job, and the ranch looks great. You should go into town and kick up your heels."

The hired hand readily agreed and went into town one Saturday night. One o'clock came, however, and he didn't return. Two o'clock, and no hired hand. He returned around two-thirty, and upon entering the room, he found the rancher's widow sitting by the fireplace with a glass of wine, waiting for him. She quietly called him over to her.

"Unbutton my blouse and take it off," she said. Trembling, he did as she directed.

"Now take off my boots." He did as she asked, ever so slowly.

"Now take off my socks." He removed each gently and placed them neatly by her boots.

"Now take off my skirt." He slowly unbuttoned it, constantly watching her eyes in the fire light.

"Now take off my bra." Again, with trembling hands, he did as he was told and dropped it to the floor.

"Now," she said, "take off my panties." By the light of the fire, he slowly pulled them down and off. Then she looked at him and said, "If you ever wear my clothes into town again, you're fired."

WILD RIDE!

A woman from Seattle is visiting friends in Spokane and decides to try horseback riding, even though she has had no lessons or prior experience.
She mounts the horse, unassisted, and the horse immediately springs into motion. It gallops along at a steady and rhythmic pace, but the lady begins to slip from the saddle. In terror, she grabs for the horse's mane, but cannot seem to get a firm grip. She tries to throw her arms around the horse's neck, but she slides down the side of the horse anyway.

The horse gallops along, seemingly impervious to its slipping rider. Finally, giving up her frail grip, the woman attempts to leap away from the horse and throw herself to safety.
Unfortunately, her foot has become entangled in the stirrup; she is now at the mercy of the horse's pounding hooves as her head is struck against the ground over and over. As her head is battered against the ground, she is mere moments away from unconsciousness when to her great fortune, Frank, the Wal-Mart greeter, sees her and unplugs the horse.

LIFE ISN'T LIKE A BOWL OF CHERRIES OR PEACHES ...

It's more like a jar of Jalapenos: What you do today, might burn your butt tomorrow!

AWAY

My mother was away all weekend at a business conference. During a break, she decided to call home collect. My six-year-old brother picked up the phone and heard a stranger's voice say, "We have a Marcia on the line. Will you accept the charges?"

Frantic, he dropped the receiver and came charging outside screaming, "Dad! They've got Mom! And they want money!"

HOW MANY CHRISTIANS DOES IT TAKE TO CHANGE A LIGHT BULB?

- Charismatic: Only one. Hand's already in the air.
- Pentecostal: Ten. One to change the bulb, and nine to pray against spirit of darkness.
- Presbyterians: None. Lights will go on and off at predestined times.
- Roman Catholic: None. Candles only.
- Baptists: At least 15. One to change the light bulb, and three committees to approve the change and decide who brings the potato salad and fried chicken.
- Episcopalians: Three. One to call the electrician, one to mix the drinks, and one to talk about how much better the old one was.
- Mormons: Five. One man to change the bulb, and four wives to tell him how to do it.
- Unitarians: We choose not to make a statement either in favor of or against the need for a light bulb. However, if in your own journey you have found that light bulbs work for you, that is fine. You are invited to write a poem or compose a modern dance about your light bulb for the next Sunday service in which we will explore a number of light bulb traditions and equally valid paths to luminescence.
- Methodists: Undetermined. Whether your light is bright, dull, or completely out, you are loved. You can be a light bulb, turnip bulb, or tulip bulb. Church-wide lighting service is planned for Sunday. Bring bulb of your choice and a covered dish.
- Nazarene: Six. One woman to replace the bulb while five men review church lighting policy.
- Lutherans: None. Lutherans don't believe in change.
- Amish: What's a light bulb?

LOGIC

Two South Texas farmers, Jim and Bob, are sitting at their favorite bar, drinking beer. Jim turns to Bob and says, "You know, I'm tired of going through life without an education. Tomorrow I think I'll go to the community college and sign up for some classes."

Bob thinks it's a good idea, and the two leave. The next day Jim goes down to the college and meets the dean of admissions, who signs him up for the four basic classes: math, english, history, and logic.

"Logic?" Jim says. "What's that?"

The dean says, "I'll show you. Do you own a weed-eater?"

"Yeah."

"Then logically because you own a weed-eater, I think that you have a yard."

"That's true, I do have a yard."

"I'm not done," the dean says. "Because you have a yard, I think logically that you would have a house."

"Yes, I do have a house."

"And because you have a house, I think that you might logically have a family."

"I have a family."

"I'm not done yet. Because you have a family, then logically you must have a wife."

"Yes, I do have a wife."

"And because you have a wife, then logically you must be a heterosexual."

"I am a heterosexual. That's amazing; you were able to find out all of that because I have a w eed-eater."

Excited to take the class now, Jim shakes the dean's hand and leaves to meet Bob at the bar. He tells Bob about his classes, how he is signed up for math, English, history and logic.

"Logic?" Bob says, "What's that?"

Jim says, "I'll show you. Do you have a weed-eater?"

"No."

"Then you're gay."

(Folks, it's just a joke on the farmer. Please don't write us, unless you're an offended farmer).

SOME PEOPLE SHOULD NOT ANSWER THE PHONE IN HOSPITALS

The famous Olympic skier Picabo Street (pronounced Peek-A-Boo) is not just an athlete, she is now a nurse currently working at the Intensive Care Unit of a large metropolitan hospital. She is not permitted to answer the hospital telephones. It caused too much confusion when she would answer the phone and say, "Picabo, ICU."

20 DEFINITIONS YOU DIDN'T KNOW YOU KNEW

1. ARBITRATOR: A cook that leaves Arby's to work at McDonalds.
2. AVOIDABLE: What a bullfighter tried to do.
3. BERNADETTE: The act of torching a mortgage.
4. BURGLARIZE: What a crook sees with.
5. CONTROL: A short, ugly inmate.
6. COUNTERFEITERS: Workers who put together kitchen cabinets.
7. ECLIPSE: What an English barber does for a living.
8. EYEDROPPER: A clumsy ophthalmologist.

9. HEROES: What a guy in a boat does.
10. LEFTBANK: What the robber did when his bag was full of money.
11. MISTY: How golfers create divots.
12. PARADOX: Two physicians.
13. PARASITES: What you see from the top of the Eiffel Tower.
14. PHARMACIST: A helper on the farm.
15. POLARIZE: What penguins see with.
16. PRIMATE: Removing your spouse from in front of the TV.
17. RELIEF: What trees do in the Spring.
18. RUBBERNECK: What you do to relax your wife.
19. SELFISH: What the owner of a seafood store does.
20. SUDAFED: Brought litigation against a government official.

BEAR ON THE ROOF!

A man wakes up in the morning to find a bear on his roof. So he looks in the Yellow Pages and sure enough, there's an ad for "Bear Removers."
He calls the number, and the remover says he'll be over in 30 minutes.
The bear remover arrives, and gets out of his van. He's got a ladder, a baseball bat, a shotgun and a mean old pit bull.
What are you going to do?" the homeowner asks.
"I'm going to put this ladder up against the roof, then I'm going to go up there and knock the bear off the roof with this baseball bat. When the bear falls off, the pit bull is trained to grab his privates and not let go. The bear will then be subdued enough for me to put him in the cage in the back of the van."
He hands the shotgun to the homeowner.
"What's this for?" asks the homeowner?
"If the bear knocks me off the roof, shoot the dog."

THE INSURANCE SALESMAN AND HIS WIFE

An insurance agent was teaching his wife to drive when the brakes suddenly failed on a steep, downhill grade.
"I can't stop!" she shrilled. "What should I do?"
"Brace yourself," advised her husband, "and try to hit something cheap."

SUBJECT: NEVER LIE TO YOUR MOTHER

Brian Hester invited his mother over for dinner. During the course of the meal, Brian's mother couldn't help but keep noticing how beautiful Brian's roommate, Stephanie, was. Mrs. Hester had long been suspicious of a relationship between Brian and Stephanie, and this had only made her more curious. Over the course of the evening, while watching the two interact, Mrs.

Hester started to wonder if there was more between Brian and Stephanie than met the eye.

Reading his mom's thoughts, Brian volunteered, "I know what you must be thinking, but I assure you Stephanie and I are just roommates."

About a week later, Stephanie came to Brian saying, "Ever since your mother came to dinner, I've been unable to find the beautiful silver gravy ladle. You don't suppose she took it, do you?"

Brian said, "Well, I doubt it, but I'll send her an e-mail just to be sure."

So he sat down and wrote: Dear Mother: I'm not saying that you "did" take the gravy ladle from the house and I'm not saying that you "did not" take the gravy ladle. But the fact remains that it has been missing ever since you were here for dinner. Love, Brian.

Several days later, Brian received an e-mail from his mother that read: Dear Son: I'm not saying that you "do" sleep with Stephanie, and I'm not saying that you "do not" sleep with Stephanie. But the fact remains that if she was sleeping in her own bed, she would have found the gravy ladle by now. Love, Mom.

LESSON OF THE DAY... NEVER LIE TO YOUR MOTHER!

I have entered the "snapdragon" part of my life.
Part of me has snapped ... and the rest of me is draggin'!

THE EXPLANATION OF LIFE

ON THE FIRST DAY, God created the dog and said, "Sit all day by the door of your house and bark at anyone who comes in or walks past. For this, I will give you a life span of twenty years."

The dog said, "That's a long time to be barking. How about only ten years and I'll give you back the other ten?"

On the second day, God created the monkey and said, "Entertain people, do tricks and make them laugh. For this, I'll give you a twenty-year life span."

The monkey said, "Monkey tricks for twenty years? That's a pretty long time to perform. How about I give you back ten like the Dog did?" And, God agreed.

On the third day, God created the cow and said, "You must go into the field with the farmer all day long and suffer under the sun, have calves and give milk to support the farmer's family. For this, I will give you a life span of sixty years."

The cow said, "That's kind of a tough life you want me to live for sixty years. How about twenty and I'll give back the other forty?" And, God agreed again.

On the fourth day, God created man and said, "Eat, sleep, play, marry, and enjoy your life. For this, I'll give you twenty years."

But man said, "Only twenty years? Could you possibly give me my twenty, the forty the cow gave back, the ten the monkey gave back and the ten the dog gave back; that makes eighty, okay?"

"Okay," God said. "You asked for it."

So, that is why the first twenty years we eat, sleep, play and enjoy ourselves. For the next forty years we slave in the sun to support our family. For the next ten years we do monkey tricks to entertain the grandchildren. And for the last ten years we sit on the front porch and bark at everyone.

Life has now been explained to you.

YOU KNOW IT'S TIME TO DIET WHEN . . .
. . . you dance and it makes the band skip.
. . . you are diagnosed with the flesh eating virus, and the doctor
   gives you 22 more years to live.
. . . you put mayonnaise on an aspirin.
. . . you go to the zoo and the elephants throw you peanuts.
. . . your driver's license says, "Picture continued on other side."
. . . you ran away and they had to use all four sides of the milk
   carton for your picture.
. . . you learn you were born with a silver shovel in your mouth.
. . . you could sell shade.
. . . your blood type is Ragu.
. . . you need an appointment to attend an 'open house'.
. . . The buttons on your shirts are declared legal weapons.
. . . You go to Sam's Tent and Awning for custom fit clothing.

WHAT IS EASTER?
Three women from Seattle died and found themselves standing before St. Peter. He told them that before they could enter the kingdom, they had to tell him what Easter was.

The first lady said, "Easter is a holiday where they have a big Feast and we give thanks and eat turkey."

St. Peter said, "noooooo," and he banished her.

The second lady said, "Easter is when we celebrate Jesus' birth and exchange gifts."

St. Peter said, "noooooo," and he banished her.

The third lady said she knew what Easter is, and St. Peter said, "So, tell me."

She said, "Easter is a Christian holiday that coincides with the Jewish festival of Passover. Jesus was having Passover feast with his disciples when he was betrayed by Judas, and the Romans arrested him. The Romans hung him on the cross and eventually he died. Then they buried him in a tomb behind a very large boulder."

St. Peter said, "verrrrrry good."

Then the woman continued, "Now every year the Jews roll away the boulder and Jesus comes out. If he sees his shadow, we have six more weeks of basketball." St. Peter fainted.

WHEN I SAY I'M BROKE, I'M BROKE!!!

A little old lady answered a knock on the door one day, only to be confronted by a well-dressed young man carrying a vacuum cleaner.

"Good morning," said the young man. "If I could take a couple of minutes of your time, I would like to demonstrate the very latest in high-powered vacuum cleaners."

"Go away!" said the old lady. "I haven't got any money!" and she proceeded to close the door.

Quick as a flash, the young man wedged his foot in the door and pushed it wide open. "Don't be too hasty!" he said. "Not until you have at least seen my demonstration." And with that, he emptied a bucket of horse manure onto her hallway carpet.

"If this vacuum cleaner does not remove all traces of this horse manure from your carpet, Madam, I will personally eat the remainder."

The old lady stepped back and said, "Well I hope you've got a darn good appetite, because they cut off my electricity this morning."

I SIGNED UP FOR AN exercise class and was told to wear loose-fitting clothing. If I HAD any loose-fitting clothing, I wouldn't have signed up in the first place!

THREE OLD LADIES

Three old ladies are sitting in a diner, chatting about various things.

One lady says, "You know, I'm getting really forgetful. This morning, I was standing at the top of the stairs, and I couldn't remember whether I had just come up or was about to go down."

The second lady says, "You think that's bad? The other day, I was sitting on the edge of my bed, and I couldn't remember whether I was going to bed or had just woken up!"

The third lady smiles smugly. "Well, my memory's just as good as it's always been, knock on wood." She raps the table. With a startled look on her face, she asks, "Who's there?"

"SO KEEP THE SINGING DOWN, OK?"

A Sunday school teacher asked her little children, as they were on the way to church service, "And why is it necessary to be quiet in church?"

One bright little girl replied, "Because people are sleeping."

THE PRESSED LEAF

A little boy opened the big and old family Bible with fascination; he looked at the old pages as he turned them. Then something fell out of the Bible and he picked up and looked at it closely. It was an old leaf from a tree that has been pressed in between pages.

"Momma, look what I found," the boy called out.

"What have you got there, dear?" his mother asked.

With astonishment in the young boy's voice he answered: "It's Adam's suit!!!!!"

"Wrinkled Was Not One of the Things I Wanted to Be When I Grew up."

My New Job

The day I started my construction job, I was in the office filling out an employee form when I came to the section that asked: Single____, Married____, Divorced____.

I marked single. Glancing at the man next to me, who was also filling out his form, I noticed he hadn't marked any of the blanks. Instead he had written, 'Yes, in that order.'

A TOUR GUIDE WAS SHOWING a tourist around Washington, D. C. The guide pointed out the place where George Washington supposedly threw a dollar across the Potomac River.

"That's impossible," said the tourist. "No one could throw a coin that far!"

"You have to remember," answered the guide, "a dollar went a lot farther in those days."

THE SILENT TREATMENT

A man and his wife were having some problems at home and were giving each other the silent treatment.

Suddenly, the man realized that the next day, he would need his wife to wake him at 5:00 AM for an early morning business flight. Not wanting to be the first to break the silence (and LOSE), he wrote on a piece of paper, "Please wake me at 5:00 AM."

He left it where he knew she would find it. The next morning, the man woke up, only to discover it was 9:00 AM and he had missed his flight.

Furious, he was about to go and see why his wife hadn't wakened him, when he noticed a piece of paper by the bed. The paper said, "It is 5:00 AM. Wake up."

Men are not equipped for these kinds of contests.

WHEN A WOMAN LIES, IT'S USUALLY GOOD

One day, when a seamstress was sewing while sitting close to a river, her thimble fell into the river. When she cried out, the Lord appeared and asked, "My dear child, why are you crying?"

The seamstress replied that her thimble had fallen into the water and that she needed it to help her husband in making a living for their family. The Lord dipped His hand into the water and pulled up a golden thimble set with pearls. "Is this your thimble?" The Lord asked.

The seamstress replied, "no."

The Lord again dipped into the river. He held out a silver thimble ringed with sapphires. "Is this your thimble?" The Lord asked.

Again, the seamstress replied, "no."

The Lord reached down again and came up with a leather thimble. "Is this your thimble?" The Lord asked.

When the seamstress replied, "yes," the Lord was pleased with the woman's honesty and gave her all three thimbles to keep.

Some years later, the seamstress was walking with her husband along the riverbank, and her husband fell into the river and disappeared under the water. When she cried out, the Lord again appeared and asked her, "Why are you crying?"

"Oh Lord, my husband has fallen into the river!"

The Lord went down into the water and came up with Mel Gibson. "Is this your husband?" The Lord asked.

"Yes," cried the seamstress.

The Lord was furious. "You lied! That is an untruth!"

The seamstress replied, "Oh, forgive me, my Lord. It is a misunderstanding. You see, if I had said 'no' to Mel Gibson, you would have come up with Tom Cruise. Then if I said 'no' to him, you would have come up with my husband. Had I then said 'yes,' you would have given me all three.

Lord, I'm not in the best of health and would not be able to take care of all three husbands, so that's why I said 'yes' to Mel Gibson."

The moral of this story is: - whenever a woman lies, it's for a good and honorable reason, and in the best interest of others.

That's our story, and we're sticking to it.

QUICKIES!
- Now that food has replaced sex in my life, I can't even get into my own pants.
- I saw a woman wearing a sweat shirt with "Guess" on it. So I said "Implants?" She hit me.
- A good friend will come and bail you out of jail...but, a true friend will be sitting next to you saying, "Wow...that was fun!"
- Why is it that our children can't read a Bible in school, but they can in prison?
- Wouldn't you know it... Brain cells come and brain cells go, but FAT cells live forever.
- Why do I have to swear on the Bible in court when the Ten Commandments cannot be displayed outside?

BUMPER STICKER OF THE YEAR:
"If you can read this, thank a teacher, and, since it's in English, thank a soldier"

AND REMEMBER:
Life is like a roll of toilet paper. The closer it gets to the end, the faster it goes.

"PLEASE TELL ME: If Barbie® is so popular,
why do you have to buy her friends?" Steven Wright

TEST FOR DEMENTIA
Below are four (4) questions and a bonus question. You have to answer them instantly. You can't take your time, answer all of them immediately.

First Question: You are participating in a race. You overtake the second person. What position are you in?

Answer: If you answered that you are first, then you are absolutely wrong! If you overtake the second person and you take his place, you are second!

Try not to screw up in the next question.

To answer the second question, don't take as much time as you took for the first question.

Second Question: If you overtake the last person, then you are...?

Answer: If you answered that you are second to last, then you are wrong again. Tell me, how can you overtake the LAST Person? You're not very good at this! Are you?

Third Question: Very tricky math! This must be done in your head only. Do NOT use paper and pencil or a calculator. Try it.
Take 1000 and add 40 to it. Now add another 1000. Now add 30. Add another 1000. Now add 20. Now add another 1000 Now add 10. What is the total?
Did you get 5000?
The correct answer is actually 4100. Don't believe it? Check with your calculator! Today is definitely not your day. Maybe you will get the last question right?
Fourth Question: Mary's father has five daughters: 1. Nana, 2. Nene, 3. Nini, 4. Nono. What is the name of the fifth daughter?
Answer: Nunu?
NO! Of course not. Her name is Mary. Read the question again
Okay, now the bonus round: There is a mute person who wants to buy a toothbrush. By imitating the action of brushing one's teeth he successfully expresses himself to the shopkeeper and the purchase is done. Now if there is a blind man who wishes to buy a pair of sunglasses, how should he express himself?
Answer: (Tell me you got THIS one right)! He just has to open his mouth and ask. So simple, don't you agree?

RED NECK?

We have enjoyed the redneck jokes for years. It's time to take a reflective look at the core beliefs of a culture that values home, family, country and God. If I had to stand before a dozen terrorists who threaten my life, I'd choose a half dozen or so rednecks to back me up. Tire irons, squirrel guns and grit -- that's what rednecks are made of. I hope I am one of those.
You might be a redneck if...
1. It never occurred to you to be offended by the phrase, "One nation, under God... "
2. You've never protested about seeing the 10 Commandments posted in public places.
3, You still say "Christmas" instead of "Winter Festival."
4. You bow your head when someone prays.
5. You stand and place your hand over your heart when they play the National Anthem and stand for "America" or "America the Beautiful."
6. You treat Viet Nam vets with great respect, and always have.
7. You've never burned an American flag.
8. You know what you believe and you aren't afraid to say so, no matter who is listening.
9. You respect your elders and expect your kids to do the same.

10. You'd give your last dollar to a friend.
11. You say Easter Vacation, Not Spring Break

WHAT'S IN A NAME?

George goes to the Birth Registration Office to register his newborn son. The man behind the counter asks the name he wants to give to the boy, and the father replies: "Euro."

The man says that such a name is not acceptable, because it's a currency.

Says George: "What? There weren't any objections when I called my first two sons Mark and Frank."

HELP YOU CAN DO WITHOUT

A hostess is making final arrangements for an elaborate reception. "Nora," she said to her veteran servant, "for the first half-hour I want you to stand at the drawing room door and call the guests' names as they arrive."

"Nora's face lit up. "Thank you, ma'am," she replied. "I've been wanting to do that to some of your friends for the last twenty years."

NEW ACCOUNTANT

Fresh out of business school, the young man answered a want ad for an accountant. Now he was being interviewed by a very nervous man who ran a small business that he had started himself. "I need someone with an accounting degree," the man said. "But mainly, I'm looking for someone to do my worrying for me."

"Excuse me?" the accountant said.

"I worry about a lot of things," the man said. "But I don't want to have to worry about money. Your job will be to take all the money worries off my back."

"I see," the accountant said. "And how much does the job pay?"

"I'll start you at eighty thousand."

"Eighty thousand dollars!" the accountant exclaimed. "How can such a small business afford a sum like that?"

"That," the owner said, "is your first worry."

DO YOU KNOW HOW MANY?

A. Stripes are on a United States flag?
B. Cards are in a standard deck?
C. Stars are on a United States flag?
D. Bones in your body?
E. Great Lakes there are?
F. Keys are on a piano?

G. Stories are in the Empire State Building?
H. Inches around a baseball?
I. Legs are on a spider?
J. Spaces are on a monopoly board?
K. Tentacles are on an octopus?
L. Sides are on a decagon?
M. Senses you have?
N. Players are on a regular soccer team?
O. Teeth an adult normally has?
P. Bones are in your foot?

ANSWERS:
A. - 13; B. - 52; C. - 50; D. - 206; E. - Five: Lake Michigan, Lake Huron, Lake Superior, Lake Erie, and Lake Ontario; F. - 88; G. - 102; H. - 9 to 9 1/4 inches; I. - 8; J. - 40 spaces; K - Eight tentacles; L. - Ten sides; M. - Five senses; N. - 11 players on one team; O. - 32 teeth; P. - 26 bones.

NAVIGATOR

The scene is sometime in the old era when cockpits had round dials plus flight engineers and navigators. The crusty old-timer captain is breaking in a brand new navigator. The captain opens his briefcase, pulls out a .38 and rests it on the glare panel. He asks the navigator, "Know what this is for?"

"No, sir," replies the newbie.

"I use it on navigators that get us lost," explains the captain, winking at his first officer.

The navigator then opens his briefcase, pulls out a .45 and sets it on his chart table.

"What's THAT for?" queries the surprised captain.

"Well, sir," replies the navigator, "I'll know we're lost before you will."

WE HAVE AN OPENING FOR YOU

A man went to apply for a job. After filling out all of his applications he waited anxiously for the outcome.

The employer read all his applications and said, "We have an opening for people like you."

"Oh, great," the man said, "What is it?"

"It's called the door!'"

DON'T UNDERESTIMATE THE POODLE

A wealthy old lady decides to go on a photo safari in Africa, taking her faithful aged poodle named Cuddles, along for the company.

One day the poodle starts chasing butterflies and before long, Cuddles discovers that she's lost. Wandering about, she notices a leopard heading rapidly in her direction with the intention of having lunch.

The old poodle thinks, "Oh, oh! I'm in deep doo-doo now!" Noticing some bones on the ground close by, she immediately settles down to chew on the bones with her back to the approaching cat.

Just as the leopard is about to leap, the old poodle exclaims loudly, "Boy, that was one delicious leopard! I wonder if there are any more around here?" Hearing this, the young leopard halts his attack in mid-strike, a look of terror comes over him and he slinks away into the trees.

"Whew!" says the leopard, "That was close! That old poodle nearly had me!"

Meanwhile, a monkey who had been watching the whole scene from a nearby tree, figures he can put this knowledge to good use and trade it for protection from the leopard. So off he goes. But the old poodle sees him heading after the leopard with great speed, and figures that something must be up. The monkey soon catches up with the leopard, spills the beans, and strikes a deal for himself with the leopard.

The young leopard is furious at being made a fool of and says, "Here, monkey, hop on my back and see what's going to happen to that conniving canine!"

Now, the old poodle sees the leopard coming with the monkey on his back and thinks, "What am I going to do now?"

But instead of running, the dog sits down with her back to her attackers, pretending she hasn't seen them yet, and just when they get close enough to hear, the old poodle says, "Where's that darn monkey? I sent him off an hour ago to bring me another leopard!"

Moral of this story. Don't mess with the old and knowledgeable, for age with wisdom will always overcome youth and skill!

GOING TO HEAVEN

Father Murphy walks into a pub in Donegal, and says to the first man he meets, "Do you want to go to heaven?"

The man said, "I do Father."

The priest said, "Then stand over there against the wall."

Then the priest asked the second man, "Do you want to go to heaven?"

"Certainly, Father," was the man's reply.

"Then stand over there against the wall," said the priest.

Then Father Murphy walked up to O'Toole and said, "Do you want to go to heaven?"

O'Toole said, "No, I don't Father."

The priest said, "I don't believe this. You mean to tell me that when you die you don't want to go to heaven?"

O'Toole said, "Oh, when I die, yes. I thought you were getting a group together to go right now."

A MAN ENTERED THE BUS with both of his front pants pockets full of golf balls, and sat down next to a beautiful woman. The puzzled woman kept looking at him and his bulging pockets. Finally, after many such glances from her, he said, "It's golf balls."

Nevertheless, the woman continued to look at him thoughtfully and finally, not being able to contain her curiosity any longer, asked, "Does it hurt as much as tennis elbow?"

CONFESSION

O'Toole worked in the lumber yard for twenty years and all that time he'd been stealing the wood and selling it. At last his conscience began to bother him and he went to confession to repent. "Father, it's 15 years since my last confession, and I've been stealing wood from the lumber yard all those years," he told the priest.

"I understand my son," says the priest. "Can you make a Novena?"

O'Toole said, "Father, if you have the plans, I've got the lumber."

CROSSING

Paddy was in New York, patiently waiting and watching the traffic cop on a busy street crossing.

The cop stopped the flow of traffic and shouted, "Okay pedestrians." Then he'd allow the traffic to pass. He'd done this several times, and Paddy still stood on the sidewalk.

After the cop had shouted "Pedestrians" for the tenth time, Paddy went over to him and said, "Is it not about time ye let the Catholics across?"

"OUR LIBERTY IS PROTECTED BY FOUR BOXES... The ballot box, the jury box, the soap box, and the cartridge box." - Anonymous

AS I MATURE ... I have learned that you cannot make someone love you. All you can do is stalk them and hope they panic and give in.

MRS. MURPHY IS LOOKING FOR the grave of her late husband (a notorious criminal) as it has been a while since she was there. She goes to the cemetery's management office and says, "I am looking for my husband's grave."

"Ok madam," says the director. "What was his name?"

"John Murphy," she answers.

He looks through his large book for quite a time and says, "Sorry, there are no John Murphys in our cemetery, nothing but one Mary Murphy."

The woman brightens up and says, "Of course, that's it; everything was in my name."

WHEN I'M 100, IF I LEAN A LITTLE ... LET ME !

The family wheeled Grandma out on the lawn, in her wheelchair, where the activities for her 100th birthday were taking place. Grandma couldn't speak very well, but she could write notes when she needed to communicate.

After a short time out on the lawn, Grandma started leaning off to the right, so some family members grabbed her, straightened her up, and stuffed pillows on her right.

A short time later, she started leaning off to her left, so again the family grabbed her and stuffed pillows on her left.

Soon she started leaning forward, so the family members again grabbed her, then tied a pillowcase around her waist to hold her up.

A grandson who arrived late came up to Grandma and said, "Hi, Grandma, you're looking good! How are they treating you?"

Grandma took out her little notepad and slowly wrote a note to her grandson, "They won't let me fart.

EAR IN THE SAWDUST

There was once a sawmill worker who bent down, got too close to the saw and cut his ear off. The ear fell down into the pile of sawdust and disappeared. The worker got down into the sawdust pit and started scratching around looking for his ear.

I walked by and saw my worker in the pit and I asked, "What you looking for?"

The worker said, "I cut my ear off and I'm down here looking for it."

"Well, hang on," I said. "I'll come down and help you."

I got down into the pit and started feeling around in the sawdust and I found the ear. "I got it," I called out. "Here it is."

The worker took hold of the ear and looked at it closely, then he threw it back down in the sawdust. "Better keep on looking," he said. "Mine had a pencil behind it."

WARNING: A WOMAN'S PERSPECTIVE

* Behind every successful woman is herself.
* A woman is like a tea bag... You don't know how strong she is until you put her in hot water.

* I have yet to hear a man ask for advice on how to combine marriage and a career.
* Coffee, chocolate, men. Some things are just better rich.
* I'm out of estrogen and I have a gun.
* Warning: I have an attitude and I know how to use it.
* Of course I don't look busy... I did it right the first time.
* Do not start with me. You will not win.
* All stressed out and no one to choke.
* If you want breakfast in bed, sleep in the kitchen.

IF RAISING CHILDREN WERE GOING TO BE EASY,
it never would have started with something called labor!

KETCHUP

A woman was trying hard to get the ketchup to come out of the jar. During her struggle the phone rang so she asked her 4-year-old daughter to answer the phone.

"It's the minister, Mommy," the child said to her mother. Then she added, "Mommy can't come to the phone to talk to you right now. She's hitting the bottle."

WORLD'S THINNEST BOOKS
HOW I SERVED MY COUNTRY by Jane Fonda
MY BEAUTY SECRETS by Janet Reno
HOW TO BUILD YOUR OWN AIRPLANE by John Denver
MY SUPER BOWL HIGHLIGHTS by Dan Marino
THINGS I LOVE ABOUT BILL by Hillary Clinton
MY LITTLE BOOK OF PERSONAL HYGIENE by Osama Bin Laden
THINGS I CANNOT AFFORD by Bill Gates
THINGS I WOULD NOT DO FOR MONEY by Dennis Rodman
FRENCH WAR HEROES by Jacques Chirac
MY WILD YEARS by Al Gore
AMELIA EARHART'S GUIDE TO THE PACIFIC
AMERICA'S MOST POPULAR LAWYERS
DETROIT : a Travel Guide
A COLLECTION of MOTIVATIONAL SPEECHES by Dr. J. Kevorkian
ALL THE MEN I HAVE LOVED BEFORE by Ellen de Generes
GUIDE TO DATING ETIQUETTE by Mike Tyson
SPOTTED OWL RECIPES by the EPA
THE AMISH PHONE DIRECTORY
MY PLAN TO FIND THE REAL KILLERS by O. J. Simpson

MY BOOK OF MORALS by Bill Clinton with an introduction by the Rev. Jessie Jackson

I WAS DRIVING with my three young children one warm summer evening when a woman in the convertible ahead of us stood up and waved. She was stark naked!

As I was reeling from the shock, I heard my 5-year-old shout from the back seat, "Mom! That lady isn't wearing a seat belt!

A LITTLE BOY got lost at the YMCA and found himself in the women's locker room. When he was spotted, the room burst into shrieks, with ladies grabbing towels and running for cover. The little boy watched in amazement and then asked, "What's the matter haven't you ever seen a little boy before?"

MY SON ZACHARY, 4, came screaming out of the bathroom to tell me he'd dropped his toothbrush in the toilet. So I fished it out and threw it in the garbage. Zachary stood there thinking for a moment, then ran to my bathroom and came out with my toothbrush. He held it up and said with a charming little smile, "We better throw this one out too then, 'cause it fell in the toilet a few days ago.

ELDERLY

While working for an organization that delivers lunches to elderly shut-ins, I used to take my 4-year-old daughter on my afternoon rounds. The various appliances of old age, particularly the canes, walkers and wheelchairs, unfailingly intrigued her. One day I found her staring at a pair of false teeth soaking in a glass. As I braced myself for the inevitable barrage of questions, she merely turned and whispered, "The tooth fairy will never believe this!"

THE PRINCESS

Once upon a time there lived a king. The king had a beautiful daughter, the PRINCESS. But there was a problem. Everything the princess touched would melt. No matter what -- metal, wood, stone -- anything she touched would melt. Because of this, men were afraid of her. Nobody would dare marry her.

The king despaired. What could he do to help his daughter? He consulted his wizards and magicians.

One wizard told the king, "If your daughter touches one thing that does not melt in her hands, she will be cured."

The king was overjoyed and came up with a plan. The next day, he held a competition. Any man that could bring his daughter an object that would not melt would marry her and inherit the king's wealth.

Three young princes took up the challenge. The first brought a sword of the finest steel. But alas, when the princess touched it, it melted. The prince went away sadly.

The second prince brought diamonds. He thought diamonds are the hardest substance in the world and would not melt. But alas, once the princess touched them, they melted. He too was sent away disappointed.

The third prince approached. He told the princess, "Put your hand in my pocket and feel what is in there."

The princess did as she was told, though she turned red. She felt something hard. She held it in her hand, and it did not melt!!!

The king was overjoyed. Everybody in the kingdom was overjoyed. And the third prince married the princess and they both lived happily ever after.

Question: What was in the prince's pants?

Answer: M&M's, of course! They melt in your mouth, not in your hand.

DRESS-UP

A little girl was watching her parents dress for a party. When she saw her dad donning his tuxedo, she warned, "Daddy, you shouldn't wear that suit."

"And why not, darling?"

"You know that it always gives you a headache the next morning."

SCHOOL

A little girl had just finished her first week of school.
"I'm just wasting my time," she said to her mother. "I can't read, I can't write and they won't let me talk!"

GAMES FOR WHEN WE ARE OLDER
1. Sag, you're It.
2. Hide and go pee.
3. 20 questions shouted into your good ear.
4. Kick the bucket .
5. Red Rover, Red Rover, the nurse says Bend Over.
6. Musical recliners.
7. Simon says something incoherent.
8. Pin the Toupee on the bald guy.

A FRIEND IS LIKE A GOOD BRA. Hard to Find, Supportive, Comfortable, And Always Close To Your Heart!

MY HUSBAND SAYS I never listen to him. At least I think that's what he said.

OLD IS WHEN:
1. Going bra-less pulls all the wrinkles out of your face.
2. You don't care where your spouse goes, just as long as you don't have to go along.
3. Getting a little action means I don't need fiber today.
4. Getting lucky means you find your car in the parking lot.
5. An all-nighter means not getting up to pee!

SIGNS OF MENOPAUSE:
1. You sell your home heating system at a yard sale.
2. You have to write post-it notes with your kids' names on them.
3. You change your underwear after a sneeze.

JUST REMEMBER...IF THE WORLD DIDN'T SUCK, we'd all fall off.

NEWS HEADLINERS!
Contributed by Zak Likarich
- Eye Drops off Shelf
- Teacher Strikes Idle Kids
- Reagan Wins on Budget, But More Lies Ahead
- Squad Helps Dog Bite Victim
- Enraged Cow Injures Farmer with Ax
- Plane Too Close to Ground, Crash Probe Told
- Miners Refuse to Work after Death
- Juvenile Court to Try Shooting Defendant
- Stolen Painting Found by Tree
- 2 Soviet Ships Collide, 1 Dies
- Two Sisters Reunited after 18 Years in Checkout Counter
- Killer Sentenced to Die for Second Time in 10 Years
- War Dims Hope for Peace
- If Strike isn't Settled Quickly, It May Last a While
- Cold Wave Linked to Temperatures
- Enfields Couple Slain; Police Suspect Homicide
- Red Tape Holds Up New Bridge
- Deer Kill 17,000
- Typhoon Rips Through Cemetery; Hundreds Dead
- Man Struck by Lightning Faces Battery Charge
- New Study of Obesity Looks for Larger Test Group
- Astronaut Takes Blame for Gas in Spacecraft
- Kids Make Nutritious Snacks

- Chef Throws His Heart into Helping Feed Needy
- British Union Finds Dwarfs in Short Supply
- Ban On Soliciting Dead in Trotwood
- Local High School Dropouts Cut in Half
- New Vaccine May Contain Rabies
- Man Minus Ear Waives Hearing
- Deaf College Opens Doors to Hearing
- Air Head Fired
- Steals Clock, Faces Time
- Prosecutor Releases Probe into Undersheriff
- Old School Pillars are Replaced by Alumni
- Hospitals are Sued by 7 Foot Doctors
- Some Pieces of Rock Hudson Sold at Auction
- Sex Education Delayed, Teachers Request Training
- Include your Children when Baking Cookies
- Something Went Wrong in Jet Crash, Expert Says
- Choir Director Shows His Organ To Church-goers
- Police Begin Campaign to Run Down Jaywalkers
- Safety Experts Say School Bus Passengers Should Be Belted
- Drunk Gets Nine Months in Violin Case
- Survivor of Siamese Twins Joins Parents
- Is There a Ring of Debris around Uranus?
- Stud Tires Out
- Panda Mating Fails; Veterinarian Takes Over

Spoiled Kids

My wife said to me, "Honey, do you think our kids are spoiled?"
I said, "Nah, I think most kids smell that way."

What's Going On?

If I had a dime for every time I didn't understand what's going on, I'd be like, "Why y'all keep giving me all these dimes?"

DURING A VISIT TO THE MENTAL ASYLUM, a visitor asked the Director what the criteria is that defines whether a patient should be institutionalized or not.

"Well," said the Director, "we fill up a bathtub with water, then we offer a teaspoon, a teacup, and a bucket to the patient and ask the patient to empty the water out of the tub."

Okay, here's your test:
1. Would you use the spoon?

2. Would you use the teacup?

3. Would you use the bucket?

"Oh, I understand," said the visitor. "A normal person would choose the bucket since it is larger than the teacup or spoon."

"No," answered the Director. "A normal person would pull out the stopper."

So how did you do? I've been committed - have a good day!

Relatively Speaking

If you find $60 to $80 to be too expensive for ancestry DNA kits, I have a cheap alternative; announce that you won the lottery and you'll quickly meet relatives you never knew you had!

I Ate At Mary Poppins Restaurant

I ate at the Mary Poppins Restaurant last night. Super cauliflower cheese but the lobster was atrocious.

Q & A

Q: What do you call a hippie's wife?
A: Mississippi.

If someone wants to say the word "motel" backwards, just letom.

Robin: The batmobile won't start.
Batman: Check the battery.
Robin: Who's Terry?

Warning

My grandfather warned people that the Titanic would sink. No one listened, but he kept on warning them nonetheless until they got sick of him and kicked him out of the movie theater.

Lumberjack

A lumberjack went to a magical forest to cut a tree. Upon arrival he started chopping at a tree.

The tree said, "Don't chop! I'm a talking tree!"

And the lumberjack replied, "And you will dialogue."

The WiFi Connection

I had terrible internet connection on my farm till I moved the modem into the barn. Now I have stable WiFi.

Peaceful Solution
My wife asked if I was going to yoga with her.
I said, "Namaste home today."

Police Record?
I got pulled over by the cops and asked if I had a police record.
I said, "No, but I've got a Sting album."

Q & A
Q: What do you call a snake that is 3.14 meters long?
A: A pi-thon.

Meditation
I recently took up meditation.
I soon realized it beats sitting around doing nothing.

Yikes!
My wife spilled her red hair coloring all over the bathroom.
It looks like somebody dyed in there.

Breakup
I told my Mom that I texted my girlfriend, Ruth, and told her that was over between us.
My Mom told me I was Ruthless.

Mix Up
I always get pickle and chutney mixed up.
It makes me chuckle.

Every One Counts
If I had a penny for every time someone said they think I have OCD I'd have 1,526 pennies.

Listen Closely
Did you know if you hold your ear up to a stranger's leg you can actually hear them say, "What the heck are you doing?"

Egg Hunt
I'm combining Easter and April Fool's day this year.
I'm sending the kids out to look for eggs I haven't hidden.

Respecting One's Privacy
      The misuse of users' Facebook data has caused Mark Zuckerberg significant emotional distress.
      He asks that you respect his privacy during this challenging time.

No Surprise
We should've known communism would fail.
There were a lot of red flags.

Aquire A Choir
"How much to buy a singing ensemble?"
You mean a choir?
"Fine, how much to acquire a singing ensemble?"

Human Pyramid
One of the Russian acrobats in our human pyramid has been deported.
We don't have Oleg to stand on.

Against The Odds
My girlfriend broke up with me because I'm a compulsive gambler.
Ever since, all I can think about is how to win her back.

Mountains Are Funny!
Mountains aren't just funny; they're hill areas!

Anger Management
I received a flyer on "Anger Management" the other day. But, then, I just lost it!

Herd Boss
"I love my job!" said the farmer.
"All you do is boss me around all day!" said one of his sheep.
"What did you say?" asked the farmer.
"You herd me," said the sheep.

I Would, Too!
If you rearrange the letters of "Postmen" they get really annoyed.

Horse With a Name
I have a horse named Mayo.
Mayo neighs.

Definition
My daughter asked me what "inexplicable" means.
I said, "It's hard to explain."

Pie Rate Sea
A slice of apple pie is $2.50 in Jamaica and $3.00 in the Bahamas.
Just an example of the pie rates of the Caribbean.

Autocorrect
We'll We'll We'll… If it isn't autocorrect…

Chicken Dating
I've started a dating site for chickens.
It's not my full-time job, I'm just doing it to make hens meet.

Issues…
I love taking photos of myself standing next to boiling water. My doctor says I've got selfie steam issues.

It's No Secret
This is top secret.
And, this is bottom secret.

Royal T
What's it called when a King and Queen have no children?
That would be a receding heir line.

Drum Roll Dad
Did you hear about the drummer who gave all his daughters the same name?
    Anna 1, Anna 2, Anna 3, Anna 4.

Heritage
I spent my whole life being proud of my British heritage until I found out that my Great Grandfather was actually from Transylvania.
Now I can't even look myself in the mirror.

All Worked Up
Someone stole 300 cans of Red Bull from my local store.
I don't know how they can sleep at night.

Yodeling Class
If you're here for the yodeling lesson please form an orderly orderly orderly orderly queue.

What Do You Say?
What do you say to your sister when she's crying?
"Are you having a crisis?"

It's OK!
I accidentally superglued my thumb and index finger together, and at first I started to panic. But then I realized that it's always going to be "OK."

Two cheese trucks ran into each other. De brie was everywhere.

You Are What You Eat
They say you are what you eat… Today I bought some ready-to-eat chicken and sure enough, I was ready to eat chicken.

Confrontation
      Bob left work one Friday evening. But, it was payday, so instead of going home, he stayed out the entire weekend partying with his friends and spending his entire paycheck.

      When he finally appeared at home on Sunday night, he was confronted by his angry wife and was barraged for nearly two hours with a tirade befitting his actions. Finally his wife stopped the nagging and said to him, "How would you like it if you didn't see me for two or three days?"

      He replied, "That would be fine with me."

      Monday went by and he didn't see his wife.

      Tuesday and Wednesday came and went with the same results.

      But on Thursday, the swelling went down just enough where he could see her a little out of the corner of his left eye.

Thief!
To the guy who stole my antidepressants… I hope you're happy.

Pillow Thief
To the thief who stole my pillow, know this… I will not rest until I find you.

Cloning Business
I quit my job to start a cloning business and it's been great. I love being my own boss.

Simple Deduction
The doctor said to me, "You have a severe iron deficiency."
I said, "How did you know? I just walked in!"
He said, "Your shirt is all wrinkled."

Q & A
Q: How many ears does Captain Kirk have?
A: Three: the left ear, the right ear, and the final frontier.

Q & A
Q: What do you call a game where Germans throw bread at each other?
A: Gluten tag.

Better Without Glasses
I told a girl she looked better without her glasses on.
She said I also look better without her glasses on.

Go Ahead
I asked the doctor if I could administer my own anesthetic.
He said, "Go ahead. Knock yourself out."

IKEA Interview
I went for a job interview at IKEA today.
When I got there, the interviewer said, "Welcome! Come in and make yourself a seat."

Religious Movement
   I accidentally drank some holy water with my laxative. I'm about to start a religious movement.

Impasse
Broken bridges really annoy me. I just can't get over them.

Take Your Pick
My wife handed me two kayak paddles and asked, "Which one do you want?"
I said I'd take either/oar.

Uninteresting
My girlfriend borrowed $100 from me. When we separated 3 years later, she returned exactly $100. I lost interest in that relationship.

Sea Turtles
A guy walks into library and asks for a book on sea turtles.
The librarian asks, "Hard back?"
The guy replies, "Yeah, little heads too."

Q & A
Q: What do you call a spider with 20 eyes?
A: Spiiiiiiiiiiiiiiiiiiider.

Silent On The Matter
A mime broke his left arm in a bar fight and got arrested.
He still has the right to remain silent.

Q & A
Q: At what frequency does laughter become painful?
A: 1 gigglehurts.

Could Have Been Me
I was crossing the street when I suddenly saw my ex getting run over by a bus!
I thought to myself, "Wow! That could have been me!"
Then I remembered I can't drive a bus.

Just a Phase
My son identifies as a crescent moon.
I'm worried, but my wife says it's just a phase.

Exactly
The doctor said to me, "Do you know you have a serious problem vocalizing your emotions?"
I said, "I can't say I'm surprised."

New Job!
I just got a new job as senior director at Old MacDonald's farm.
I'm the CIEIO.

50th Birthday Card
As I handed my Dad his 50th birthday card, he looked at me with tears in his eyes and said, "You know, one card would have been enough."

I haven't owned a watch for I don't know how long.

Q & A
Q: How does an Eskimo build his house?
A: Igloos it together.

No Cure!
The doctor said to me, "Your brain seems to have deleted all information about 80s pop music!"
I said, "Yikes, what's The Cure?"
He said, "Oh my God, it's worse than I thought!"

Funny Word
Asparagus is a funny word.
It sounds like an Italian guy begging you not to kill someone named Gus.
Go ahead, say it and see what I mean!

Q & A
Q: What do you call birds that stick together?
A: Velcrows.

Q & A
Q: Why do bees stay in the hive in the winter?
A: Swarm.

The Case of the Missing Bag
A man filed a report to the police that his bag was stolen.
Upon leaving the man's apartment, the officer found the man's bag at the bottom of the stairwell. It was a brief case.

Alphabet Soup
When I was little my Dad used to feed me alphabet soup, claiming that I loved it.
I didn't really – he was just putting words in my mouth.

I Need To Speak To The Wheel Boss!
I rang the bicycle factory and asked to speak to whoever was in charge of wheels.
The person who answered said they weren't there.
I said, "Okay, who are you?"
They said, "His spokes person."

Ad In Paper
I'm giving away my chimney for free. Come and get it. It's on the house.

Only When It Gets Really Bad
I have kleptomania, but when it gets bad I take something for it.

Marriage Phobia
The doctor told me I might have a marriage phobia and asked if I thought I had any symptoms.
I said, "I can't say I do."
He said, "Yeah, that's the main one."

Broken Finger
I broke my finger today.
But on the other hand I'm completely fine.

Hit or Miss
Have you ever tried blind folded archery?
You don't know what you're missing.

Remember When It Was Free?
Remember as a child when air for your bike was free? Now it's $1.50!
I asked the gas station attendant why and he said, "Inflation."

Career Quandry
I'm not having much luck with jobs lately:
I couldn't concentrate in the orange juice factory.
I wasn't suited to be a tailor.
The muffler factory was just exhausting.
I couldn't cut it as barber.
I didn't have the patience to be a doctor.
I didn't fit in the shoe factory even though I put my soul into it.
The paper shop folded.
Pool maintenance was too draining.
I got fired from the cannon factory.
And I just couldn't see any future as a historian.

A Day Off
Two factory workers are talking to each other one day.
The woman says, "I can make the boss give me the day off."
The man replies, "Oh yeah? And how would you do that?"
The woman says, "Just wait and see."
She then hangs upside down from the ceiling.
The boss comes in and says, "What are you doing?"

The woman replies, "I'm a light bulb."

The boss then says, "You've been working so much that you've gone crazy. I think you need to take the day off."

As the woman leaves, the man starts to follow her and the boss says, "Where are you going?"

The man says, "I'm going home, too. I can't work in the dark."

Job Opportunity

A man is hiring for an accounting position, and is conducting interviews for each of the hopefuls.

The first accountant walks in and starts to introduce himself, "I'm here for the accounting position."

The boss asks him, "What's 2+2?"

"4" replies the accountant.

The boss tells him to get out. Sad, disappointed, and a little confused, the accountant slowly leaves.

The next candidate then enters and the boss asks him, "What's 2+2?".

"4" replies the accountant.

The boss tells him to get out.

Just as confused as the first accountant, the second one leaves thinking that if the boss is that stupid he doesn't want to work there anyway.

The next candidate then enters and the boss asks him, "What's 2+2?".

The accountant replies, "Anything you want it to be."

The boss says, "You're hired."

Parting Words

An employee is getting to know her new co-workers when the topic of her last job comes up.

"Why did you leave that job?" asked one co-worker.

"It was something my boss said," the woman replied.

"Why? What did he say?" the co-worker asked.

"You're fired."

Strengths and Weaknesses

I went for a job interview today and the interviewer asked me, "What would you consider to be your main weaknesses and strengths?"

I said, "Well my main weakness would be my issues with reality, telling what's real from what's not."

They then asked, "And your strengths?"

I said, "I'm Batman."

Starting Salary

I went for an interview for an office job today.

The interviewer told me I'd start on $2,000 a month and then after 6 months I'd be on $2,500 a month.

I told them I'd start in 6 months.

The 3 Envelopes

A new manager spends a week at his new office with the manager he is replacing.

On the last day, the departing manager tells him, "I've left three numbered envelopes in the desk drawer. Open an envelope if you encounter a crisis you can't solve."

Three months down the road there is a major drama in the office and the manager feels very threatened by it all.

He remembers the parting words of his predecessor and opens the first envelope.

The message inside says "Blame your predecessor!"

He does this and gets off the hook.

About half a year later, the company is experiencing a dip in sales, combined with serious product problems.

The manager quickly opens the second envelope.

The message read, "Reorganize!"

He starts to reorganize and the company quickly rebounds.

Three months later, at his next crisis, he opens the third envelope.

The message inside says, "Prepare three envelopes."

Best Kept Secret!

A salesman dropped in to an office to see a business customer.

Not a soul was in the office except a big dog emptying the waste baskets.

The salesman stared at the animal, wondering if his imagination could be playing tricks on him.

The dog looked up and said, "Don't be surprised. This is just part of my job."

"Incredible!" exclaimed the man. "I can't believe it! Does your boss know what a prize he has in you? An animal that can talk!"

"Please don't tell him!" said the dog. "If he finds out I can talk, he'll make me answer the phone, too!"

I Love My Job!

I love my job.Colleagues have been writing names on the food in the office fridge - I'm currently eating a sandwich called Susan. How cute!

Two Windmills

Two windmills are standing in a field. One asks the other, "What kind of music do you like?"

The other one says, "I'm a big metal fan."

A man showed up for a duel armed only with a pencil and paper.
He then proceeded to draw his weapon.

I bought a dog off a blacksmith today.
As soon as I got it home it made a bolt for the door.

Thanks for explaining the word "many" to me. It means a lot.

I left my Adderall in my Ford Fiesta. Now it's a Ford Focus.

Thank you, student loans for getting me through college.
I don't think I can ever repay you.

There's a fine line between a numerator and a denominator.
Only a fraction of people will find this funny.

My astronaut girlfriend has dumped me. She said she needs space.

Every single morning I get hit by the same bike. It's a vicious cycle.

My wife asked me to pass her lip balm.
I accidentally gave her superglue instead. She's still not talking to me.

The Trucker
A truck driver stopped at a roadside diner one day to grab some lunch. He ordered a cheeseburger, a coffee and a slice of apple pie.
Just as he was about to eat them, three big hairy bikers walked in.
The first biker grabbed the trucker's cheeseburger and took a big bite from it.
The second biker picked up the trucker's coffee and downed it in one gulp.
The third biker ate the trucker's apple pie.
The truck driver didn't do anything or say a word as all this went on.
When they finished, he just paid the waitress and left.
The first biker said to the waitress, "He ain't much of a man, is he?"
"He's not much of a driver, either," the waitress replied. "He's just backed his 18-wheeler over three motorbikes."

Instructor, Teach Me!
I said to the gym instructor, "Can you teach me to do the splits?"
He said, "How flexible are you?"
I said, "I can't make Tuesdays."

Doctor, Doctor!
"Doctor, doctor, I can't stop singing The Green, Green Grass Of Home."
"That sounds like Tom Jones syndrome."
"Is it common?"
"It's not unusual."

"Q & A"
Q: What does homework stand for?
A: Half Of My Energy Wasted On Random Knowledge.

Stuck
    A trucker gets lost one day and as luck would have it he comes to a low bridge and gets stuck under it. The cars are backed up for miles behind him.
    Eventually, a cop car pulls up. The cop gets out and walks around to the truck driver. He puts his hands on his hips and says to him, "Got stuck huh, sir?"
    The trucker replies, "No, I was delivering this bridge and ran out of gas."

Directions
    I was walking down the street today when the driver of a repair truck pulled up alongside me and said, "Excuse me, I'm looking for the accident site involving a van carrying a load of cutlery."
    "No problem," I said. "Go straight down this road for 1 mile, then take the first left, and when you get to the fork in the road you're there."

Out of Season But Still Funny!
    A trucker stops for a red light one day and notices a lady in the car behind with a California license plate. She jumps out of her car, runs up to his truck, and knocks on the door. The trucker lowers the window, and the lady says to him, "Hi, my name's Julie and I thought you should know you're losing some of your load."
    The trucker just ignores her, raises the window and proceeds down the street as the light changes. A short while later he has to stop for another red light. The lady in the car is still behind him. Again, she jumps out of her car, runs up and knocks on the door. Again, the trucker lowers the window.

As if they've never spoken before, the lady says brightly, "Hi my name's Julie and I thought you should know you're losing some of your load!"

The trucker shakes his head but apart from this he ignores her again. He raises the window and drives on as the red light changes.

At the third red light, the same thing happens again.

At the fourth red light the trucker jumps out of his truck, and runs back to the lady's car. He knocks on the window and she lowers it.

The trucker says, "Hi, my name's Steve, it's winter here in Stevens County, and I'm driving the salt truck!"

The Engineer

An Engineer was fed up with his job and so he decided to switch careers.

He'd always enjoyed tinkering with truck engines, so he enrolled in a school for truck mechanics.

After the class ended, the students were given their final exam. The task was to strip a truck engine completely and reassemble it in perfect working order.

The engineer did his best - and was amazed to find he scored 150%.

He asked the instructor, "150%? How did I possibly score that?"

"Well," replied the instructor, "I gave you 50% for taking the engine apart. Then I gave you 50% for reassembling it perfectly. And then I gave you a 50% bonus for doing it all through the exhaust pipe."

LOL! NOT.

A young executive is leaving the office late one evening, when he finds the CEO standing in front of a shredder with a piece of paper in his hand.

"Listen," says the CEO, "this is a very sensitive and important document here, and my secretary has gone for the night. Can you make this thing work for me?"

"Sure," the young executive says.

He turns the machine on, inserts the paper, and presses the start button.

"Excellent, excellent!" says the CEO as his paper disappears inside the machine. "I just need one copy."

I Need A Raise!

Bill walks into his boss's office one day and says, "Sir, I'll be straight with you, I know the economy isn't great, but I've got three companies after me, and I'd like to respectfully ask for a raise."

After a few minutes of haggling, the boss finally agrees to give him a 5% raise, and Bill happily gets up to leave.

"By the way," asks the boss as Bill is leaving his office, "which three companies are after you?"

Bill replies, "The electric company, water company, and phone company."

"I got fired at work today. My boss said my communication skills were awful. I didn't know what to say to that."

Our computers went down at work today, so we had to do everything manually. It took me twenty minutes to shuffle the cards for Solitaire.

Busted!
My boss phoned me today.
He said, "Is everything okay at the office?"
I said, "Yes, it's all under control. It's been a very busy day, I haven't stopped."
"Can you do me a favor?" he asked.
I said, "Of course, what is it?"
He said, "Hurry up and take your shot, I'm behind you on the 7th hole."

Ha, Ha, Ha, Ha, Ha!
When I got to work this morning, my boss stormed up to me and said, "You missed work yesterday, didn't you?"
I said, "No, not particularly."

Honey Do-NOT!
An employee goes to see his supervisor in the front office.
"Boss," he says, "we're doing some heavy house-cleaning at home tomorrow, and my wife needs me to help with the attic and the garage, moving, and hauling stuff."
"Sorry, but we're short-handed," the boss replies. "I can't give you the day off."
"Thanks, boss," says the employee. "I knew I could count on you!"

Fake It Till U Make It
A young businessman had just started his own firm. He rented a beautiful office and had it furnished with antiques. Sitting there, he saw a man come into the outer office. Hoping to look like a hot shot, the businessman picked up the phone and started to pretend he was working on a big, important business deal.

He threw huge figures around and made giant commitments. Finally he hung up and asked the visitor, "Can I help you?"

The man said, "Yeah, I've come to hook up your phone lines."

Heh, Heh, Heh (sigh!)
My boss asked me today, "Do you believe in life after death and the supernatural?"
I replied, "Yes, I think so."
"I thought you would," he said. "Yesterday after you left to go to your grandmother's funeral, she phoned up to talk to you."

You Can't Have Mine!
I was walking through the park today when this girl came up to me and asked me if she could have my number.
I said, "Get lost! Get your own number!"

Date With Librarian
I went on a date with a librarian last night. It cost me a fortune.
My own fault really; keeping her out too long.

What Women Want
Scientists have finally discovered what women really want.
Trouble is, now they've changed their minds…

Wonderland
I said to my friend, "My girlfriend keeps asking me if I'm an Alice in Wonderland character, and it's getting really annoying!"
He said, "Are you mad at her?"
I said, "Geez! Don't you start, too!"

Ruined Her Birthday?
My girlfriend isn't talking to me because apparently I ruined her birthday.
I'm not sure how I did that – I didn't even know it was her birthday…

Watch This!
I was at a party the other day when I lost my watch.
A bit later I saw a guy standing on it while harassing a girl.
I walked up to the guy and punched him in the face.
No one does that to a girl... not on my watch.

Unintended Message
    A new small business was opening and one of the owner's friends arranged for flowers to be sent to mark the occasion and wish the owner luck.
    The flowers duly arrived at the new business site and the business owner read the accompanying card to find it said, "Rest in Peace."

The business owner rang his friend and told him what the card read. The friend was angry and called the florist to complain.

After he had told the florist of the obvious mistake and how angry he was, the florist said, "Sir, I'm really sorry for the mistake, but rather than getting angry you should consider this... somewhere there's a funeral taking place today, and they have flowers with a note saying, 'Congratulations on your new location.'"

Never laugh at your girlfriend's choices. You're one of them.

My new girlfriend works at the zoo. I think she's a keeper.

Late For Work

Bill struggled to get up early in the morning and as a result was always late for work. His boss got fed up of his constant lateness and so threatened to fire him if he didn't get his act together.

So, Bill went to see his doctor who gave him a pill and told him to take it just before going to bed.

Bill did this, and slept very well and actually beat the alarm clock by two hours. So he fixed himself a nice breakfast and drove happily to work, in plenty of time for the start of the work day.

When he got there, he said, "Boss, that pill the doctor gave me actually worked!"

His boss said, "That's all very well, but where were you yesterday?"

"Q" and "A"

Q: What's the difference between love and marriage?
A: Love is blind. Marriage is an eye-opener.

"Q" and "A"

Q: Why did the burglar retire?
A: He just couldn't take it anymore.

My boss asked me to make a presentation and said I should start it with a joke. So I put my payslip on the first slide.

An Offer You Can't Refuse

A very successful businessman went to visit his new son-in-law.

He said to him, "I love my daughter, and now I welcome you into the family. To show you how much we care for you, I'm making you a 50-50 partner in my business. All you have to do is go to the factory every day and learn how everything works."

The son-in-law said, "That's very kind of you but I hate factories. I can't stand the noise."

"Oh, I see," said the father-in-law. "In that case, you can work in the office and take charge of some of the operations there."

"That's very kind of you but I hate office work too," said the son-on-law. "I can't stand being stuck behind a desk in an office all day, every day."

"Wait a minute," said the father-in-law who was getting a little annoyed now. "I just made you half-owner of a huge money-making organization, but you don't like factories and you won't work in a office. What am I going to do with you?"

"Easy," said the young man. "Buy me out."

Fifty Years From Now

These three old retired guys were talking about what their grandchildren would be saying about them in fifty years' time.

The first old guy says, "I'd like my grandchildren to say, 'He was successful in business.'"

The second old guy then says, "Fifty years from now, I want my grandchildren to say, 'He was a faithful and loving family man.'"

The first old guy then turns to the third and asks him, "So what do you want your grandchildren to say about you in fifty years' time?"

The third old guy replies "Me? I just want them all to say, 'He looks good for his age!'"

Discreet Harry

Six old retired guys are sat playing poker at Joe's house one evening when George loses $500 on a single hand. At the shock of this he clutches his chest and then drops dead from a heart attack.

Bill asks, "Who's going to go and tell his wife?"

None of them want this horrible job so they finally decide to cut the pack, and lowest card loses and has to go tell her. Harry draws a three and loses so he's the one who has to go and break the bad news. The others tell him to be discreet and gentle so as not to make a bad situation even worse.

Harry says, "Discreet? I'm the most discreet person you'll ever meet - discretion is my middle name. Leave it to me, not a problem."

He drives over to George's house and knocks on the door. George's wife answers and asks Harry what he wants.

Harry replies, "I'm sorry to have to tell you this but your husband just lost $500 playing cards and is afraid to come home. He's asked me to come over here and apologize to you."

George's wife is mad and shouts, "You tell him I said drop dead!"

Harry doesn't bat an eyelid and says, "Ok, I'll go tell him."

If you think that no-one cares you're alive,
just try missing a couple of mortgage payments.

My real estate agent did such a good job describing my house in their listing that I've decided to keep it.

Realtors need closure, too.

Every Scooby-Doo episode would literally be two minutes long if the gang went to the mask store first and asked a few questions.

Probably the worst thing you can hear when you're wearing a bikini is "Good for you!"

Shocking News
I finally managed to get rid of that nasty electrical charge I've been carrying. I'm ex-static!

Walks Into A Bar
So, this superconductor walks into a bar. The bartender says, "Get out! We don't serve your kind here."
The superconductor left without resistance.

Grilled
This electrician arrives home at 3am.
His wife asks him, "Wire you insulate?"
He replies, "Watt's it to you? I'm Ohm, aren't I?"

Dear God!
My niece Katrina tailgates other cars and it makes me nervous. I just can't get it through her head that she does this and that it's very dangerous. One good thing is that I sometimes find myself drawing closer to the Lord when I ride with her.

Recently, when I greeted my coworker, she said, "You look so gorgeous, I didn't recognize you."

"Q" and "A"
Q: What do you call someone who can't stick with a diet?
A: A desserter.

Marc With a "C"
When asked for his name by the coffee shop clerk, my brother-in-law answered, "Marc, with a C."
Minutes later, he was handed his coffee with his name written on the side: Cark.

It's amazing how a person can complement and insult you at the same time.

Married Life
I once gave my husband the silent treatment for an entire week, at the end of which he declared, "Hey, we're getting along pretty great lately!"

Free Advice
I've been working on my PhD in engineering for the past five years, but my kids don't necessarily see that as work. As we were driving past Walmart one day, my son spotted a "Now Hiring" sign and suggested that I could get a job there.
Hoping to make a point, I asked, "Do you think they're looking for an engineer?"
"Oh, sure," he said. "They'll hire anybody."

"Q" and "A"
Q: Did you hear about the wooden tractor?
A: It had wooden wheels, wooden engine, wooden transmission, and wooden work.

Farmer and the Frog
An old farmer was walking down the path to the pond one day when he came across a frog. He reached down, picked the frog up, and started to put it in his pocket.
As he did so, the frog said, "Kiss me on the lips and I'll turn into a beautiful farmers wife."
The old farmer carried on putting the frog in his pocket.
The frog said, "Didn't you hear what I said?"
The farmer looked at the frog and said, "At my age I'd rather have a talking frog."

Farmer and His Dog
A farmer took his cross-eyed dog to the vet.

The vet picked the dog up to examine him and said, "Sorry, I'm going to have to put him down."
The farmer said "Oh no! It's not that bad is it?"
The vet said, "No, he's just very heavy."

Farmer and His Gal
A farmer and his girlfriend were out for a stroll in the fields when they came across a cow and a calf rubbing noses.
"Boy," said the farmer, "that sure makes me want to do the same."
"Well, go ahead," said his girlfriend. "It's your cow."

Uninteresting Relationship
My girlfriend borrowed $100 from me.
When we separated 3 years later, she returned exactly $100.
I lost interest in that relationship

"Q" and "A"
Q: What happened when the farmer crossed a chili pepper, a shovel, and a terrier?
A: He got a hot-diggity-dog.

Mad Wife
My wife is still mad at me because I accidentally put superglue on her pen a few days ago.
She just can't seem to let it go.

Split Up
My wife and I have split up over my obsession with horoscope jokes.
In the end it Taurus apart.

Chemist Arrest
Why was the chemist arrested?
He threw sodium chloride at his wife. That's a salt.
I've never been married. But I've had a few near Mrs.

Mud Pack
I tried to have a conversation with my wife when she was applying a mud pack.
You should have seen the dirty look she gave me.

Compulsive Gambler
My girlfriend broke up with me because I'm a compulsive gambler.
Ever since, all I can think about is how to win her back.

FBI Agent
If you were dating an FBI agent and you broke up... He would be your fed ex.

Just a Game!
My wife sighed, "Why does everything have to be a game with you?"
I replied, "An excellent question, my dear. But next time, please use the buzzer!"

Not Paying Attention!
My wife said to me, "You're shirtless and also covered in... oil?"
I said, "Well, you're always saying I never glisten so I thought I'd do something about it."
My wife said, "Listen! You never listen!"

It's All Relative
My wife accused me of hating her family and relatives.
I said, "No, I don't hate your relatives. In fact, I like your mother-in-law a lot better than I like mine."

It Must Have Been The Way I Said Them
While my wife was in labor I read her jokes to distract her from the pain, but she didn't seem amused.
It must have been the delivery.

Marriage on My Mind
I'm seriously thinking about asking my ex-wife to remarry me; but, I'm pretty sure she'll figure out I'm just after my money.

Wait!
My girlfriend told me she was leaving me because I keep pretending to be a Transformer.
I said, "No, wait! I can change."

Have a Nice Time
My wife left me because I'm too insecure.
No wait, she's back. She just went to make a cup of tea.

The last time I was someone's type... I was donating blood.

A Conference Call is the best way for a dozen people to say "bye" 300 times.

Note On Fridge Door
My girlfriend left a note on the fridge.
It said, "It's not working. I can't take it anymore. I'm going to my mom's."
I opened the fridge door, the light came on, the beer was cold. What the heck did she mean?

Act Your Age
My girlfriend keeps telling me to act my age, but I don't know how.
I've never been this old before.

Like a Detective
My girlfriend said, "You're always acting like a detective. I want to split up."
I said, "Good idea, we can cover more ground that way."

The Twins
I've been dating this really cute girl who's a twin.
My friend asked me how I tell them apart.
I said, "That's easy – her brother has a beard."

Barbie
Ralph is driving home one evening, when he suddenly realizes that it's his daughter's birthday and he hasn't bought her a present.

He drives to the mall, runs to the toy store, and says to the shop assistant, "How much is that Barbie in the window?"

The assistant says, "Which Barbie?" She continues, "We have Barbie Goes to the Gym for $19.95, Barbie Goes to the Ball for $19.95, Barbie Goes Shopping for $19.95, Barbie Goes to the Beach for $19.95, Barbie Goes Nightclubbing for $19.95, and Divorced Barbie for $265.00."

Ralph asks, "Why is the Divorced Barbie $265.00 when all the others are only $19.95?"

"That's obvious," the saleslady says. "Divorced Barbie comes with Ken's house, Ken's car, Ken's boat, Ken's furniture..."

What's the Password?
I was doing an overnight at a hotel away from home. I took my computer down to the snack bar to do some data entries. I sat down and asked the cashier "What's the WiFi password?"

The cashier says, "You need to buy a sandwich first."

So, I said, "Okay, I'll have a sandwich."

Cashier replied, "We have BLT, Tuna, Club, or Reuben."

I said, "I'll have a BLT. How much is that?"

Cashier says, "$6.00."
I say, "Ok. Here you are. What's the WiFi password?"
Cashier, "you need to buy a sandwich first, no spaces and all lowercase,"

Q: Is Google male or female?
A: Female, because it doesn't let you finish a sentence before making a suggestion.

Q: What did the duck say when he bought lipstick?
A: "Put it on my bill."

Q: What's the difference between a hippo and a zippo?
A: One is really heavy, and the other is a little lighter.

"I told my girlfriend she drew her eyebrows too high. She seemed surprised."

My friend says to me, "What rhymes with orange?" I said, "No it doesn't."

What's orange and sounds like a parrot? A carrot.

People in Dubai don't like the Flintstones. But people in Abu Dhabi do!

It's hard to explain puns to kleptomaniacs. They always take things literally.

How many opticians does it take to change a lightbulb?
Is it one or two? One... or two?

Where does a cat go if it's lost it's tail? The Retail Store.

"Any pizza is a personal pizza if you believe in yourself"

So what if I don't know what Armageddon means?
It's not the end of the world.

Newlyweds!
The newlywed wife said to her husband, "I have great news for you. Pretty soon, we're going to be three in this house instead of two."
Her husband ran to her with a smile on his face and delight in his eyes.
He was glowing of happiness and kissing his wife when she said, "I'm glad that you feel this way since tomorrow morning, my mother moves in with us."

Police Stop

At 2:00 a.m. Ron Chestna, 79 years of age, was stopped by the police and was asked where he was going at that time of night.
Ron replied, "I'm on my way to a lecture about alcohol abuse and the effects it has on the human body, as well as smoking and staying out late."
The officer asked, "Really? Who's giving that lecture at this time of night?"
Ron replied, "That would be my wife.

You Haven't Heard?

Joe: Have you heard about Murphy's Law?
Sam: Yes. Anything that can go wrong will go wrong.
Joe: How about Cole's Law?
Sam: No.
Joe: It's julienned cabbage in a creamy dressing.

I got my husband a fridge for his birthday. His face lit up when he opened it.

Q: Which rock group has four guys who can't sing or play instruments?
A: Mount Rushmore.

Q: Why does Humpty Dumpty love autumn?
A: Because he always has a great fall.

Q: What should you do if you're attacked by a group of clowns?
A: Go straight for the juggler.

My teachers told me I'd never amount to much because I procrastinate so much. I told them, "Just you wait!"

NEWSFLASH!

A cement mixer and a prison bus crashed on the highway. Police are advising citizens to look out for a group of hardened criminals.

Q: Why did the taxi driver get fired?
A: Passengers didn't like it when he went the extra mile.

This is a Library!

A man walks into a library and orders a hamburger.
The librarian says, "This is a library."
The man apologizes and whispers, "I'd like a hamburger, please."

I think I want a job cleaning mirrors.
It's just something I could really see myself doing.

If you ever get cold, just stand in a corner for a while.
They're usually around 90 degrees.

Q: Did you hear about the two guys who stole a calendar?
A: They each got 6 months.

Cowboy and His Brothers

A cowboy walks into a bar in Texas and orders three beers. He sits at the bar, drinking a sip out of each glass in turn.

This goes on for a few weeks till the bartender says "You know beer goes flat after pouring - why don't you just buy them one at a time?"

The cowboy replies, "Well, you see, I have two brothers. One is in Arizona, the other is in Colorado. When they left our home we promised that we'd drink this way to remember the days when we drank together. So I'm drinking one beer for each of my brothers and one for myself."

The bartender admits that this is a nice custom, and leaves it there. The cowboy becomes a regular in the bar and always drinks the same way.

One day, he comes in and only orders two beers. All the regulars take notice and fall silent.

When he comes back to the bar for the second round, the bartender says, "I don't want to intrude on your grief, but I wanted to offer my condolences on your loss."

The cowboy looks quite puzzled for a moment, then a light dawns in his eyes and he laughs. "Oh, no, everybody's just fine," he explains, "It's just that my wife made me quit drinking but it hasn't affected my brothers though."

Nervous Crew

A very nervous first time crew member says to the skipper, "Do yachts like this sink very often?"

"Not too often," replied the skipper. "Usually only once."

ConSEAquences

An old sea captain was sitting on a bench near the wharf when a young man walked up and sat down. The young man had spiked hair and each spike was a different color... green, red, orange, blue, and yellow.

The young man noticed that the captain was staring at him.

"What's the matter old timer—never done anything wild in your life?"

The old captain snorted. "Got drunk once and married a parrot. I was just wondering if you were my son!"

Q: How much does it cost a pirate to pierce his ears?
A: A Buccaneer!

Q: What's a pirate's favorite letter?
A: You may think it's the RRRRR, but it's the C that they're in love with! Aye.

Q: What lies at the bottom of the ocean and twitches?
A: A nervous wreck!

"BOAT FOR SALE"

Thibodaux marches right up to Beaudreaux's front porch and wraps hard on the door. Beaudreaux opens it.

Thibodaux say, "Beaudreaux! How long we ban frands?"
Beaudreaux say, "Well......... All our lives Thibodeaux."
Thibodaux say, "Why don't you told me you gotta boat?"
Beaudreaux say, "I ant gotta boat !"
Thibodaux say, "Da' sign say; "BOAT FOR SALE."
Beaudreaux say, "OH-NO Thibodaux! See dat old '72 Ford pickem'up truck over-dare?"
Thibodaux say, "yas, I see dat old pickem'up truck."
Beaudreaux say, "See dat '76 Chevro-lay Cee-dan?"
Thibodaux say, "yas, I see dat Ce-dan."
Beaudreaux say, "Well, dey boat for sale!"

Radio Conversation

This is a transcript of a radio conversation between a British Navy ship and the Irish Coastguard, off the coast of Kerry:

Irish. Please divert your course 15 degrees to the south, to avoid collision.

British. We are recommending you divert your course 15 degrees to the north, to avoid collision

Irish. Negative. You will have to divert your course 15 degrees to the south to avoid collision.

British. This is the Captain of a British Navy Ship. I say again, divert YOUR course.

Irish. Negative. I say again, you will have to divert YOUR course

British. This is the largest ship in the british fleet. We are accompanied by 3 destroyers, 3 cruisers, and numerous support ships. I demand that you change your course 15 degrees to the north, or countermeasures will be taken to ensure the safety of this flotilla.

Irish. This is a lighthouse. Your call!

Famous Captain

Once upon a time there was a famous sea captain. This captain was very successful at what he did; for years he guided merchant ships all over the world.

Never did stormy seas or pirates get the best of him. He was admired by his crew and fellow captains. However, there was one thing different about this captain. Every morning he went through a strange ritual. He would lock himself in his captain's quarters and open a small safe. In the safe was an envelope with a piece of paper inside. He would stare at the paper for a minute, and then lock it back up. After, he would go about his daily duties.

For years this went on, and his crew became very curious. Was it a treasure map? Was it a letter from a long lost love? Everyone speculated about the contents of the strange envelope.

One day the captain died at sea. After laying the captain's body to rest, the first mate led the entire crew into the captains' quarters. He opened the safe, got the envelope, opened it and... The first mate turned pale and showed the paper to the others. Four words were on the paper:
"Port Left - Starboard Right"

HOOYAH!

One morning, a grandmother was surprised to find that her 7-year-old grandson made her coffee. Smiling, she choked down the worst cup of her life. When she finished, she found three little green Army men at the bottom. Puzzled, she asked, "Honey, what are these Army men doing in my coffee?"

Her grandson answered, "Like it says on TV, Grandma. 'The best part of waking up is soldiers in your cup.'"

Goodbye, Mother

"A young man was walking through a supermarket to pick up a few things when he noticed an old lady following him around. Thinking nothing of it, he ignored her and continued on. Finally, he went to the checkout line, but she got in front of him.

"Pardon me," she said, "I'm sorry if my staring at you has made you feel uncomfortable. It's just that you look just like my son, who just died recently."

"I'm very sorry," replied the young man, "is there anything I can do for you?"

"Yes," she said, "As I'm leaving, can you say 'Goodbye, Mother? It would make me feel so much better."

"Sure," answered the young man.

As the old woman was leaving, he called out, "Goodbye, Mother!"

As he stepped up to the checkout counter, he saw that his total was $127.50.

"How can that be?" he asked, "I only purchased a few things!"

"Your mother said that you would pay for her," said the clerk."

Q: Did you hear about the painter who was hospitalized?
A: Reports say it was due to too many strokes.

Q: Why did the robber take a bath?
A: Because he wanted to make a clean getaway.

Q: What happens if life gives you melons?
A: You're dyslexic.

Q: What did the ties say to the hat?
A: You go on ahead and I'll hang around.

Q: What washes up on very small beaches?
A: Microwaves!

Q: Why did the cross-eyed teacher lose her job?
A: Because she couldn't control her pupils.

Q: What stays in the corner and travels all over the world?
A: A stamp.

Q: What do you call a man with no body and just a nose?
A: Nobody nose.

Q: What do you call a computer that sings?
A: A-Dell.

Q: Did you hear about the angry pancake?
A: He just flipped!

Q: What do you call a cow with a twitch?
A: A beef jerky!

Volume 3

Hang On To Your Pigtails For Some Cowpoke Humor...

A COWBOY RIDES into town in the Wild West and shoots an artist.
    The sheriff asks him, "Why did you do that?"
    The cowboy says, "I thought he was going to draw."

I believe a lot of conflict in the Wild West could have been avoided completely if cowboy town planners had just made their towns big enough for everyone.

A YOUNG COWBOY walks into the saloon.
    He sits at the counter and notices an old cowboy with his arms folded, staring blankly at a full bowl of chowder.
    After fifteen minutes of just sitting there staring at it, the young cowboy bravely asked the old cowboy, "If you ain't gonna eat that, mind if I do?"
    The older cowboy slowly turns his head toward the young wrangler and in his best cowboy manner says, "Nah, go ahead."

Eagerly, the young cowboy reaches over and slides the bowl over to his place and starts spooning in it with delight. He gets nearly down to the bottom and notices a dead mouse. The sight was shocking and he immediately "empties" the chowder back into the bowl.

The old cowboy quietly says, "Yep, that's as far as I got, too."

Q: Where do cowboys cook their meals?
A: On the range.

AN OLD BLIND cowboy wanders into an all-girl biker bar by mistake...

He finds his way to a bar stool and orders a shot of Jack Daniels.

After sitting there for a while, he yells to the bartender, "Hey, you wanna hear a blonde joke?"

The bar immediately falls absolutely silent.

In a very deep, husky voice, the woman next to him says, "Before you tell that joke, Cowboy, I think it is only fair, given that you are blind, that you should know five things: The bartender is a blonde girl with a baseball bat. The bouncer is a blonde girl with a 'Billy Club.' I'm a 6-foot tall, 175-pound blonde woman with a black belt in karate. The woman sitting next to me is blonde and a professional weight lifter. The lady to your right is blonde and a professional wrestler. Now, think about it seriously, Cowboy.... Do you still wanna tell that blonde joke?"

The blind cowboy thinks for a second, shakes his head and mutters, "No... not if I'm gonna have to explain it five times."

A COWBOY appeared before St. Peter at the Pearly Gates.

"Have you ever done anything of particular merit?" St. Peter asked.

"Well, I can think of one thing," the cowboy offered.

"On a trip to the Big Horn Mountains out in Wyoming, I came upon a gang of bikers who were threatening a young woman. I told them to leave her alone, but they wouldn't listen. So, I approached the largest and most tattooed biker and smacked him in the face, kicked his bike over, ripped out his nose ring, and threw it on the ground. Then I yelled, 'Now, back off or I'll beat you all unconscious.'"

Saint Peter was impressed, "When did this happen?"

"Couple of minutes ago."

A cowboy walks into a German car showroom and says, "Audi!"

ONE DAY THE LONE Ranger and Tonto are riding in a canyon when suddenly they are completely surrounded and cut off by angry natives.

The Lone Ranger turns to Tonto and says, "Well, this looks like the end for us, old friend."

Tonto replies, "What you mean by 'us,' paleface?"

A TOUGH OLD cowboy from Texas one day told his granddaughter that if she wanted to live a long life, the secret was to sprinkle a pinch of gun powder on her oatmeal every morning.

The granddaughter did this religiously until the age of 103, when she died.

She left behind 14 children, 30 grandchildren, 45 great-grandchildren, 25 great-great-grandchildren, and a 40-foot hole where the crematorium used to be.

I worked in a record factory making cowboy records. I quit because when I told my friends what I did, they would tell me, "Howdy Pressing."

What did the cowboy say when his dog ran away?
"Doggone!"

I'm directing a cowboy film called "The Sun." It's set in the west.

A COWBOY AND A biker are on death row, and are due to be executed on the same day.

The day comes, and they are brought to the gas chamber. The warden asks the cowboy if he has a last request, to which the cowboy replies, "Ah shore do, wardn. Ah'd be mighty grateful if'n yoo'd play 'Achy Breaky Heart' fur me bahfore ah hafta go."

"Sure enough, cowboy, we can do that," says the warden. He turns to the biker, "And you, biker, what's your last request?"

"That you kill me first."

THE OLD COWBOY came riding into town on a hot, dry, dusty day. The local sheriff watched from his chair in front of the saloon as the cowboy wearily dismounted and tied his horse to the rail a few feet in front of the sheriff.

"Howdy, stranger..."

"Howdy, Sheriff..."

The cowboy then moved slowly to the back of his horse, lifted its tail, and placed a big kiss were the sun don't shine.

He dropped the horse's tail, stepped up on the walk, and aimed towards the swinging doors of the saloon.

"Hold on, Mister..." said the sheriff.

"Sheriff?"

"Did I just see what I think I just saw?"

"Reckon you did, Sheriff. I got me some powerful chapped lips..."

"And that cures them?"

"Nope, but it keeps me from lickin' em."

A COWBOY WAS trying to buy a health insurance policy and the insurance agent was going down the list of standard questions.

"Ever have an accident?"

"Nope, nary a one."

"None? You've never had any accidents."

"Nope. Ain't never had one. Never."

"Well, you said on this form you were bitten by a snake once. Wouldn't you consider that an accident?"

"Heck, no. That dang varmint bit me on purpose."

AN OLD RANCHER had a small ranch that he worked for many many years. Then one year, the IRS claimed that he was not paying proper wages to his workers and sent an agent out to interview him.

"I need a list of your employees and how much you pay them," demanded the IRS agent.

"Well," replied the rancher, "There's my ranch hand who has been with me for about 3 years. I pay him $600 a week plus free room and board."

"Any others?" asked the agent.

"Well, the cook has been here for 18 months ever since my wife passed away. I pay her $500 a week plus free room and board." answered the old rancher.

"Is that everyone? You realize that making false statements to the IRS can mean a fine, jail time, or a confiscation of your land and equipment!" said the IRS agent trying to intimidate the old rancher.

"Well," thought the old rancher, "there's the half-wit who works about 18 hours every day and does about 90% of all the work around here. He makes about $10 per week, pays his own room and board and I buy him a glass or two of bourbon every Saturday night as a reward."

"That's the guy! I want to talk to the half-wit!" demanded the agent.

"That would be me," replied old rancher.

Genie in a Bottle

A woman found a magic lamp on the beach, rubbed it, and out popped a genie.

"Ask me anything and it's yours!"

She thought a moment and said, "I want my husband to pay more attention to me, to protect me, to take me out frequently, to sleep close to me, and to be more caring, even if I get a tiny scratch."

"No problem." And poof! she was a smartphone!"

Dads That Help

When I was a child, my dad tried to force-feed me. After a while, my mom said, "Just use a freaking spoon, Bob. You're not a Jedi."

OMG!!!

I was in the public restroom. I was barely sitting down when I heard a voice in the other stall.
Stall: "Hi, how are you?"
Me: embarrassed, "Doin' fine!"
Stall: "So what are you up to?"
Me: "Uhhh, I'm like you, just sitting here."
Stall: "Can I come over?"
Me: (attitude) "No, I'm a little busy right now!!"
Stall: "Listen, I'll have to call you back. There's an idiot in the other stall who keeps answering all my questions!"

A Sandwich in a Bar

A Sandwich walks into a bar. The bartender says, "Sorry, we don't serve food in here."

I Bean There

A teacher asked her students to use the word "beans" in a sentence.
"My father grows beans," said one girl.
"My mother cooks beans," said a boy.
A third student spoke up, "We are all human beans."

Lookin' Good!

What did the duck say when he bought lipstick?
"Put it on my bill."

Let's Google It

Is Google male or female?
Female, because it doesn't let you finish a sentence before making a suggestion.

Addicted To My Phone

I forgot my cell phone when I went to the toilet yesterday. We have 245 tiles.

Simple Math
How many gorillas can fit into a car? Eight.
How many chickens can fit into the car?
None, the car is already full of gorillas.

Silly Wabbit
A lady opened her refrigerator and saw a rabbit sitting on one of the shelves.
"What are you doing in there!?" she asked.
The rabbit replied, "This is a Westinghouse, isn't it?"
The lady confirmed, "Yes."
"Well," the rabbit said, "I'm westing."

Where's the Paper?
I asked my daughter if she'd seen my newspaper. She told me that newspapers are old school. She said that people use tablets nowadays and handed me her iPad. The fly didn't stand a chance.

Husband: "Oh the weather is beautiful today. Shall we go out for a quick jog?"
Wife: "Hahaha, I love the way you pronounce 'Shall we go out and have a cake'!"

"I'm not going to vacuum 'til Sears makes one you can ride on."
Roseanne Barr

Allergy
As part of the admission procedure in the hospital where I work, I ask the patients if they are allergic to anything. If they are, I print it on an allergy band placed on the patient's wrists.

Once when I asked an elderly woman if she had any allergies, she said she couldn't eat bananas. Imagine my surprise when several hours later a very irate son came out to the nurses' station demanding, "Who's responsible for labeling my mother 'bananas'?"

No one is ever totally useless. They can always serve as a bad example.

Assault & Battery
Did you hear about the snail that got beat up by two turtles?
At the police station they asked him, "Did you get a good look at the turtles that did this?"
He said, "No, it all happened so fast."

Wanted

A group of elementary school students were on a field trip to the local police station. Several of the children were fascinated by the wanted posters on the wall.

Little Billy raised his hand and asked the police officer giving them the tour who the people on the wall were.

"Those are pictures of criminals we are looking for," answered the policeman. "We call those wanted posters."

Little Billy looked puzzled. His hand shot back up into the air. "Well," he wondered, "why didn't you just keep them when you took their picture?"

"Start by doing what's necessary, then do what's possible, and suddenly you are doing the impossible." St. Francis of Assisi

"If you go out looking for friends, you're going to find they are very scarce. If you go out to be a friend, you'll find them everywhere." Zig Zigler

Courage doesn't always roar. Sometimes courage is the little voice at the end of the day that says... I'll try again tomorrow.

Motel Rates

When the follow called a motel and asked how much they charged for a room, the clerk told him that the rates depended on room size and number of people.

"Do you take children?' the man asked.

"No, sir" replied the clerk. "Only cash and credit cards."

He who blames others has a long way to go on his journey. He who blames himself is halfway there. He who blames no one has arrived.

"Happiness is a perfume which you cannot pour on someone without getting some on yourself." Ralph Waldo Emerson

A government big enough to give you everything you want is a government big enough to take from you everything you have.
"What you think of me is none of my business." Terry Cole-Whittaker

"Always remember, others may hate you, but those who hate you don't win unless you hate them —and then you destroy yourself." Richard Nixon

How do you drown a hipster? In the mainstream.

*"At age 20 we worry about what others think of us.
At 40 we don't care what they think of us.
At 60 we discover they haven't been thinking of us at all."* Ann Landers

"Be who you are and say what you feel because those who mind don't matter and those who matter don't mind." Dr. Seuss

*"Courage is doing what you're afraid to do.
There can be no courage unless you're scared."* Eddie Rickenbacker

"People forget how fast you did a job - but they remember how well you did it." Howard Newton

If Life Were Like A Computer...
You could add/remove someone in your life using the control panel.
You could put your kids in the recycle bin and restore them when you feel like it!
You could click on "find" (Ctrl, F) to recover your lost remote control and car keys.
You could always press "Ctrl, Alt, Delete" and start all over!"

Ollie Goes Ice Fishing
Ollie wants to go ice fishing, so he goes to the ice and cuts a hole in it.
He hears, "THERE ARE NO FISH IN HERE."
He leaves and goes to another spot on the ice.
He hears, "THERE ARE NO FISH IN HERE."
Baffled, the guy asks, "Is this God?"
The voice responds, "No, this is the announcer! You're at a hockey rink!"

Dayvorce
A farmer walks into a lawyer's office and says, "I'd like to get one of them-thar day-vorce-ees."

"Yes sir, I believe I can help you," replied the lawyer. "Do you have any grounds?"

"Oh shore do!" exclaimed the farmer. "Got me bout a 140 acres out back a the house thar."

"No no, I mean do you have a case?" asked the lawyer.

"No sur," replied the farmer, "I drive one of them John Deers."

"You don't understand," said the lawyer, "You need something like a grudge."

"Oh!!" said the farmer, "I got me one uh dem! That's what I park muh Deer in!"

The lawyer, a bit frustrated responded, "Sir, you've got to have a reason to divorce your wife. Does she beat you up or anything?"

"No sur," replied the farmer, "I purt near get outta bed afore her ever mornin."

Finally the exasperated lawyer shouted, "WHY do you want a divorce?"

"Oh, well," replied the farmer, "She says we jus can't communicate!!"

Don't be afraid of opposition;
Remember a kite rises against, not with the wind.

Remedy

Little Emily was complaining to her mother that her stomach hurt.

Her mother replied, "That's because it's empty. Maybe you should try putting something in it."

The next day, the pastor was over at Emily's family's house for lunch. He mentioned having his head hurt, to which Emily immediately replied, "That's because it's empty. Maybe you should try putting something in it."

Little Pete

Little Pete came home from the playground with a bloody nose, black eye, and torn clothing. It was obvious he'd been in a bad fight and lost.

While his father was patching him up, he asked his son what happened.

"Well, Dad," said Pete, "I challenged Larry to a duel. And, you know, I gave him his choice of weapons."

"Uh-huh," said the father, "that seems fair."

"I know, but I never thought he'd choose his sister!"

Skeeters!

Some boy scouts from the city were on a camping trip. The mosquitoes were so fierce, the boys had to hide under their blankets to avoid being bitten.

Then one of them saw some lightning bugs and said to his friend, "We might as well give up. They're coming after us with flashlights!"

Sound Like A Frog

A little boy went up to his grandfather and asked, "Grandpa, can you make a sound like a frog?"

When the grandfather asked why, the boy replied, "Because daddy said when you croak we're all going to Disneyland."

It Is

"I am." is the shortest complete sentence in the English language.

It's scary when you start making the same noises as your coffee maker.

I used to have Saturday Night Fever...
Now I just have Saturday Night hot flashes.

A smooth sea never made a skillful mariner.

A goal without a plan is just a wish.

Betcha Didn't Know This...
The only 15 letter word that can be spelled without repeating a letter is "uncopyrightable."

Or, This...
Each king in a deck of playing cards represents a great king from history.
Spades - King David,
Clubs - Alexander the Great,
Hearts - Charlemagne,
and Diamonds - Julius Caesar.

A pessimist is someone who looks at the land of milk and honey
and sees only calories and cholesterol.

Signs
• In the front yard of a funeral home, "Drive carefully, we'll wait."
• In a nonsmoking area, "If we see you smoking, we will assume you are on fire and take appropriate action."
• On a maternity room door, "Push, Push, Push."
• On a front door, "Everyone on the premises is a vegetarian except the dog."
• At an optometrist's office, "If you don't see what you're looking for, you've come to the right place."
• On a taxidermist's window, "We really know our stuff."
• On a butcher's window, "Let me meat your needs."
• On a fence, "Salesmen welcome. Dog food is expensive."
• At a car dealership, "The best way to get back on your feet -- miss a car payment."
• Outside a muffler shop, "No appointment necessary. We'll hear you coming."
• On a desk in a reception room, "We shoot every 3rd salesman, and the 2nd one just left."
• In a veterinarian's waiting room, "Be back in 5 minutes. Sit! Stay!"

- In a Beauty Shop, "Dye now!"
- On the side of a garbage truck, "We've got what it takes to take what you've got." (Burglars please copy.)
- In a restaurant window, "Don't stand there and be hungry, come in and get fed up."
- Inside a bowling alley, "Please be quiet. We need to hear a pin drop."
- In a cafeteria, "Shoes are required to eat in the cafeteria. Socks can eat any place they want."

The man who fell into an upholstery machine is fully recovered.
"Enjoy the little things, for one day you may look back and realize they were the big things."~ Robert Brault

A lot of money is tainted - It taint yours and it taint mine.

I love to sleep. It really is the best of both worlds.
You get to be alive and unconscious.

"Now they show you how detergents take out bloodstains, a pretty violent image there. I think if you've got a T-shirt with a bloodstain all over it, maybe laundry isn't your biggest problem. Maybe you should get rid of the body before you do the wash."

Memory

A man goes to see his doctor because of a problem he is having concerning his memory. The man tells the doctor "I have been having lots of problems remembering things that happened in the past couple of hours, you know, my short term memory."

The doctor replies "How long has this been going on?"

The puzzled man looks back at the doctor and says "How long has what been going on?"

...wait. Have we published this before?

Bringing Home A Second

When our second child was on the way, my wife and I attended a pre-birth class aimed at couples who had already had at least one child. The instructor raised the issue of breaking the news to the older child. It went like this:

"Some parents," she said, "tell the older child, 'We love you so much we decided to bring another child into this family.' But, think about that. Ladies, what if your husband came home one day and said, 'Honey, I love you so much I decided to bring home another wife.'"

One of the women spoke up immediately. "Does she cook???"

Bar-be-que (bar*bi*q) n. You bought the groceries, washed the lettuce, chopped the tomatoes, diced the onions, marinated the meat and cleaned everything up, but he "made the dinner."

If you don't learn to laugh at trouble,
you won't have anything to laugh at when you are old.

If you are not big enough to lose you are too small to win.

"In matters of style, swim with the current; in matters of principle, stand like a rock." ~ Thomas Jefferson

"Here is a test to find whether your mission on earth is finished: if you're alive, it isn't." ~ Richard Bach

It is not what you are that holds you back,
it is what you think you are not. ~ Denis Waitley

Life is not measured by the number of breaths we take
but by the moments that take our breath away.

Obstacles are those frightful things you see
when you take your eyes off your goal. ~ Henry Ford

"The best way to predict your future is to create it." ~ Stephen Covey

Give the Frog a Loan

A frog goes into a bank and hops up to a teller. He can see from her name plate that she is called Patricia Whack, so he says "Ms. Whack, I'd like to borrow $30,000, please."

The teller asks for his name and the frog replies that he is Kermit Jagger, son of Mick Jagger, and a personal friend of the bank manager.

Unconvinced, Ms. Whack explains she will need some identity and also some security against his loan.

The frog produces a tiny pink porcelain elephant and hands it to her.

The confused teller says she will have to consult with her manager.

"There's a frog called Kermit Jagger at the counter who wants to borrow $30,000," she tells her boss. "And what do you think this elephant is about?"

The manager looks back at her and says, "It's a knick-knack, Patti Whack, give the frog a loan. His old man's a Rolling Stone."

The Outhouse

Once there was a boy, and he had a very old outhouse in his back yard. Just downhill from the outhouse was a little lake. So, one day when he was bored, the boy decides to slide the outhouse right into the lake.

That night the boy's father tells him the story of George Washington chopping down the cherry tree.

The boy is so impressed, he decides to confess. He tells his father, "I'm the one who slid the outhouse into the lake."

You can imagine the boy's surprise when his father begins spanking him. He asks his father, "I told the truth like President Washington; so, why are you spanking me?'

His father said, "George Washington's father wasn't in the cherry tree, when George chopped it down."

A Frog's Future

A boy frog telephones the Psychic Hotline and his Personal Psychic Advisor tells him: "You are going to meet a beautiful young girl who will want to know everything about you."
The frog is thrilled, "This is great! Will I meet her at a party?"
"No," says his Advisor, "in her biology class."

Cat Romance

A tom cat and a tabby were courting on a back fence one night.
The tom leaned over to the tabby with pent up passion and purred, "I'd die for you!"
The tabby gazed at him from under lowered eye lids and asked, "How many times?"

Oh Oh

Two snake buddies were slithering along through the grass.
One snake asked his friend, "Thay, are we poithonouth?"
His friend answered, "Yes, very. Why do you ask?"
The first snake explained, "I jutht bit my thongue."

Why do scientists call it "re"search when looking for something new?

Nurse: How is the girl who swallowed the quarter?
Doctor: No change yet!

Pa is Gonna Be Mad

A farm boy accidentally overturned his wagon load of corn. The farmer who lived nearby heard the noise and rushed right over.

"Hey Willis!!" the farmer yelled. "Forget it for now. It's dinnertime. Come eat with us, and then we'll come back and I will help you turn the wagon back up."

"That's mighty nice of you," Willis answered, "but, I don't think Pa would like me to."

"Aw, come on," the farmer insisted, "you have to eat! We'll get back to the wagon soon."

"Well okay," the boy finally agreed, and added, "But, Pa won't like it."

After a hearty dinner, Willis thanked his host. "I feel a lot better now, but I know Pa is going to be real upset."

"Don't be foolish." the neighbor said with a smile. "By the way, where is your Pa?"

Willis replied, "Under the wagon."

Young Patients

A pediatrician in town always plays a game with some of his young patients to put them at ease and test their knowledge of body parts.

One day, while pointing to a Little boy's ear, the doctor asked him, "Is this your nose?"

Immediately the little boy turned to his mother and said, "Mom, I think we'd better find a new doctor!"

Training Your Puppy

Puppy owners should get a newspaper and roll it up very tight. Secure it with a rubber band and leave it on the coffee table.

Then, when the puppy piddles in the house, chews up a slipper, or does anything he's not supposed to do, simply take the newspaper and bang it on the top of YOUR head very hard while repeating... "I should have been watching the puppy! I should have been watching the puppy!"

Can't Make This Stuff Up

A group of unicorns is called a "blessing."
Twelve or more cows are known as a "flink."
A group of frogs is called an "army."
A group of rhinos is called a "crash."
A group of kangaroos is called a "mob."
A group of whales is called a "pod."

A group of geese is called a "gaggle."
A group of ravens is called a "murder."
A group of officers is called a "mess."
A group of larks is called an "exaltation."
A group of owls is called a "parliament."

Now consider a group of baboons. They are the loudest, most dangerous, most obnoxious, most viciously aggressive, and least intelligent of all primates. And what is the proper collective noun for a group of baboons? A "Congress."

Play With The Boys?
A little girl asked her mother, "Can I go outside and play with the boys?" Her mother replied, "No, you can't play with the boys, they're too rough." The little girl thought about it for a few moments and asked, "If I can find a smooth one, can I play with him?"

The Concept of Marriage
The child was a typical four-year-old girl, cute, inquisitive, and bright as a new penny. When she expressed difficulty in grasping the concept of marriage, her father decided to pull out the wedding photo album, thinking visual images would help. One page after another, he pointed out the bride arriving at the church, the entrance, the wedding ceremony, the recessional, the reception, etc.
"Now do you understand?" he asked.
"I think so," she said, "So that's when mommy came to work for us?"

The Nun
An old nun who was living in a convent next to a construction site noticed the coarse language of the workers and decided to spend some time with them to correct their ways. She decided she would take her lunch, sit with the workers, and talk with them. She put her sandwich in a brown bag and walked over to the spot where the men were eating. She walked up to the group and with a big smile said, "Do you men know Jesus Christ?"
They shook their heads and looked at each other.
One of the workers looked up into the steelwork and yelled, "Anybody up there know Jesus Christ?"
One of the steelworkers asked, "why."
The foreman yelled, "His wife is here with his lunch!"

Uh-Oh, Joe
When the usher noticed a man stretched across three seats in the movie theater, he walked over and whispered "Sorry sir, but you are allowed only one seat."

The man moaned but didn't budge.

"Sir," the usher said more loudly, "if you don't move, I'll have to call the manager."

The man moaned again but stayed where he was.

The usher left and returned with the manager, who, after several attempts at dislodging the fellow, called the police.

The cop looked at the reclining man and said, "All right, what's your name, joker?"

"Joe," he mumbled.

"And where are you from, Joe?"

Joe responded painfully, "The balcony!"

Listen to Your Mother!

A mother was anxiously awaiting her daughter's plane. She had just come back from a faraway and seeking adventure.

As the daughter was exiting the plane, the mother noticed a man directly behind her daughter. He was dressed in feathers with exotic markings all over his body and he was carrying a shrunken head.

The daughter introduced the man as her new husband.

The mother gasped in disbelief and disappointment and screamed, "You never listen to me! I said for you to marry a RICH Doctor! a RICH Doctor!"

Protocol!

The lieutenant wanted to use a pay phone but didn't have change for a dollar. He saw a private mopping the floors and asked him, "Soldier, do you have change for a dollar?"

"I sure have, buddy," the private answered.

Giving him a mean stare, the lieutenant said, "That's no way to address an officer! Let's try it again. Private, do you have change for a dollar?"

"NO, SIR!" replied the private.

Motel

When the fellow went into a motel to ask how much they charged for a room, the clerk told him that the rates depended on room size and number of people. The man asked the clerk, "Do you take children?"

"No, sir" replied the clerk. "only cash and credit cards."

Wacky Warning Labels

• Warning on a bottle of drain cleaner: If you do not understand, or cannot read, all directions, cautions and warnings, do not use this product.

- On a snow sled: Beware: sled may develop high speed under certain snow conditions.
- Third place: On a 12-inch-high storage rack for compact discs: Do not use as a ladder.
- Fourth place: A 5-inch fishing lure with three nasty steel hooks advises it is "Harmful if swallowed." Too bad fish can't read!
- A warning on an electric router made for carpenters cautions, "This product not intended for use as a dental drill."
- A warning label found on a baby stroller cautions the user: Remove child before folding.
- A bottle of prescription sleeping pills says, "Warning: May cause drowsiness."
- A sticker on a toilet at a public facility in Ann Arbor, Michigan actually warns: "Recycled flush water unsafe for drinking."
- A CD player carries this unusual warning: "Do not use the Ultradisc2000 as a projectile in a catapult."
- An "Aim-n-Flame" fireplace lighter cautions, "Do not use near fire, flame, or sparks."
- A label on a hand-held massager advises consumers not to use "while sleeping or unconscious."

Ultimatum

One day, a cowboy rode into a Wild, Wild West town. The people in the town love to play jokes on visitors. After tying his horse to the pole outside a bar, the cowboy went in.

"A cup of milk please." he said to the bartender.

After drinking, he went out, only to find his horse missing. Knowing that the villagers did it, he went back into the bar and said to everybody, "I am going to have another drink and when I finish it, I want to see my horse outside! Or else, I will have to do what I did in Texas - HERE!"

The people were very frightened. When he finished his drink, he went outside and saw his horse. The villagers had put it back. Curious, the bartender asked the cowboy, "What did you do in Texas?"

The Cowboy replied, "Well, I had to walk home."

All In One

While shopping for vacation clothes, my husband and I passed a display of bathing suits. It had been at least ten years and twenty pounds since I had even considered buying a bathing suit, so I sought my husband's advice.

"What do you think?" I asked. "Should I get a bikini or an all-in-one?"

"Better get a bikini," he replied. "You'd never get it all in one."

Obituary

The local newspaper funeral notice telephone operator received a phone call. The woman on the other end asked, "How much do funeral notices cost?"

"$5.00 per word, Ma'am," came the response.

"Good, do you have a paper and pencil handy?"

"Yes, Ma'am."

"OK, write this: 'Cohen died.'"

"I'm sorry, Ma'am; I forgot to tell you there's a five-word minimum."

"Hmmph," came the reply, "You certainly did forget to tell me that."

A moment of silence. "Got your pencil and paper?"

"Yes, Ma'am."

"OK, print this: 'Cohen died, Cadillac for sale.'"

"I have yet to hear a man ask for advice on how to combine marriage and a career." ~Gloria Steinem

"I am a marvelous housekeeper.
Every time I leave a man I keep his house." ~Zsa Zsa Gabor

Car-napper!

While Mark was shopping for pet supplies, one of the salespeople came running up to him. "Mark! Mark! I just saw someone driving off with your BMW!"

"Dear God! Did your try to stop him?"

"No," said the clerk, "but don't worry. I got the license plate number!"

"In politics, if you want anything said, ask a man
--if you want anything done, ask a woman." ~Margaret Thatcher

"The phrase 'working mother' is redundant."
-Jane Sellman-

"A man's got to do what a man's got to do.
A woman must do what he can't."-Rhonda Hansome-

"I'm not offended by all the dumb blonde jokes because I know I'm not dumb... and I'm also not blonde. -Dolly Parton-

Here's Your Sign
- In the front yard of a funeral home, "Drive carefully, we'll wait."
- In a nonsmoking area, "If we see you smoking, we will assume you are on fire and take appropriate action."

- On a maternity room door, "Push, Push, Push."
- At an optometrist's office, "If you don't see what you're looking for, you've come to the right place."
- On a taxidermist's window, "We really know our stuff."
- On a butcher's window, "Let me meat your needs."
- On a fence, "Salesmen welcome. Dog food is expensive."
- At a car dealership, "The best way to get back on your feet -- miss a car payment."
- Outside a muffler shop, "No appointment necessary. We'll hear you coming."
- On a desk in a reception room, "We shoot every 3rd salesman, and the 2nd one just left."
- In a veterinarian's waiting room, "Be back in 5 minutes. Sit! Stay!"
- In a Beauty Shop, "Dye now!"
- On the side of a garbage truck, "We've got what it takes to take what you've got."
- In a restaurant window, "Don't stand there and be hungry, come in and get fed up."
- Inside a bowling alley, "Please be quiet. We need to hear a pin drop."
- In a cafeteria, "Shoes are required to eat in the cafeteria. Socks can eat any place they want."

"When women are depressed they either eat or go shopping.
Men invade another country."~ Elayne Boosler

My mother asked me to hand out invitations for my brother's surprise birthday party. That's when I realized he was her favorite twin.

Silly Wabbit
A lady opened her refrigerator and saw a rabbit sitting on one of the shelves, "What are you doing in there?" she asked.
The rabbit replied, "This is a Westinghouse, isn't it?"
The lady confirmed, "Yes."
"Well," the rabbit said, "I'm westing."

Surgery
A man is recovering from surgery when a nurse asks him how he is feeling.
"I'm okay, but I didn't like the four-letter-word the doctor used in surgery," he answered.
"What did he say," asked the nurse.
"Opps!" replied the man.

Assault
Did you hear about the snail that got beat up by two turtles?
At the police station they asked him, "Did you get a good look at the turtles that did this?"
He said, "No, it all happened so fast."

"Behind every successful man is a surprised woman." ~Maryon Pearson

Divine
Did you hear about the baby mouse that saw a bat?
He ran home and told his mother he'd seen and angel.

Mom Logic: "If you fall off that swing and break your neck, you can't go to the store with me."
Mom Humor: "When that lawn mower cuts off your toes, don't come running to me."
Mom Justice: "One day you'll have kids, and I hope they turn out just like you. Then you'll see what it's like!"

Mom Advice
A couple of hours into a visit with my mother she noticed I hadn't lit up a cigarette once.
"Are you trying to kick the habit?"
"No," I replied, "I've got a cold and I don't smoke when I'm not feeling well."
"You know," she observed, "you'd probably live longer if you were sick more often."

Fast Food
Two robins were lying on their backs, basking in the sun. A mama cat and her kitten were walking by.
The kitten complained, "Mama, I'm so hungry, what can we eat?"
To which the mama cat, spying the two robins, replied, "How about some Baskin Robbins?"

Texting acronyms can stump even the best parents:
Mom: Your great-aunt just passed away. LOL.
Son: Why is that funny?
Mom: It's not funny, David! What do you mean?
Son: Mom, LOL means Laughing Out Loud.
Mom: I thought it meant Lots of Love. I have to call everyone back.

Texting Mom
Mom: What do IDK, LY & TTYL mean?
Son: I don't know, love you, talk to you later.
Mom: OK, I will ask your sister.

My Great-Grandma
"My great-grandma gave me this money," said my three-year-old, happily clutching a $20 bill he'd received as a present.
"That's right," I said. "How did you know that?"
Pointing to Andrew Jackson's face in the middle, he said, "Because her picture is on it."

What's the Deal?
My nephew asked, "Why does Nana have so many Bibles?"
I said, "She's studying for finals."

Being A Mom
I was not thrilled with the idea of letting my clueless 13-year-old son babysit his younger sisters, even though he begged me to.
"What about a fire?" I asked, referring to my No. 1 concern.
"Mom," he said, rolling his eyes, "I'm a Boy Scout. I know how to start a fire."

Birthday Present
Fresh out of gift ideas, a man buys his mother-in-law a large plot in an expensive cemetery. On her next birthday, he buys her nothing, so she lets him have it.
"What are you complaining about?" he fires back.
"You still haven't used the present I gave you last year."

Mom's Turn
On the day I received my learner's permit, my mom agreed to take me out for a driving lesson.
With a big grin, she hopped in behind the driver's seat.
"Why aren't you sitting up front on the passenger's side?" I asked.
"Kirsten, I've been waiting for this ever since you were a little girl," Mom replied. "Now it's my turn to sit back here and kick the seat."

Oh, Dad
My father was completely lost in the kitchen and never ate unless someone prepared a meal for him. When Mother was ill, however, he volunteered to go to the supermarket for her. She sent him off with a carefully numbered list of seven items.

Dad returned shortly, very proud of himself, and proceeded to unpack the grocery bags. He had one bag of sugar, two dozen eggs, three hams, four boxes of detergent, five boxes of crackers, six eggplants, and seven green peppers.

Oh, Dad - 2

A wife asks her husband, "Could you please go shopping for me and buy one carton of milk and, if they have avocados, get six."

A short time later, the husband returns with six cartons of milk.

"Why did you buy six cartons of milk?" his wife asks.

He replies, "They had avocados."

Visiting Mom

My mom moved into a new condo, and I went to visit for a couple of days. Searching for a coffee cup one morning, I sighed, "It seems like I'm always looking for something in your kitchen."

"That's good," Mom said. When I looked confused, she explained, "Because when you know where to look, it's time to go home."

My Mom

"Why doesn't your mother like me?" a woman asked her boyfriend.

"Don't take it personally," he assures her. "She's never liked anyone I've dated. I once dated someone exactly like her, and that didn't work out at all."

"What happened?"

"My father couldn't stand her."

Etiquette

While flying from Denver to Kansas City, Kansas, my mother was sitting across the aisle from a woman and her eight-year-old son. Mom couldn't help laughing as they neared their destination and she heard the mother say to the boy, "Now remember — run to Dad first, then the dog."

Not What I Meant, Guv'na

My daughter said something to me that I didn't think was very polite. I told her she needed to say it again in a nicer way—so she repeated it with a British accent.

Work for Mother?

My coworker at the hotel was miserable at his job and was desperately searching for a new one.

"Why don't you work for your mother?" I suggested.

He shook his head. "I can't," he said. "Her company has a very strict policy against hiring relatives."

"Who made up that ridiculous rule?"

"My mother."

Early Start

I was sound asleep when the telephone jarred me awake.

"Hi!" It was my peppy mother-in-law. She proceeded to rattle on about the busy day she had ahead and all the things that awaited her the rest of the week.

"Mom," I interrupted. "It's five in the morning."

"Really? What are you doing up so early?"

Raisin Em Up!

After my three-year-old begged and begged, I gave in and let her attend a concert with her older sister and brother.

As we took our seats, I handed programs to the kids. Following the lead of her siblings, my three-year-old opened her program and announced, "I'll have the chicken."

Lucas

After catching her five-year-old son Lucas trying to pull a fast one, his mother demanded, "Do you think I have idiot written on my forehead?"

Lucas answered, "I don't know. I can't read."

Family Nite IN

My husband and I both work, so our family eats out a lot. Recently, when we were having a rare home-cooked meal, I handed a glass to my three-year-old and told her to drink her milk.

She looked at me bewildered and replied, "But I didn't order milk."

Dinner Prayer

A couple invited some people to dinner. At the table, the wife turned to their six-year-old daughter and said, "Would you like to say the blessing?"

"I wouldn't know what to say," the girl replied.

"Just say what you hear Mommy say," the wife answered.

The daughter bowed her head and said, "Lord, why on earth did I invite all these people to dinner?"

Family Night Out

The night we took our three young sons to an upscale restaurant for the first time, my husband ordered a bottle of wine.
The server brought it over, began the ritual uncorking, and poured a small amount for me to taste.

My six-year-old piped up, "Mom usually drinks a lot more than that."

Call Your Mother!

My mother, a master of guilt trips, showed me a photo of herself waiting by a phone that never rings.

"Mom, I call all the time," I said. "If you had voicemail, you'd know." Soon after, my brother set it up for her.

When I called the next time, I got her message: "If you are a salesperson, press one. If you're a friend, press two. If you're my daughter who never calls, press 911 because the shock will probably give me a heart attack."

Teen Wisdom

I mentioned to my sons that some teens used Facebook to plan a robbery at a local mall.

"How did the NSA miss that?" my 21-year-old asked.

"I told you guys," said my 17-year-old. "No one uses Facebook anymore."

Do for others with no desire of returned favor.
We all should plant some trees we'll never sit under.

Nobody can make you feel offended without your permission.
~ Eleanor Roosevelt

Those who get too big for their britches will be exposed in the end.

Forgiveness does not change the past, but it does enlarge the future
~ Paul Boese

Enjoy the little things, for one day you may look back and realize they were the big things. ~ Robert Brault

Don't make me come down there ~ God

Courage is what it takes to stand up and speak; courage is also what it takes to sit down and listen.

Discipline is remembering what you want. ~ David Campbell

Character is what you are when nobody's looking. ~ Anonymous

An obstacle is something you see when you take your eyes off the goal.

A smooth sea never made a skillful mariner. ~ English Proverb

A truth spoken before its time is dangerous.

A wish changes nothing. A decision changes everything!

Always keep your words soft and sweet, just in case you have to eat them.

A man who trims himself to suit everybody will soon whittle himself away. ~ Charles Schwab

Having A Bad Day?
    A woman came home to find her husband in the kitchen shaking frantically, almost in a dancing frenzy, with some kind of wire running from his waist towards the electric kettle. Intending to jolt him away from the deadly current, she whacked him with a handy plank of wood, breaking his arm in two places. Up to that moment, he had been happily listening to his iPod.

What Memory Problem?
    A man goes to see his doctor because of a problem he is having concerning his memory.
    The man tells the doctor, "I have been having lots of problems remembering things that happened in the past couple of hours, you know, my short term memory."
    The doctor replies, "How long has this been going on?"
    The puzzled man looks back at the doctor and says, "How long has what been going on?"

Ten Dollars
    Johnny and his wife went to the State Fair every year. Every year Johnny would say, "I'd like to ride in that airplane."
    Every year his wife would say, "I know, Johnny, but that airplane ride costs ten dollars, and ten dollars is ten dollars."

This year Johnny and his wife went to the fair and Johnny said, "I'm 71 years old. If I don't ride that airplane this year I may never get another chance."

"That airplane ride costs ten dollars, and ten dollars is ten dollars," replied his wife.

The pilot overheard them and said, "Folks, I'll make you a deal. I'll take you both up for a ride. If you can stay quiet for the entire ride and not say one word, I won't charge you, but if you say one word it's ten dollars."

Johnny and his wife agree and up they go. The pilot does all kinds of twists and turns, rolls and dives, but not a word is heard. He does all his tricks over again, but still not a word.

They land and the pilot turns to Johnny, "By golly, I did everything I could think of to get you to yell out, but you didn't."

Johnny replied, "Well, I was gonna say something when my wife fell out, but ten dollars is ten dollars."

Hermit

Last year authorities in Washington State discovered that a hermit had been living in an old Forest Service cabin, and they were concerned about his wellbeing. They decided to send up a team of experts from different fields to analyze his living arrangements, and to make sure that he was okay.

First, they decided on a Psychologist, to make sure that the man was mentally handling his isolation.

Next, they decided on an Engineer, to make sure that the cabin is still structurally sound and safe.

Finally, they decided on a Theological professor from the UW, to make sure that the man's spiritual needs were being fulfilled.

The team made its way up the treacherous terrain in three days, but they were truly exhausted. Finally, on the evening of the third day, they spotted the cabin. From the outside, it appeared all was well.

The area around the cabin was clean, the ground almost appearing as though it had been swept often. There was smoke coming from the stove pipe chimney, and the door was slightly ajar.

Cautiously, they walked inside. Inside the cabin everything appeared neat and tidy. The only thing that stood out, and this immediately caught the attention of all three men, was that the stove was suspended 18 inches off of the floor by about a hundred wires attached to the ceiling. The pattern of the wires was very intricate, cutting this way and that, and it appeared to be a very sturdy arrangement.

At first, all three men did not know what to make of the arrangement. Finally with a loud, "Oh yes!" the Psychologist spoke. "This very clearly explains this man's desire to return to the womb. He has arranged the stove so that he can crawl underneath to, once again, feel the warmth of the womb."

"Nonsense!" exclaimed the Engineer. "This serves a very clear and definite thermodynamic purpose. He has lifted the stove so as to reduce the zone which the heat has to permeate, allowing the cold air to remain within the cabin, locking the heat in place. This man is a genius."

The Theological Professor stayed quiet a moment longer, but then he too spoke. "I hate to disappoint you both, but I believe you are both wrong. The placement of fire on raised altars has always been a significant emblem of the existence of faith and religion in cultures of the past and present. It would clearly be that this man has created an altar for whatever faith he has clung onto or, worse yet, created."

At this, the three men argued until there was a loud knock at the door, and the three men turned to see that the hermit had returned to his home.

Immediately, the three men approached him and demanded to know the significance of the placement of the stove.
The hermit stared at the three men long enough to hush them up, and then he spoke.

"Simple... had to fix stove pipe. Had plenty of wire and not enough stove pipe."

Bum In Need Of Food

One afternoon, a man was riding in the back of his limousine when he saw two men eating grass by the road side. He ordered his driver to stop and he got out to investigate.

"Why are you eating grass?" he asked one man.

"We don't have any money for food." The poor man replied.

"Oh, come along with me then."

"But sir, I have a wife with two children!"

"Bring them along! And you, come with me too!" he said to the other man.

"But sir, I have a wife with six children!" The second man answered.

"Bring them as well!"

They all climbed into the car, which was no easy task, even for a car as large as the limo. Once underway, one of the poor fellows says, "sir, you are too kind. Thank you for taking all of us with you."

The rich man replied "No, you don't understand, the grass at my home is about three feet tall!"

A lot of money is tainted - It taint yours and it taint mine.

You know you are getting old when everything either dries up or leaks.

Home In No Time

A woman was waiting in the checkout line at a shopping center. Her arms were laden with a mop and broom and other cleaning supplies. By her actions and deep sighs, it was obvious she was in an extreme hurry, and was not happy about the slowness of the line.

When the cashier called for a price check on a box of soap, the woman remarked indignantly, "Well, I'll be lucky to get out of here and home before Easter!"

"Don't worry, ma'am," replied the clerk. "With that wind kicking up out there and that brand new broom, you'll be home in no time."

I Am Going To Shop

"Cash, check or charge?" I asked after folding items the woman wished to purchase.

As she fumbled for her wallet I notice a remote control for a television set in her purse.

"Do you always carry your TV remote?" I asked.

"No," she replied. "But, my husband refused to come shopping with me, so I figured this was the most evil thing I could do to him."

The Texan and the New Yorker

A Texan had a business meeting with a NY Banker. The Texan hit it off with the banker real well.

He told the banker, "My son has a 100,000 acre ranch, stocked with cattle, exotic game, and horses. I'm going to have my jet come up to NYC and pick you up and fly you down to Texas. We'll have a big BBQ and go riding and hunting."

The banker replied, "Your son has done real good for himself. How old is your son?"

The Texan said, "He's 8."

The banker was shocked and asked, "What did an 8-year-old do to get a 100,000 acre ranch?"

The Texan said, "He got 4 A's and a B on his report card."

Rookie Officer

A rookie police officer pulled a biker over for speeding and had the following exchange:
- Officer: May I see your driver's license?
- Biker: I don't have one. I had it suspended when I got my 5th DUI.

- Officer: May I see the owner's card for this vehicle?
- Biker: It's not my bike. I stole it.
- Officer: The motorcycle is stolen?
- Biker: That's right. But come to think of it, I think I saw the owner's card in the tool bag when I was putting my gun in there.
- Officer: There's a gun in the tool bag?
- Biker: Yes sir. That's where I put it after I shot and killed the dude who owns this bike and stuffed his dope in the saddle bags.
- Officer: There's drugs in the saddle bags too?!?!?
- Biker: Yes, sir.

Hearing this, the rookie immediately called his captain. The biker was quickly surrounded by police, and the captain approached the biker to handle the tense situation:

- Captain: Sir, can I see your license?
- Biker: Sure. Here it is. (It was valid).
- Captain: Who's motorcycle is this?
- Biker: It's mine, officer. Here's the registration.
- Captain: Could you slowly open your tool bag so I can see if there's a gun in it?
- Biker: Yes, sir, but there's no gun in it.

(Sure enough, there was nothing in the tool bag).

- Captain: Would you mind opening your saddle bags? I was told you said there's drugs in them.
- Biker: No problem. (The saddle bags were opened; no drugs).
- Captain: I don't understand it. The officer who stopped you said you told him you didn't have a license, stole this motorcycle, had a gun in the tool bag, and that there were drugs in the saddle bags.
- Biker: Yeah, I'll bet he told you I was speeding, too.

Responsible Individual

A young man applied for a job at a new factory being built in a nearby town. He entered the main office, where the receptionist directed him down the hall to an office where he was to be interviewed by the Personnel Officer.

After several minutes of describing and explaining all about the new factory, the Personnel Officer told the young man, "We need individuals who are totally responsible."

The young man grinned and responded: "Well, I sure qualify. Everywhere I've worked, when something went wrong, I was always responsible!"

"My dad's a writer. His favorite expression is 'The pen's mightier than the sword,' which I believed for a long time until I moved into the city, and I got

into a fight with this guy. He cut me up real bad, and I drew a mustache on his face... and then I wrote him a nasty letter."
--Kevin Brennan

The Lawn Mower

Last year, when the power mower was broken and wouldn't run, I kept hinting to my husband that he ought to get it fixed; but, somehow the message never sank in.

Finally, I thought of a clever way to make the point. When my husband arrived home that day, he found me seated in the tall grass, busily snipping away with a tiny pair of sewing scissors. He watched silently for a short time and then went into the house.

He was gone only a few moments when he came out again. He handed me a toothbrush and said, "When you finish cutting the grass, you might as well sweep the sidewalks."

The doctors say he will probably live, but it will be quite a while before the cast comes off!

Kids Answers:

Why did God make mothers?
- She's the only one who knows where the scotch tape is.
- Mostly to clean the house.
- To help us out of there when we were getting born.

How did God make mothers?
- He used dirt, just like for the rest of us.
- Magic plus super powers plus a lot of stirring.
- God made my mom just the same as He made me, He just used bigger parts.

What are mothers made of?
- God makes mothers out of clouds and angel hair and everything nice in the world and one dab of mean.
- They had to get the start from men bones, then they mostly use string I think.

Why did God give you your mother and not some other mom?
- We're related.
- God knows she likes me a lot more than other people's moms like me.

What kind of little girl was your mom?
- My mom has always been my mom and none of that little girl stuff.
- I don't know because I wasn't there, but my guess would be pretty bossy.
- They say she used to be nice.

What did mom need to know about dad before she married him?
- His last name.

• She had to know his background. Like is he a crook? Does he get drunk on beer? Does he make at least $800 a year? Did he say no to drugs and yes to chores?

Contest

There was a group of scientists and they were all sitting around discussing which one of them was going to go to God and tell Him that they didn't need him anymore. One of the scientists volunteered and went to go tell God he was no longer needed.

The scientist says to God, "God, you know, a bunch of us have been thinking and I've come to tell you that we really don't need you anymore. I mean, we've been coming up with great theories and ideas, we've cloned sheep, and we're on the verge of cloning humans. So as you can see, we really don't need you."

God nods understandingly and says. "I see. Well, no hard feelings. But, before you go, let's have a contest. What do you think?"

The scientist says, "Sure. What kind of contest?"

God says, "A man-making contest."

The scientist says, "Sure! No problem."

The scientist bends down and picks up a handful of dirt and says, "Okay, I'm ready!"

God replies, "No, no, no... You go get your own dirt."

The Dog

As I drove into a parking lot, I noticed that a pickup truck with a dog sitting behind the wheel was rolling toward a female pedestrian.

She seemed oblivious; so, I hit my horn to get her attention. She looked up just in time to jump out of the way of the truck's path, and the vehicle bumped harmlessly into the curb and stopped.

I rushed to the woman's side to see if she was all right.

"I'm fine," she assured me, "but, I don't know WHAT would have happened if that dog hadn't honked!"

When Mother Theresa received her Nobel Prize, she was asked, "What can we do to promote world peace?" She replied, "Go home and love your family."

Dog Tired

Submitted by Paul Jacob

An older, tired-looking dog wandered into my yard. I could tell from his collar and well-fed belly that he had a home and was well taken care of. He calmly came over to me. I gave him a few pets on his head. He then followed me into my house, slowly walked down the hall, curled up in the corner, and fell asleep. An hour later, he went to the door, and I let him out.

The next day he was back, greeted me in my yard, walked inside and resumed his spot in the hall. And, again, he slept for about an hour. This continued on and off for several weeks.

Curious, I pinned a note on his collar: "I would like to find out who the owner of this wonderful sweet dog is and ask if you are aware that almost every afternoon your dog comes to my house for a nap."

The next day he arrived for his nap with a different note pinned to his collar: "He lives in a home with 6 children -- 2 under the age of 3. He's trying to catch up on his sleep. Can I come with him tomorrow?"

Relationship Tip for Men
When a woman says, "Correct me if I'm wrong but..." DON'T DO IT! IT'S A TRAP! Do NOT, I repeat, do NOT correct that woman!

Health Tip
Once you lick the frosting off a cupcake it becomes a muffin... and muffins are healthful. You're welcome.

NAVY Seal
After a reporter discussed what countries a NAVY Seal had been deployed, she asked him if he had to learn any of the languages.

He replied, "Oh, no ma'am, we don't go there to talk."

Air Space
Conversation overheard on the VHF Guard (emergency) frequency 121.5 MHz while flying from Europe to Dubai.
Iranian Air Defense Site: 'Unknown aircraft you are in Iranian airspace. Identify yourself.'
Aircraft: 'This is a United States aircraft. I am in Iraqi airspace.'
Air Defense Site: 'You are in Iranian airspace. If you do not depart our airspace we will launch interceptor aircraft!'
Aircraft: 'This is a United States Marine Corps FA-18 Fighter. Send 'em up, I'll wait!'
Air Defense Site: (... total silence)

"As I hurtled through space, one thought kept crossing my mind -- every part of this rocket was supplied by the lowest bidder." ~ John Glenn

Israel

A Jewish businessman in Brooklyn decided to send his son to Israel to absorb some of the culture of the homeland. When the son returned, the father asked him to tell him about his trip.

The son said, "Pop, I had a great time in Israel. By the way, I converted to Christianity."

"Oh, my," said the father. "What have I done?"

He decided to go ask his friend Jacob what to do.

Jake said, "Funny you should ask. I too sent my son to Israel, and he also came back a Christian. Perhaps we should go see the rabbi and ask him what we should do."

So, they went to see the rabbi.

The rabbi said, "Funny you should ask. I too sent my son to Israel. He also came back a Christian. What is happening to our young people? Perhaps we should go talk to God and ask him what to do."

The three of them prayed and explained what had happened to their sons and asked God what to do.

Suddenly, a voice came loud and clear from Heaven. The Voice said, "Funny you should ask. I, too, sent my Son to Israel…"

Irish Priest Who Was Transferred to Texas

Father O'Malley rose from his bed one morning. It was a fine spring day in his new west Texas mission parish. He walked to the window of his bedroom to get a deep breath of the beautiful day outside. He then noticed there was a donkey lying dead in the middle of his front lawn. He promptly called the local police station.

"Good morning. This is Sergeant Jones. How might I help you?"

"And the best of the day te yerself. This is Father O'Malley at St. Ann's Catholic Church. There's a donkey lying dead in me front lawn and would ye be so kind as to send a couple o'yer lads to take care of the matter?"

Sergeant Jones, considering himself to be quite a wit and recognizing the foreign accent, thought he would have a little fun with the good father, replied, "Well now Father, it was always my impression that you people took care of the last rites!"

There was dead silence on the line for a long moment.

Father O'Malley then replied, "Aye, 'tis certainly true; but, we are also obliged to notify the next of kin first, which is the reason for me call."

"After the game, the King and the pawn go into the same box." ~ Italian proverb

"When a man opens a car door for his wife, it's either a new car or a new wife." ~ Prince Philip

"A computer once beat me at chess, but it was no match for me at kickboxing." ~ Emo Philips.

"Wood burns faster when you have to cut and chop it yourself." ~ Harrison Ford

"We are here on earth to do well unto others. What the others are here for, I have no idea." ~ WH Auden

"The first piece of luggage on the carousel never belongs to anyone." ~ George Roberts

"I tried cooking supper with wine tonight. It didn't go so well. After 5 glasses I forgot why I was even in the kitchen."

HUH???
Alabama's Heather Whitestone was selected as Miss America 1995
Host: If you could live forever, would you and why?
Miss Whitestone: "I would not want to live forever, because we should not live forever, because if we were supposed to live forever, then we would live forever, but we cannot live forever, which is why I would not live forever."

"Whenever I watch TV and see those poor starving kids all over the world, I can't help but cry. I mean I'd love to be skinny like that, but not with all those flies and death and stuff." Mariah Carey

"Smoking kills. If you're killed, you've lost a very important part of your life," Brooke Shields, during an interview to become spokesperson for federal anti-smoking campaign.

"I've never had major knee surgery on any other part of my body," Winston Bennett, University of Kentucky basketball forward.

"Outside of the killings, Washington has one of the lowest crime rates in the country," Mayor Marion Barry, Washington, DC.

"Half this game is ninety percent mental." Philadelphia Phillies manager, Danny Ozark.

"**It isn't pollution that's** harming the environment. It's the impurities in our air and water that are doing it." Al Gore

"**Traditionally, most of** Australia's imports come from overseas." Keppel Enderbery

"**If somebody has a bad** heart, they can plug this jack in at night as they go to bed and it will monitor their heart throughout the night. And the next morning, when they wake up dead, there'll be a record." Mark S. Fowler, FCC Chairman

"Remember to hold on tight to the ones you love. And then tickle them!"

Laughter is the shortest distance between two people.

Q: What do you get when you cross poison ivy with a four-leaf clover?
A: A rash of good luck.

Q: Why can't you borrow money from a leprechaun?
A: Because they're always a little short.

Q: What's Irish and stays out all night?
A: Paddy O'furniture

Q: Why do people wear shamrocks on St. Patrick's Day?
A: Because regular rocks are too heavy.

Q: Why did St. Patrick drive all the snakes out of Ireland?
A: He couldn't afford plane fare.

On St. Patty's Day...
I went out drinking on St Patrick's Day, so I took a bus home.
That may not seem like a big deal to you, but I've never driven a bus before.

Irish Priest
An Irish priest is driving and gets stopped for speeding. The state trooper smells alcohol on the priest's breath. He sees an empty wine bottle in the car.
The trooper says, "Sir, have you been drinking?"
"Just water," says the priest.
The trooper says, "Then why do I smell wine?"
The priest looks at the bottle and says, "Good Lord! He's done it again!"

The Headstone
Reilly is walking through a graveyard when he comes across a headstone with the inscription, "Here lies a politician and an honest man."
"Faith now," exclaims Reilly, "I wonder how they got the two of them in one grave."

Finnegan's Donkey
Finnegan sells Michael a donkey. Some weeks later they met in a pub in Killarney and Michael says, "Hey, Finnegan, that donkey you sold me went and died."
Finnegan just sips his Guinness slowly and retorts, "Bejabbers, Michael, it never done that on me."

Me Head!
Kieran O'Connor always slept with his gun under his pillow. Hearing a noise at the foot of the bed, he shot off his big toe.
"Thank the Lord I wasn't sleeping at the other end of the bed," Kieran said to his friends in Donegal's pub. "I would have blown my head off."

Between Diplomats
"Why do you Irish always answer a question with a question?" asked President Franklin D. Roosevelt.
"Do we now?" came New York Mayor Al Smith's reply.

The Verdict
O'Gara was arrested and sent for trial for armed bank robbery.
After due deliberation, the jury foreman stood up and announced, "Not guilty."
"That's grand," shouted O'Gara, "Does that mean I get to keep the money?"

Digging a Hole
A passer-by watched two Irishmen in a park. One was digging holes and the other was immediately filling them in again.
"Tell me," said the passer-by, "What on earth are you doing?"
"Well," said the digger, "Usually there are three of us. I dig, Fergal plants the tree, and Sean fills in the hole. Today Fergal is away unwell, but that doesn't mean Sean and I have to take the day off, does it?"

How Many Ducks?
On the bus Paddy got chatting to Murphy who was carrying a bag on his back.
"What's in the bag?" asked Paddy.

"I'm not going to tell," replied Murphy.
"Go on, do!" pleaded Paddy.
"Ah, all right then, it's ducks." announced Murphy.
"If I guess how many ducks you have in the bag, will you give me one of them?" inquired Paddy.
"Look," said Murphy, "If you guess the correct number, I'll give you both of them."
"Five!" said Paddy triumphantly.

It's All in The Name

A pregnant Irish woman from Dublin gets in a car accident and falls into a deep coma. Asleep for nearly 6 months, she wakes up she sees that she is no longer pregnant and frantically asks the doctor about her baby.

The doctor replies, "Ma'am you had twins! a boy and a girl. Your brother from Cork came in and named them."

The woman thinks to herself, "Oh No, not my brother... he's an idiot!" She asks the doctor, "Well, what's the girl's name?"

"Denise."

"Wow, that's not a bad name, I like it! What's the boy's name?"

"Denephew."

Priest Walks into a Bar

Father O'Connor walks into a pub and says to the first man he meets, "Do you want go to heaven?"

The man replies, "Yes, Father."

Father O'Connor then says, "Leave this bar right now, and go outside."

O'Connor proceeds to another man, and asks him the same thing. The chap also answers, "Yes."

Father O'Connor asks him too to go out.

The Reverend Father goes to the third man and asks, "Would you like to go to heaven?"

This time the reply is, "No, thank-you Father,"

Surprised, Father O'Connor asks, "Why not?"

The man opines, "I mean I do, but only after I die."

Father O'Connor explains, "That's what I am talking about."

The man says, "Oh, I thought you are getting a group ready right now."

Mrs. Irwin's Watch

"Ah, good morning, Mrs Irwin, and how is everything?"
"Sure and I'm having a great time of it between my husband and the fire. If I keep my eye on the one, the other is sure to go out."

No Hiding Place

Walking into the bar, Shamus said to O'Heir the bartender, "Pour me a stiff one - just had another fight with the little woman."

"O, bejabbers," said O'Heir, "And how did this one end?"

"Hah! When it was over," Shamus replied, "she came to me on her hands and knees."

"Really!" cried O'Heir, "now that's a switch! What did she say?"

She said, "Come out from under the bed, Shamus, you little chicken."

French

"Shay, do you understand French?"
"I do if it's spoken in Irish."

Good Mrs. O'Leary

"Murphy, why don't you give up the drinking, smoking, and carousing?" said Mrs O'Leary.

"It's too late," replied Murphy.

"It's never too late," assured the virtuous Mrs O'Leary.

"Well, there's no rush then," smiled Murphy.

Irish Astronauts

After the Americans went to the Moon, Paddy and Seamus announced that the Kerry Men would go one better and send a man to the Sun.

Murphy objected. "If you send a man to the Sun, he will burn up!"

"What do you think we are, stupid?" Seamus replied. "We'll send our man at night!"

You Can't Believe Everything You Read

Dermot McCann opened the morning newspaper and was dumbfounded to read in the obituary column that he had died. He quickly phoned his best friend, Reilly.

"Did ye see the paper?" asked Dermot. "They say I died."

"Yes, I saw it." replied Reilly. "Where are ye callin' from?"

So when dogs see a police dog do they go, "oh, great, there's the cops?"

ON MY FIRST DAY at the gas station, I watched a co-worker measure the level of gasoline in the underground tanks by lowering a giant measuring stick down into them.

"What would happen if I threw a lit match into the hole?" I joked.

"It would go out," he answered very matter-of-factly.

"Really?" I asked, surprised to hear that. "Is there a safety device that would extinguish it before the fumes are ignited?"

"No," my co-worker replied. "The force from the explosion would blow the match out."

TWO ELDERLY LADIES had been friends for many decades. Over the years they had shared all kinds of activities and adventures. Lately, their activities had been limited to meeting a few times a week to play cards.

One day they were playing cards when one looked at the other and said, "Now don't get mad at me ... I know we've been friends for a long time ... but I just can't think of your name! I've thought and thought, but I can't remember it. Please tell me what your name is."

Her friend glared at her. For at least three minutes she just stared and glared at her. Finally, she said, "How soon do you need to know?"

A WOMAN FROM SEATTLE HEARD that milk baths would make her beautiful. She left a note for her milkman to leave 15 gallons of milk.

When the milkman read the note, he felt there must be a mistake. He thought she probably meant 1.5 gallons so he knocked on the door to clarify the point.

The lady came to the door and the milkman said, "I found your note to leave 15 gallons of milk. Did you mean 1.5 gallons?"

The lady said, "I want 15 gallons. I'm going to fill my bathtub up with milk and take a milk bath."

The milkman asked, "Do you want it Pasteurized?"

The lady said, "No, just up to my belly button. I can splash it in my eyes."

AT MY GRANDDAUGHTER'S WEDDING, the DJ polled the guests to see who had been married longest. It turned out to be my husband and me who had been.

The DJ asked us, "What advice would you give to the newly-married couple?"

I said, "The three most important words in a marriage are, 'You're probably right.'"

Everyone then looked at my husband. He said, "She's probably right."

TWO GIRLS, living in Seattle were sitting on a bench one evening when one asked the other, "What do you think is farther, Florida or the moon?"

The other girl gave a puzzled look and replied, "Helloooooooo--Can you see Florida?!"

PROPER ATTIRE is required in the cafeteria at the University of Maine. To enforce that rule, the management posted this notice: "Shoes are required to eat in this cafeteria."

Next to it, a student added, "Socks can eat wherever they want."

MY ITALIAN AMERICAN FRIEND is very self-conscious about his height, or lack thereof. So I always steer clear of the subject. One day, he and I went to lunch at a Sub shop.

"I'll take the Italian," he said to the guy behind the counter. "Salami, Provolone, and peppers."

"Do you want a full hero or half one?" came the reply.

"Ah... gimme a half," my friend says.

After placing our orders, we took our seats. A few minutes later, my friend grimaced when we heard... "Small Italian, your order is up!"

A MOTHER AND FATHER were chatting with their eight-year-old son about his future. The youngster said he'd like to attend Cornell, as his parents and other members of the family had.

Pleased with his response, they pressed on. "What would you like to take when you attend college?" they asked the little boy.

After giving it some thought and glancing around the kitchen, he replied, "The refrigerator, if you can get along without it."

A FRIEND ASKED ME to replace the rotted post that her mailbox sat on, but to save the beloved old box. I managed to extract all but one of the rusty nails in the bottom of the mailbox. To free the last nail, I wrapped my arms around the box in a bear hug and started yanking up.

Just then a truck came by, and the driver stuck his head out the window and said, "I tried that, but the bills just keep on coming."

A WOMAN FROM SEATTLE IS TAKING the driving portion of her driver's license exam. She handles most of the maneuvers quite well. She has a little trouble parallel parking, however, and winds up a couple of feet from the curb.

"Could you get a little closer?" the examiner asks.

She then unbuckles her seat belt and slides over toward the examiner. "Now what?"

A WOMAN MEANT TO call a record store, but dialed the wrong number and got a private home instead. "Do you have 'Eyes of Blue' and 'A Love Supreme?'" she asked.

"Well, no," answered the puzzled homeowner. "But I have a wife and eleven children."

"Is that a record?" she inquired, puzzled in her turn.

"I don't think so," replied the man, "but it's as close as I want to get."

AFTER A TRIAL HAD BEEN going on for three days, Finley, the man accused of committing the crimes, stood up and approached the judge's bench. "Your Honor, I would like to change my plea from 'innocent' to 'guilty' of the charges."

The judge angrily banged his fist on the desk. "If you're guilty, why didn't you say so in the first place and save this court a lot of time and inconvenience?" he demanded.

Finley looked up wide-eyed and stated, "Well, when the trial started I thought I was innocent, but that was before I heard all the evidence against me."

AS A JET WAS FLYING over Arizona on a clear day, the copilot was providing his passengers with a running commentary about landmarks over the PA system. "Coming up on the right, you can see the Meteor Crater, which is a major tourist attraction in northern Arizona. It was formed when a lump of nickel and iron, roughly 150 feet in diameter and weighing 300,000 tons, struck the earth 50,000 years ago at about 40,000 miles an hour, scattering white-hot debris for miles in every direction. The hole measures nearly a mile across and is 570 feet deep."

The lady next to me said, "Wow, look! It just missed the highway!"

ONE DAY A CHILD at my four-year-old's preschool class told her classmates that she needed a 'damp towel.' Some of the other kids thought she said a naughty word and told on her.

The teacher stepped in to explain, "If your mommy asked you to bring her a damp towel, what does she want?"

A little girl blurted out, "She means she wants that towel right now!"

THE TEACHER ASKED LITTLE JOHNNY if he knew his numbers.

"Yes," he said, "I do. My father taught me."

"Good. What comes after three?"

"Four," answers the boy.

"What comes after six?"

"Seven."

"Very good," says the teacher. "Your dad did a fine job. What comes after ten?"
"A jack."

THERE IS A GENTLEMEN'S CLUB where the man at reception who cloaks the members' hats, coats, umbrellas, gloves has a reputation for an infallible memory. In thirty years, he is reputed never to have given the wrong coat, hat, gloves or umbrella to any member when they leave the club.

One day, a member decided to test it out. As he left the club and was handed his coat, he asked the concierge, "How do know this is my coat?"

"I don't, sir," came the reply.

"Well, why did you give it to me?"

"Because, sir, you gave it to me."

QUESTION: What animal should you never play cards with?
ANSWER: A cheetah.

QUESTION: What shellfish lifts weights?
ANSWER: Mussels.

AFTER BEING AWAY ON BUSINESS, Tim thought it would be nice to bring his wife a little gift. "How about some perfume?" he asked the cosmetics clerk. She showed him a bottle costing $50.00. "That's a bit much," said Tim, so she returned with a smaller bottle for $30.00. "That's still quite a bit," Tim complained. Growing annoyed, the clerk brought out a tiny $15.00 bottle. "What I mean," said Tim, "is I'd like to see something really cheap." The clerk handed him a mirror.

HAVE YOU EVER BEEN guilty of looking at others your own age and thinking, surely I can't look that old? Well ...

I was sitting in the waiting room for my first appointment with a new dentist. I noticed his DDS diploma, Which bore his full name. Suddenly, I remembered a tall, handsome, dark-haired boy with the same name had been in my high school class some 40-odd years ago. Could he be the same guy that I had a secret crush on, way back then?

Upon seeing him, however, I quickly discarded any such
thought. This balding, gray-haired man with the deeply lined face was way too old to have been my classmate. Or could he?

After he examined my teeth, I asked him if he had attended Lincoln High School.

"Yes. Yes, I did. I'm a mustang," he gleamed with pride.

"When did you graduate?" I asked.

He answered, "In 1957. Why do you ask?"

"You were in my class!" I exclaimed.

He looked at me closely. Then, that ugly, old, wrinkled so-and-so asked, "Oh really, what did you teach?"

SENIOR SOLDIERS
Submitted by the author's Dad, Charles M. Cook, retired United States Air Force Officer and U.S. Veteran (R.I.P.)

I'm over 60 now and the Armed Forces say I'm too old to track down terrorists. You can't be older than 35 to join the military.

They've got the whole thing backwards. Instead of sending 18-year-olds off to fight, they ought to take us old guys. You shouldn't be able to join until you're at least 35.

For starters: Researchers say 18-year- olds think about sex every 10 seconds. Old guys only think about sex a couple of times a day, leaving us more than 28,000 additional seconds per day to concentrate on the enemy.

Young guys haven't lived long enough to be cranky, and a cranky soldier is a dangerous soldier. If we can't kill the enemy we'll complain them into submission. "My back hurts!" "I'm hungry!" "Where's the remote control?"

An 18-year-old hasn't had a legal beer yet and you shouldn't go to war until you're at least old enough to legally drink. An average old guy, on the other hand, has consumed 126,000 gallons of beer by the time he's 35 and a jaunt through the desert heat with a backpack and M-60 would do wonders for the old beer belly.

An 18-year-old doesn't like to get up before 10 a.m. Old guys get up early every morning to relieve themselves.

If old guys are captured we couldn't spill the beans because we'd probably forget where we put them. In fact, name, rank, and serial number would be a real brainteaser.

Boot camp would actually be easier for old guys. We're used to getting screamed and yelled at and we actually like soft food. We've also developed a deep appreciation for guns and rifles. We like them almost better than naps.

They could lighten up on the obstacle course however. I've been in combat and I didn't see a single 20-foot wall with rope hanging over the side, nor did I ever do any pushups after completing basic training. I can hear the Drill Sergeant now, "Get down and give me...er..one."

And the running part is kind of a waste of energy. I've never seen anyone outrun a bullet.

An 18-year-old has the whole world ahead of him. He's still learning to shave, to actually carry on a conversation, and to wear pants without the top of his butt crack showing and his boxer shorts sticking out.

He's still hasn't figured out that a pierced tongue catches food particles, and that a 400-watt speaker in the back seat of a Honda Accord can rupture an eardrum.

These are all great reasons to keep our sons at home to learn a little more about life before sending them off to possible death.

Let us old guys track down those dirty rotten cowards who attacked our hearts on September 11. The last thing the enemy would want to see right now is a couple of million old fogies with attitudes.

CLEANING OUT THE AVIARY at a run-down zoo, the keeper finds two finches that have died of old age. He picks them up and places them in a sack. After cleaning the cage he puts the sack in his wheelbarrow and moves on to the next cage. When he reaches the primate cage he finds two chimps that have also died of natural causes. "Waste not, want not," he says, as puts them in the sack with the finches. Later at feeding time, he flips the dead animals from the sack, into the lions' cage.

"Oh, no!" roars the lion. "Not finch and chimps again!"

AN ARKANSAS HILLBILLY came to town carrying a jug of moonshine in one hand and a shotgun in the other. He stopped a man on the street, saying to him, "Here friend, take a drink outta my jug."

The man protested, saying he never drank.

The hillbilly leveled his shotgun at the stranger and commanded, "Drink!"

The stranger drank, shuddered, shook, shivered and coughed. "Gee! That's awful stuff you've got there."

"Ain't it, though?" replied the hillbilly. "Now, you hold the gun on me while I take a swig."

MY NIECE, TONYA, BOUGHT HER MOM a really nice Spinet Piano for her birthday. A few weeks later, I asked Tonya how her mom was doing.

"Oh," said Tonya, "I persuaded her to switch to a clarinet."

"How come?" I asked.

"Well," Tonya answered, "because with a clarinet, she can't sing...."

A YOUNG MAN WALKS INTO A CAFE with a shotgun in one hand pulling a male buffalo with the other and says to the waiter, "Coffee please." The waiter says, "Sure thing, coming right up." He gets the young man a tall mug of coffee. After drinking the coffee down in one gulp, the young man turns and blasts the buffalo with the shotgun, then just walks out of the place! The next morning the young man returns. He has his shotgun in one hand, pulling another male buffalo with the other. He walks up to the counter and says to the waiter, "Coffee please!" The waiter says, "Whoa, mister! We're still cleaning up your mess from yesterday. What the heck is all this about, anyway?" The young man smiles and proudly says, "Training for upper management. Come in, drink coffee, shoot the bull, leave the mess for others to clean up, and disappear for rest of day."

JONES CAME INTO THE OFFICE AN HOUR LATE for the third time in one week and found the boss waiting for him. "What's the story this time, Jones?" he asked sarcastically. "Let's hear a good excuse for a change." Jones sighed, "Everything went wrong this morning, Boss. The wife decided to drive me to the station. She got ready in ten minutes, but then the drawbridge got stuck. Rather than let you down, I swam across the river -- look, my suit's still damp -- ran out to the airport, got a ride on Mr. Thompson's helicopter, landed on top of Radio City Music Hall, and was carried here piggyback by one of the Rockettes." "You'll have to do better than that, Jones," said the boss, obviously disappointed. "No woman can get ready in ten minutes."

A COUPLE HAD BEEN MARRIED FOR 45 YEARS and had raised a brood of 11 children and were blessed with 22 grandchildren. When asked the secret for staying together all that time, the wife replies, "Many years ago we made a promise to each other: the first one to pack up and leave has to take all the kids...."

2 LITTLE OLD LADIES were sitting in church one Sunday during service, when one turns to the other and says, "Mabel, my butt has gone to sleep!" Mabel replies, "I know it did. I heard it SNORING!"

A WOMAN FROM SEATTLE was sitting on the train reading the newspaper. The headline blared, "12 Brazilian Soldiers Killed."
She shook her head at the sad news, then turned to the stranger sitting next to her and asked, "How many is a Brazilian?"

A SHOCKING GIFT

An elderly carpenter was ready to retire. He told his employer, a building contractor, of his plans to leave the house building business and live a more leisurely life with his wife enjoying his extended family. He would miss the paycheck, but he needed to retire. They could get by.

His employer was sorry to see his good worker go and asked if he could build just one more house as a personal favor. The carpenter said, "yes," but it was easy to see that his heart was no longer in his work. He had lost his enthusiasm and had resorted to shoddy workmanship and used inferior materials. It was an unfortunate way to end his career.

When the carpenter finished his work and his boss came to inspect the new house, the contractor handed the front- door key to the carpenter. "This is your house," he said, "my gift to you."

What a shock! What a shame! If he had only known he was building his own house, he would have done it all so differently. Now he had to live in the home he had built none too well.

So it is with us. We build our lives in a distracted way, reacting rather than acting, willing to put up less than the best. At important points we do not give the job our best effort. Then with a shock we look at the situation we have created and find that we are now living in the house we have built for ourselves. If we had realized, we would have done it differently.

Think of yourself as the carpenter. Think about your house. Each day you hammer a nail, place a board, or erect a wall. Build wisely. It is the only life you will ever build. Even if you live it for only one day more, that day deserves to be lived graciously and with dignity.

A plaque on a wall reads, "Life is a do-it-yourself project."

Who could say it more clearly? Your life today is the result of your attitudes and choices in the past. Your life tomorrow will be the result.

SOME REDNECK HUMOR
(We don't intend to pick on a particular group of people ... that's why we picked some from several different states. Hey, we're redneck in E. WA, too).

- A North Carolina redneck passed away and left his entire estate in trust, consisting of a1982 Ford pickup, a Remington shotgun, 6 1/2 books of Green Stamps and $18.37 due from the mill for his last week's work for his beloved widow. However, she can't touch it until she turns 14.
- Folks in Georgia now go to some movies in groups of 18 or more. They were told 17 and under are not admitted.
- The minimum drinking age in Tennessee has been raised to 32. It seems they want to keep alcohol out of the high schools.
- In Mississippi, reruns of "Hee Haw" are called documentaries.
- How can you tell if a West Virginia redneck is married? There's dried tobacco spit on both sides of his pickup truck.
- Tennessee has a new $3,000,000 State Lottery. The winner gets $3 a year for a million years.
- Recently, the Governor's Mansion in Little Rock burned down. In fact, it took out the whole trailer park.
- The best thing to ever come out of Arkansas is Interstate 40.

• An Alabama State Trooper stopped a pickup truck. He asked the driver, "Got any ID?" The driver said, "'Bout what?"

AN EXHAUSTED DEER HUNTER out in the wilderness stumbled into a hunting camp. "Am I ever glad to see you!" said the deer hunter. "I've been lost for 3 days."

"Don't get too excited," the other hunter replied. "I've been lost for 3 weeks."

A PRETTY YOUNG LADY FROM TACOMA was stopped by a very good looking Seattle patrolman. When asked for her drivers license she nervously went through her purse but could only find credit cards.

Impatiently the officer told her in a dry voice, "It's the one with your picture on it."

Digging a little further she came up with a small mirror, handed it to the officer who said, "Why didn't you tell me you were a patrolman? I never would have stopped you!"

A DEER HUNTER FROM SEATTLE bagged a big buck. Just about that time, the game warden arrived and asked the hunter if he had a hunting license and deer tag.

The hunter said he didn't have a license or a tag, so the game warden had to take the hunter and the deer to town.

The game warden helped the hunter drag the 200 plus pound deer out to the road.

Now that the hard work was done, the hunter exclaimed, "I just remembered, I do have a hunting license and deer tag after all."

AN OLD DEER HUNTER GOES TO THE DOCTOR for his yearly physical, with his wife tagging along.

When the doctor enters the examination room, he tells the old hunter, "I need a urine sample, and a stool sample."

The old hunter, being hard of hearing, looks at his wife and yells, "What's he want?"

His wife yells back, "He wants your underwear."

TWO MEN GO DEER HUNTING. They settle down in their stand and start waiting for the deer. This gets rapidly boring for one of them so he reaches into his backpack and withdraws a bottle of 100 proof scotch.

"Want some?" he asks his deer hunting partner.

"No, I've got to concentrate on watching for deer."

"Okay..." he says and happily drains the bottle.

They go back to watching for deer. Again, the man gets bored and gets from his backpack another bottle of scotch. "Want some?" he asks again.

"No, thanks." is his reply.

"Your loss." he says and happily drains the bottle.

He's pretty sloshed by now, but goes back to help his friend watch for deer. A minute later, a single deer walks up to their stand.

"Bang!!!" goes his partners rifle.

"Dang, missed it." his partner says.

The sloshed hunter waves his rifle in the general direction of the fleeing deer. "Bang!!!" his rifle goes. He kills the deer straight out.

"Wow," his partner said, "how did you do that?"

"Well," he replied, "when there's a whole herd of deer, you can hardly miss, can you?"

THIS DEER HUNTER IS STRANDED on a desert island, all alone for ten years. One day he sees a speck on the horizon. He thinks to himself, "It's not a ship." The speck gets a little closer and he thinks to himself, "It's not a boat." The speck gets even closer and he thinks to himself, "It's not a raft." Then coming out of the surf was this gorgeous woman, wearing a wet suit and scuba gear.

She comes up to the guy and asks, "How long has it been since you've had a cigarette?"

"Ten years!" He said.

She then reaches over, unzips this waterproof pocket on her left sleeve and pulls out a fresh pack of cigarettes.

He reaches over and takes one, lights it, takes a long drag and says, "Man, oh man! Is that good!"

Then she asked, "How long has it been since you had a good drink of whiskey?"

"He replies, "Ten years!"

She then reaches over and, unzips her waterproof pocket on her right sleeve and pulls out a flask and, gives it to the guy.

He then takes a long drink and says, "Wow, that's fantastic!"

Then she asks, "And how long has it been since you've had some REAL fun?"

The man replies, "Oh, my! Don't tell me that you've got a deer rifle in there!"

A CARLOAD OF DEER HUNTERS, looking for a place to hunt, pulled into a farmer's yard. The driver went up to the farmhouse to ask permission to hunt on his land.

The old farmer said, "Sure you can hunt, but would you do me a favor? That old mule over there is 20 years old and sick with cancer, but I don't have the heart to kill her. Would you do it for me?"

The hunter said, "Sure," and headed for the car.

Walking back, however, he decided to pull a trick on his deer hunting buddies. He got into the car and when they asked if the farmer said it was "OK," he said, "No, we can't hunt here, but I'm going to teach that old cuss a lesson."

With that, he rolled down his window, stuck his rifle out and blasted the mule. Then he exclaimed, "There, that will teach him!"

A second shot rang out from the passenger side and one of his deer hunting buddies shouted, "I got his cow, lets get out of here!!!"

FARMER JOHN LIVED ON A QUIET rural highway. But, as time went by, the traffic built up at an alarming rate. The traffic was so heavy and so fast that his chickens were being run over at a rate of three to six a day.

So one day Farmer John called the sheriff's office and said, "You've got to do something about all of these people driving so fast and killing all of my chickens."

"What do you want me to do?" asked the sheriff.

"I don't care, just do something about those crazy drivers!"

So the next day he had the county workers go out and erected a sign that read: SLOW: SCHOOL CROSSING.

Three days later Farmer John called the sheriff and said, "You've got to do something about these drivers. The 'school crossing' sign seems to make them go even faster."

So, again, the sheriff sends out the county workers and they put up a new sign: SLOW: CHILDREN AT PLAY.

That really sped them up.

So Farmer John called and called and called every day for three weeks.

Finally, he asked the sheriff, "Your signs are doing no good. Can I put up my own sign?"

The sheriff told him, "Sure thing, put up your own sign." He was going to let Farmer John do just about anything in order to get him to stop calling every day to complain. The sheriff got no more calls from Farmer John.

Three weeks later, curiosity got the best of the sheriff and he decided to give Farmer John a call. "How's the problem with those drivers. Did you put up your sign?"

"Oh, I sure did. And not one chicken has been killed since then. I've got to go. I'm very busy." He hung up the phone.

The sheriff was really curious now and he thought to himself, "I'd better go out there and take a look at that sign... it might be something that WE could use to slow down drivers.."

So, the sheriff drove out to Farmer John's house, and his jaw dropped the moment he saw the sign. It was spray-painted on a sheet of wood: "NUDIST COLONY -- Go slow and watch out for the chicks."

THE TEENAGER LOST A CONTACT LENS while playing basketball in his driveway. After a fruitless search, he told his mother the lens was nowhere to be found. Undaunted, she went outside and in a few minutes, returned with the lens in her hand.

"How did you manage to find it, Mom?" the teenager asked.

"We weren't looking for the same thing," she replied. "You were looking for a small piece of plastic. I was looking for $150."

ONE DAY A MAN WAS WALKING IN THE WOODS when he got lost. For two days he roamed around trying to find a way out. He had not eaten anything during this period and was famished. Over on a rock ledge he spotted a bald eagle, killed it, and started to eat it. Surprisingly, a couple of park rangers happen to find him at that moment, and arrested him for killing an endangered species.

At court, he plead innocent to the charges against him claiming that if he didn't eat the bald eagle he would have died from starvation. The judge ruled in his favor.

In the judge's closing statement he asked the man, "I would like you to tell me something before I let you go. I have never eaten a bald eagle, nor ever plan on it. What did it taste like?"

The man answered, "Well, it tasted like a cross between a whooping crane and a spotted owl!"

STOPPING TO PICK UP MY DAUGHTER at kindergarten, I found out that the topic of "Show and Tell" that day had been parents' occupations.

The teacher pulled me aside. Whispering, she advised, "You might want to explain a little bit more to your daughter what you do for a living."

I work as a training consultant and often conduct my seminars in motel conference rooms.

When I asked why, the teacher explained, "Your daughter told the class she wasn't sure what you did, but said you got dressed real pretty and went to work at motels."

A WOMAN FROM SEATTLE calls her best friend one day and she is very upset. "I can't get this jigsaw puzzle put together and I've been trying for weeks," she cried. "Can you please come over and help me before I go crazy?"

"What kind of puzzle is it?" asks the friend.

The panicked woman says, "Well there is a rooster on the box. But there's so many pieces and it's so confusing, I just don't know where to start!"

Her friend is the compassionate sort and says, "I'll be right over."

Off to the friend's house she goes. When she gets there, she takes one look at the table and turns to her friend and says: "Put the corn flakes back in the box."

AN EASTERN WASHINGTON farmer passed away and left 17 mules to his three sons. The instructions left in the will said that the oldest boy was to get one-half, the second oldest one-third, and the youngest one-ninth. The three sons, recognizing the difficulty of dividing 17 mules into these fractions, began to argue.

Their uncle heard about the argument, hitched up his mule and drove out to settle the matter. He added his mule to the 17, making 18.

The oldest therefore got one-half, or nine, the second oldest got one-third, or six, and the youngest son got one-ninth, or two. Adding up 9, 6 and 2 equals 17.

The uncle, having settled the argument, hitched up his mule and drove home.

"A RAMBLING ROSE BY ANY OTHER NAME"

A man takes a lady out to dinner for the first time. Later they go on to a show. The evening is a huge success and as he drops her at her door he says, "I have had a lovely time. You looked so beautiful, you remind me of a beautiful rambling rose. May I call on you tomorrow?"

She agrees and a date is made. The next night he knocks on her door and when she opens it she slaps him hard across the face.

He is stunned. "What was that for?" he asked.

She said, "I looked up rambling rose in the encyclopedia last night and it said 'Not well suited to bedding but is excellent for rooting up against a garden wall.'"

TWO GALS FROM SEATTLE were walking down the road and the first one says, "Look at that dog with one eye!"

The other gal covers one of her eyes and says, "Where?"

"Some folks are wise and some are otherwise." --Tobias George Smolett

"THAT WAS NICE OF YOU to set up a blind date for your ex-boyfriend."
"I know, but I don't hold any grudges."
"I'm surprised he trusted you enough to agree to go out with her."
"Well, I had to swear to him she's Jennifer Lopez's double."
"Wow! Is that true?"
"I wouldn't lie. She's twice her weight and twice her age."

WHILE PROUDLY SHOWING OFF his new apartment to friends one night Ted led the way to his bedroom where pride of place was given to a large brass gong.
"What's that big brass gong for?" one of the guests asked.
"Why, that's the speaking clock,'" Ted replied.
"How does it work?"
"I'll show you," Ted said, giving it an ear-shattering blow with an unpadded dodger.
Suddenly, someone on the other side of the wall screamed, "For goodness sake you idiot, it's 2 o'clock in the morning!"

MY LITTLE NIECE, KELLY, went with a neighbor girl to church for First Communion practice. The pastor has the children cup their hands, and when he gives them the "Host," in this case, a piece of bread, he says, "God be with you."

Apparently this made quite an impression on my niece. She came home and told her mother to cup her hands and bend down. Kelly took a piece of bread from her sandwich, placed it in her mother's hands, and whispered, in her most angelic voice, "God will get you."

A MINISTER HAD JUST FINISHED an excellent fried chicken dinner at the home of a congregation member when he saw a rooster come strutting through the yard. "That's certainly a proud-looking rooster," the minister commented.

"Yes, sir," replied the farmer. "He has reason to be proud-- one of his sons just entered the ministry."

A VISITOR TO NEW YORK rushed from the airport into a waiting taxi, trying to keep dry in the heavy downpour. "Can you think of anything worse," grumbled the visitor, "than raining cats and dogs in New York?"

"Sure," said the cab driver. "Hailing taxis!"

MUSHROOM

Question: What did the boy mushroom tell the girl mushroom?
Answer: I don't know why you are not interested in me, I am really a FUN GUY. (fungi)

VISITATION

Pastor Jones was out on Wednesday night visitation. He had decided to visit Mrs. Smith, an elderly widow who had been housebound for many years.

As he sat talking with her, he kept helping himself to the dish of peanuts on the coffee table. After an hour of conversation he realized he'd eaten all the peanuts from the dish.

"I'm so sorry Mrs. Smith, I didn't mean to eat all your peanuts."

"That's perfectly okay." she said. "Ever since I got these new dentures, the best I've been able to do is suck the chocolate off them."

OUTSTANDING IN HIS FIELD

Ders a feller who lives down the road who is kinda dense named Rabbit. One day I wuz driving to Wacahoota and I seed Rabbit standing in his watermellon field doing nothing. Just standing there. I stopped and asked Rabbit what he was doing just standing there.

He says that he was a tryin to win a Nobel Prize.

"Nobel Prize? I dont understand."

And then Rabbit tole me that this feller on TV said that they wuz givin these Nobel Prizes to peoples who wuz outstanding in their field!

Who Knows If These Really Are "Actual Ads," as Claimed – They are funny anyway! Enjoy!

1) FREE YORKSHIRE TERRIER. 8 years old. Hateful little dog. Bites.
2) FREE PUPPIES; 1/2 Cocker Spaniel, 1/2 sneaky neighbor's dog.
3) FREE PUPPIES ... Part German Shepherd, part stupid dog.
4) GERMAN SHEPHERD 85 lbs. Neutered. Speaks German.
5) FOUND; DIRTY WHITE DOG. Looks like a rat ... been out awhile. Better be a reward.
6) NORDIC TRACK 300 Hardly used, call Chubby.
7) GEORGIA PEACHES, California grown - 89 cents lb.
8) NICE PARACHUTE; Never opened - used once.
9) FOR SALE BY OWNER; Complete set of Encyclopedia Britannica. 45 volumes. Excellent condition. 1,000 or best offer. No longer needed. Got married last month. Wife knows everything.

IN HEAVEN ITS ALL FREE

This 85-year-old couple, having been married almost 60 years, had died in a car crash. They had been in good health the last ten years, mainly due to her interest in health food and exercise. When they reached the pearly gates, St. Peter took them to their mansion, which was decked out with a beautiful kitchen and master bath suite and jetted tub. As they 'ooohed and aaahed' the old man asked Peter how much all this was going to cost.

"It's free," Peter replied, "this is Heaven."

Next, they went out back to see the championship golf course that the home backed up to. They would have golfing privileges every day and each week the course changed to a new one representing the great golf courses on earth.

The old man asked, "What are the green fees?"

Peter replied, "This is heaven, you play for free."

Next they went to the clubhouse and saw the lavish buffet lunch with the cuisines of the world laid out.

"How much to eat?" asked the old man.

"Don't you understand yet? This is heaven. It is free!" Peter replied.

"Well, where are the low fat and low cholesterol foods?" the old man asked timidly.

"That's the best part -- you can eat as much as you like of whatever you like and you never get fat and you never get sick. This is Heaven."

The old man looked at his wife and said, "You and your bran muffins. I could have been here ten years ago!"

A COLVILLE WOMAN WAS DRIVING DOWN HIGHWAY 395

about 75 miles an hour, when she noticed a motorcycle policeman following her. Instead of slowing down, she picked up speed.

When she looked back again, there were two motorcycles following her. She shot up to 90 miles an hour. The next time she looked around, there were three cops following her.

Suddenly, she spotted a gas station ahead in Loon Lake. She screeched to a stop and ran into the ladies' room. Ten minutes later, she innocently walked out.

The three cops were standing there waiting for her.

Without batting an eye, she said coyly, "I'll bet none of you thought I would make it."

GONNA BE A BEAR!

In this life I'm a woman. In my next life, I'd like to come back as a bear. When you're a bear, you get to hibernate. You do nothing but sleep for six months. I could deal with that.

Before you hibernate, you're supposed to eat yourself stupid. I could deal with that, too.

When you're a bear girl, you birth your children (who are the size of walnuts) while you're sleeping and wake to partially grown, cute, cuddly cubs. I could definitely deal with that.

If you're a mama bear, everyone knows you mean business. You swat anyone who bothers your cubs. If your cubs get out of line, you swat them, too. I could deal with that.

If you're a bear, your mate EXPECTS you to wake up growling. He EXPECTS that you will have hairy legs and excess body fat.

Yup, gonna be a bear!

SOUTHERN AND NORTHERN ZOOS

Question: What is the difference between a southern zoo and a northern Zoo?
Answer: The southern Zoo has a discription of the animal and a recipe.

"HOW TO PAY YOUR TAX BILL"

Dear IRS,

Enclosed is my 2006 Tax Return & payment. Please take note of the attached article from the USA Today newspaper. In the article, you will see that the Pentagon is paying $171.50 for hammers and NASA has paid $600.00 for a toilet seat.

Please find enclosed four toilet seats (value $2,400) and six hammers (value $1,029). This brings my total payment to $3,429.00.

Please note the overpayment of $22.00 and apply it to the "Presidential Election Fund," as noted on my return.

Might I suggest that you send the above mentioned fund a "1.5 inch screw." (See attached article ... HUD paid $22.00 for a 1.5 inch Phillips Head Screw).

It has been a pleasure to pay my tax bill this year, and I look forward to paying it again next year. I just saw an article about the Pentagon and "screwdrivers."

I SHALL SEEK AND FIND YOU

I shall seek and find you ... I shall take you to bed and have my ... way with you ... I will make you ache, shake and sweat until you moan and groan. I will make you beg for mercy... beg for me to stop. I will exhaust you to the point that you will be relieved when I'm finished with you, and you will be weak for days.

All my love,
THE FLU

"78 YEAR OLD'S CHECK UP"

You're in incredible shape," the doctor said. "How old are you again?"

"I am 78." The man said.

"78?" asked the doctor. "How do you stay so healthy? You look like a 60 year old."

"Well, my wife and I made a pact when we got married that whenever she got mad she would go into the kitchen and cool off and I would go outside to settle down." the man explained.

"What does that have to do with it?" asked the doctor.

"I've pretty much lived an outdoor life."

MOST OF US HAVE A BAD HABIT we are constantly trying to break. For me, it's biting my fingernails. One day I told my husband about my latest solution: press-on nails.

"Great Idea, Honey," he smiled. "You can eat them straight out of the box."

MASTERING THE COMPUTER

Using a new painting program on my computer, I managed to come up with a very credible still life of fruit. I made a color printout and sent it to my daughter, a graphic designer. She called when it arrived. "Isn't it good?" I asked.

She chuckled, and in a tone that echoed mine from years ago, replied, "Mom, it's beautiful. We put it on the refrigerator."

ON MY FOUR-YEAR-OLD DAUGHTER'S first trip to Disneyland, she couldn't wait to get on Mr. Toad's Wild Ride. As the car zoomed through the crazy rooms, into the path of a speeding train, and through walls that fell away at the last second, she clutched the little steering wheel in front of her. When the ride was over, she said to me a little shakily, "Next time, you drive. I didn't know where I was going."

FRESH OUT OF BUSINESS SCHOOL, the young man answered a want ad for an accountant. Now he was being interviewed by a very nervous man who ran a small business that he had started himself.

"I need someone with an accounting degree," the man said. "But mainly, I'm looking for someone to do my worrying for me."

"Excuse me?" the accountant said.

"I worry about a lot of things," the man said. "But I don't want to have to worry about money. Your job will be to take all the money worries off my back."

"I see," the accountant said. "And how much does the job pay?"

"I'll start you at eighty thousand."

"Eighty thousand dollars!" the accountant exclaimed. "How can such a small business afford a sum like that?"

"That," the owner said, "is your first worry."

"THIS HOTEL STINKS!" a guest complained when he showed up at the front desk to check out.

"What's wrong?" I asked. "I got no sleep. Every 15 minutes this loud banging sound woke me up!"

I apologized for the noise and checked him out. A few minutes later, a couple showed up. Again, I made the mistake of asking how their stay was.

"Terrible!" they said. "The guy in the next room was snoring so loudly that we had to bang on the wall every 15 minutes to wake him up!"

AT LONG LAST THE GOOD-HUMORED BOSS was compelled to call Fisk into his office. "It has not escaped my attention," he pointed out, "that every time there's a home game at the stadium you have to take your aunt to the doctor."

"You know you're right, sir," exclaimed Fisk. "I didn't realize it. You don't suppose she's faking it, do you?"

RECENTLY, OUR 18-YEAR-OLD DAUGHTER started hunting for her first real job. She spent an afternoon filling out applications, leaving them on the kitchen table to finish later. As I walked by, a section of the application on top jumped out at me. Under "Previous Employment" she wrote, "Baby sitting." In answer to "Reason for Leaving" she wrote, "Parents came home."

A GUY TRAVELING THROUGH THE PRAIRIES of the USA stopped at a small town and went to a bar. He stood at the end of the bar and lit up a cigar. As he sipped his drink, he stood there quietly blowing smoke rings.

After he blew nine or ten smoke rings into the air, an angry American Indian approached him and said, "Now listen, buddy, if you don't stop calling me that I'll take your cigar from you!"

A MAN WROTE A LETTER TO A SMALL HOTEL in a Midwest town, which he planned to visit on his vacation. He wrote, "I would very much like to bring my dog with me. He is well groomed and very well behaved. Would you be willing to permit me to keep him in my room with me at night?"

An immediate reply came from the hotel owner, who said, "I've been operating this hotel for many years. In all that time, I've never had a dog steal towels, bedclothes, silverware or pictures off the walls. I've never had to evict a dog in the middle of the night for being drunk and disorderly. And I've never had a dog run out on a hotel bill. Yes, indeed, your dog is welcome at my hotel, and if your dog will vouch for you, you're welcome to stay here, too!"

"STARBUCKS SAYS THEY ARE GOING TO start putting religious quotes on cups. The very first one will say, 'Jesus! This cup is expensive!'" --Conan O'Brien

"HOMELAND SECURITY CHIEF Michael Chertoff said that he wants to expel all illegal immigrants from the United States. Which would reduce the population of Los Angeles to 142 people." --Jay Leno

"The average man's idea of a good sermon is one that goes over his head and hits a neighbor."

"If all the people in church were laid end to end, they would be ... more comfortable."

"He was said to be a good preacher -- at the close of every sermon there was a great awakening."

"Be a peacemaker ... always remember that's it's hard to shake hands with a clenched fist."

"If absence makes the heart grow fonder, then a huge bunch of people sure love their church."

CAR TROUBLE
A Bothel woman pushes her BMW into a gas station. She tells the mechanic it died. After he works on it for a few minutes, it is idling smoothly.
The woman asks, "What's the story?"
He replies, "Just crap in the carburetor."
She asks, "How often do I have to do that?"

SPEEDING TICKET
A police officer stops a Bellevue woman for speeding and asks her very nicely if he could see her license.
She replies in a huff, "I wish you guys would get your act together. Just yesterday you take away my license and then today you expect me to show it to you!"

RIVER WALK

There's this Auburn lady out for a walk. She comes to a river and sees a Kent lady on the opposite bank. "Yoo-hoo!" she shouts, "How can I get to the other side?"

The Kent lady looks up the river then down the river and shouts back, "You ARE on the other side."

KNITTING

A King County sheriff pulled alongside a speeding car on the I-5 freeway. Glancing at the car, he was astounded to see that the woman behind the wheel was knitting!

Realizing that she was oblivious to his flashing lights and siren, the officer cranked down his window, turned on his bullhorn and yelled, "PULL OVER!"

"NO!" the woman yelled back, "IT'S A SCARF!"

REDMOND WOMAN ON THE SUN

A Russian, an American, and a Redmond woman were talking one day. The Russian said, "We were the first in space!"

The American said, "We were the first on the moon!"

The Redmond woman said, "So what? A Redmond woman is going to be the first on the sun!"

The Russian and the American looked at each other and shook their heads. "You can't land on the sun, you idiot! You'll burn up!" said the Russian.

To which the Redmond woman replied, "We're not stupid, you know. We're going at night!"

IN A VACUUM

A Renton woman was playing Trivial Pursuit one night. It was her turn. She rolled the dice and she landed on Science & Nature.
Her question was, "If you are in a vacuum and someone calls your name, can you hear it?"
She thought for a time and then asked, "Is it on or off?"

A STEVENS COUNTY WOMAN AND A KENT WOMAN

A woman from Stevens County is visiting a woman from Kent. They are walking along in a park.
The woman from Stevens County says suddenly, "Awwwe, look at the dead bird."
The woman from Kent stops, looks up, and says, "Where?"

A MAN GOES INTO A RESTAURANT sits down at a table and an attractive young waitress comes for his order. He gives her a smile and says, "I want a quickie."

She turns red in the face and ahems, "Sir, I don't know what kind of restaurant you're used to eating in, but I can assure you you're not going to get a quickie here!"

"How disappointing," the man replied. "Could you ask the chef to make an exception?"

"He doesn't have anything to do with it!" says the waitress indignantly.

"Hmmm," do you know anywhere around here where I could get a quickie?"

"I'm SURE I don't know," answers the waitress loudly.

A patron from the next table leans over and taps the man on the shoulder, "I think it's pronounced QUICHE."

DRIVING AND LONG HAIR

A young boy had just gotten his driving permit. He asked his father, who was a minister, if they could discuss the use of the car.

His father took him to his study and said to him, "I'll make a deal with you. You bring your grades up, study your bible a little and get your hair cut and we'll talk about it."

After about a month the boy came back and again asked his father if they could discuss use of the car.

They again went to the father's study where his father said, "Son, I've been real proud of you. You have brought your grades up, you've studied your bible diligently, but you didn't get your hair cut!"

The young man waited a moment and replied, "You know Dad, I've been thinking about that. You know, Samson had long hair, Moses had long hair, Noah had long hair, and even Jesus had long hair...."

To which his father replied... "Yes, and they WALKED everywhere they went!"

ENGLISH FOR TOURISTS ... OR ... EVER NOTICE HOW SOME THINGS CAN BE LOST IN TRANSLATION? Read on:

Cocktail lounge, Norway: "LADIES ARE REQUESTED NOT TO HAVE CHILDREN IN THE BAR."

On an Athi River highway: "TAKE NOTICE: WHEN THIS SIGN IS UNDER WATER, THIS ROAD IS IMPASSABLE."

In a City restaurant: "OPEN SEVEN DAYS A WEEK AND WEEKENDS."

Hotel, Japan: "YOU ARE INVITED TO TAKE ADVANTAGE OF THE CHAMBERMAID."

In the lobby of a Moscow hotel across from a Russian Orthodox monastery: "YOU ARE WELCOME TO VISIT THE CEMETERY WHERE FAMOUS RUSSIAN AND SOVIET COMPOSERS, ARTISTS, AND WRITERS ARE BURIED DAILY EXCEPT THURSDAY."

Taken from a menu, Poland: "SALAD A FIRM'S OWN MAKE; LIMPID RED BEET SOUP WITH CHEESY DUMPLINGS IN THE FORM OF A FINGER; ROASTED DUCK LET LOOSE; BEEF RASHERS BEATEN IN THE COUNTRY PEOPLE'S FASHION."

Supermarket, Hong Kong: "FOR YOUR CONVENIENCE, WE RECOMMEND COURTEOUS, EFFICIENT SELF-SERVICE."

From the "Soviet Weekly:" "THERE WILL BE A MOSCOW EXHIBITION OF ARTS BY 15,000 SOVIET REPUBLIC PAINTERS AND SCULPTORS. THESE WERE EXECUTED OVER THE PAST TWO YEARS."

On the door of a Moscow hotel room: "IF THIS IS YOUR FIRST VISIT TO MOSCOW, YOU ARE WELCOME TO IT."

A laundry in Rome: "LADIES, LEAVE YOUR CLOTHES HERE AND SPEND THE AFTERNOON HAVING A GOOD TIME."

SOME QUICKIES ...
AT HIS 103RD BIRTHDAY party, my grandfather was asked if he planned to be around for his 104th. "I certainly do," he replied. "Statistics show that very few people die between the ages of 103 and 104."

ON A WHIM A MAN DECIDED to get his wife a dozen roses and surprise her after work. The minute he opened the door, his wife took one look at the flowers in his hand and started screaming, "This is the worst day that I have EVER had! The kids have been terrible. They got in a food fight, the washing machine broke and flooded the basement, I burned dinner, the dog chewed up my best pair of shoes...AND NOW YOU'VE GOT THE NERVE TO COME HOME DRUNK!"

SOME CAUSE HAPPINESS wherever they go; others whenever they go.

SKYDIVERS ARE GOOD to the last drop.

MARRIAGE MEANS commitment. Of course, so does insanity.

IF GOD WANTED US to be thin, food wouldn't taste so good.

IF IT'S THE THOUGHT that counts, think money.

THE BIGGEST DISADVANTAGE to being poor is that it's so expensive.
MANY OF OUR AMBITIONS are nipped in the budget.

A LADY WAS PICKING THROUGH the frozen turkeys at the grocery store, but couldn't find one big enough for her family.
She asked the stock boy, "Do these turkeys get any bigger?"
The stock boy answered, "No ma'am, they're dead."

QUESTION: Where did the first corn come from?
ANSWER: The stalk brought it

AN ATHEIST COMPLAINED TO A FRIEND, "Christians have their special holidays, such as Christmas and Easter; and Jews celebrate their holidays, such as Passover and Yom Kippur; Muslims have their holidays. EVERY religion has its holidays. But we atheists," he said, "have no recognized national holidays. It's an unfair discrimination."
His friend replied, "Well, why don't you celebrate April first?"

I FEEL LIKE MY BODY has gotten totally out of shape, so I got my doctor's permission to join a fitness club and start exercising. I decided to take an aerobics class for seniors. I bent, twisted, gyrated, jumped up and down, and perspired for an hour. But, by the time I got my leotards on, the class was over.

REPORTERS INTERVIEWING a 104-year-old woman: "And what do you think is the best thing about being 104?" the reporter asked.
She simply replied,"No peer pressure."

THE NICE THING about being senile is you can hide your own Easter eggs.

MY MEMORY'S not as sharp as it used to be. Also, my memory is not as sharp as it used to be.

KNOW HOW TO prevent sagging? Just eat till the wrinkles fill out.

I'VE STILL GOT IT, but nobody wants to see it.

I'M GETTING INTO swing dancing. Not on purpose. Some parts of my body are just prone to swinging.

IT'S SCARY WHEN you start making the same noises as your coffeemaker.

DON'T LET AGING get you down. It's too hard to get back up!

QUESTIONS TO PONDER
- Why do we put suits in garment bags and garments in a suitcase?
- If I melt dry ice, can I take a bath without getting wet?
- Why is it that bullets ricochet off of Superman's chest, but he ducks when the empty gun is thrown at him?
- When your pet bird sees you reading the newspaper, does he wonder why you're just sitting there, staring at carpeting?
- Why do tourists go to the tops of tall buildings and then put money into telescopes so they can see things on the ground close-up?
- After eating, do amphibians have to wait one hour before getting out of the water?
- Why do we press harder on a remote control when we know the batteries are getting weak?
- Why do banks charge a fee on "insufficient funds" when they know there is not enough?
- Why does someone believe you when you say there are four billion stars, but check when you say the paint is wet?
- Why doesn't glue stick to the bottle?
- Why doesn't Tarzan have a beard?
- Why do Kamikaze pilots wear helmets?
- Whose idea was it to put an "S" in the word "lisp?"
- If people evolved from apes, why are there still apes?
- Why is it that no matter what color bubble bath you use the bubbles are always white?
- Is there ever a day that mattresses are not on sale?
- Why do people constantly return to the refrigerator with hopes that something new to eat will have materialized?

- Why do people keep running over a string a dozen times with their vacuum cleaner, then reach down, pick it up, examine it, then put it down to give the vacuum one more chance?
- Why is it that no plastic bag will open from the end you first try?
- Why is it that whenever you attempt to catch something that's falling off the table you always manage to knock something else over?
- In winter why do we try to keep the house as warm as it was in summer when we complained about the heat?

GROWING OLDER WITH DIGNITY

I'VE SURE GOTTEN OLD! I've had two bypass surgeries, a hip replacement, new knees. Fought prostate cancer and diabetes. I'm half blind, can't hear anything quieter than a jet engine, take 40 different medications that make me dizzy, winded, and subject to blackouts. Have bouts with dementia. Have poor circulation, hardly feel my hands and feet anymore. Can't remember if I'm 85 or 92. Have lost! all my friends. But, thank God, I still have my driver's license.

AN ELDERLY WOMAN decided to prepare her will and told her preacher she had two final requests. First, she wanted to be cremated, and second, she wanted her ashes scattered over Wal-Mart.
"Wal-Mart?" the preacher exclaimed. "Why Wal-Mart?"
"Then I'll be sure my daughters visit me twice a week."

REMEMBER: YOU DON'T STOP LAUGHING because you grow old, You grow old because you stop laughing.

THE SENILITY PRAYER : Grant me the senility to forget the people I never liked anyway, the good fortune to run into the ones I do, and the eyesight to tell the difference.

IN MID-LIFE WOMEN NO LONGER have upper arms, we have wing spans. We are no longer women in sleeveless shirts, we are flying squirrels in drag.

IN MY SOCIOLOGY CLASS, we were instructed to write down answers to some questions the teacher was asking. "Next question," announced the instructor. "How would you like to be seen by the opposite sex?"
I was thinking about my answer when the young woman next to me turned and asked, "How do you spell 'intellectual?'"

What does a nosey pepper do? It gets jalapeno business!

HARD OF EAR-ING

Bob was in a terrible accident at work. He fell through a floor tile and ripped off both of his ears. Since he was permanently disfigured, he settled with the company for a rather large sum of money and went on his way. One day, Bob decided to invest his money in a small, but growing telecom business. After weeks of negotiations, he bought the company outright. But, after signing on the dotted line, he realized that he knew nothing about running such a business and quickly set out to hire someone who could do that for him.

The next day he had set up three interviews. The first guy was great. He knew everything he needed to and was very interesting. At the end of the interview, Bob asked him, "Do you notice anything different about me?"

The gentleman answered, "Why yes, I couldn't help but notice you have no ears."

Bob got very angry and threw him out. The second interview was with a woman, and she was even better than the first guy. He asked her the same question, "Do you notice anything different about me?"

She replied, "Well, you don't have any ears." Bob again was upset and tossed her out.

The third and last interview was the best of all three. It was with a very young woman who was fresh out of college. She was smart. She was well-spoken. And she seemed to be a better businessperson than the first two put together. Bob was anxious, but went ahead and asked the young woman the same question: "Do you notice anything different about me?"

And to his surprise, the young woman answered, "Yes. You wear contact lenses."

Bob was shocked, and said, "What an incredibly observant young woman. How in the world did you know that?"

The young woman replied, "Well, it's pretty hard to wear glasses with no ears!"

"RESPECTFUL LITTLE JOHNNY"

One Sunday morning, the pastor noticed Little Johnny was staring up at the large plaque that hung in the foyer of the church. The seven-year-old had been staring at the plaque for some time, so the pastor walked up, stood beside the boy, and said quietly, "Good morning, son."

"Good morning, Pastor" replied the young man, focused on the plaque. "Sir, what is this?" Little Johnny asked.

"Well son, these are all the people who have died in the service," replied the pastor.

Soberly, they stood together, staring at the large plaque. Little Johnny's voice barely broke the silence when he asked quietly, "Which one, sir, the 8:30 or the 10:30 service?"

RIVER WATER

A southern minister was completing a temperance sermon. With great expression he said, "If I had all the beer in the world, I'd take it and pour it into the river." With even greater emphasis he said, "And if I had all the wine in the world, I'd take it and pour it into the river." And then finally, he said, "And if I had all the whiskey in the world, I'd take it and pour it into the river." Sermon complete, he then sat down.

The song leader stood very cautiously and announced with a smile, "For our closing song, let us sing Hymn #365: 'Shall We Gather at the River.'"

PLAYING THE PART

A little boy was in his sister's wedding. As he was coming down the aisle he would take two steps, stop, and turn to the crowd (alternating between bride's and groom's side). While facing the crowd, he would put his hands up like claws and roar ... so it went ... step, step, ROAR ... step, step, ROAR ... all the way down the aisle.

As you can imagine, the crowd was near tears from laughing so hard by the time he reached the pulpit. The little boy, however, was getting more and more distressed from all the laughing, and was nearly in tears by the time he reached the pulpit. When asked what he was doing, the child sniffed and said, "I was being the Ring Bear."

NAME TAG

A pastor was assigned to a new church. He was worried how he would be received. At a reception for the pastor, he was given a name tag. Under his name was written, "Hog caller." The pastor responded by saying, "I'm usually called 'shepherd of the sheep', but you know your congregation better than I do!"

IRISH CLERGY

An English Clergyman turned to a Scotchman and asked: "What would you be if you were not Scot?"

The Scotchman said, "Why, an Englishman, of course!"

Then the clergyman turned to a gentleman from Ireland and asked him, "And what would you be were you not an Irishman?"

The man thought then said, "I'd be ashamed of myself!"

What do you call an alligator in a vest? An investigator.

GOOD NEWS, BAD NEWS...

A man gets a telephone call from a doctor. The doctor says, "About this medical test I did on you, I have some good news and some bad news."

The man asks for the good news first.

"The good news is that you have 24 hours to live," says the doctor.

Horrified, the man asked, "If that is the good news, then what is the bad news?!"

"I couldn't reach you yesterday."

NUMBER OF WORK DAYS IN A YEAR ...

The year is made of 365 days having 24 hours, 12 of which are night time hours which add up to 182 days. This leaves you with 183 days of work minus 52 Sundays which leaves you 131 days to work minus 52 Saturdays which leaves you 79 days to work and there are four hours each day set aside for eating which adds to 60 days which leaves you 19 days for working, and are entitled to 15 days for your vacation which leaves you 4 days left for work minus 3 days usually taken off due to illness or other emergencies, which leaves you one day to work which happens to be a Labor day, which is a holiday.

INSANE QUESTIONS
• If you take an Oriental person and spin him around several times, does he become disoriented? {For the record, rugs are Oriental; people are Asian}
• If people from Poland are called Poles, why aren't people from Holland called Holes?
• If you mixed vodka with orange juice and milk of magnesia, would you get a Philip's screwdriver?
• If a pig loses its voice, is it disgruntled?
• If love is blind, why is lingerie so popular?
• When someone asks you, "A penny for your thoughts" and you put your two cents in, don't you think you should get change back?
• Why is the man who invests all your money called a broker?
• Why do croutons come in airtight packages? It's just stale bread to begin with.
• When cheese gets its picture taken, what does it say?
• Why is a person who plays the piano call a pianist, but a person who drives a race car not called a racist?
• Why are a wise man and a wise guy opposite things?
• If horrific mean to make horrible, doesn't terrific mean to make terrible?
• Why isn't 11 pronounced onety-one?
• "I am." is reportedly the shortest sentence in the English language. Could it be that "I do." is the longest sentence?

- If lawyers are disbarred and clergymen are defrocked, doesn't it follow that electricians can be delighted, musicians denoted, cowboys deranged, models deposed, tree surgeons debarked and dry cleaners depressed?
- Do Roman paramedics refer to IVs as 4s?
- Why is it that if someone tells you that there are 1 billion stars in the universe you will believe them, but if they tell you a wall has wet paint, you will have to touch it to be sure?
- If only the good die young then what does that say about senior citizens?
- Why are the first Ten Commandments the hardest?

"Give a person a fish and you feed them for a day; teach that person to use the Internet and they won't bother you for weeks."

SHORTIES
- Only one shopping day left until tomorrow!
- A retired husband is a wife's full time job.
- Don't do for others what, given the chance, they wouldn't do for themselves.
- If you are willing to admit you are wrong when you are wrong, then you are all right.
- Happiness is the place between too little and too much.
- Even at a Mensa convention, someone is the dumbest person in the room.
- Money can't buy everything . .but then again, neither can no money.
- I work for a living, I don't live for working.
- With fuel prices skyrocketing, they should now call them gasp pumps!
- Buffet is a French term, It means "get up and get it yourself."
- Without geometry, life is pointless.
- To a worm, digging in the hard ground is more relaxing than going fishing.
- If people talk behind your back, it only means you are two steps ahead.
- Yes, I'm lost . . . but I'm making GREAT time!
- Psychiatry enables us to correct our faults by confessing our parents' shortcomings.

THE PRICE OF GAS

Did you hear about the guy in Paris who almost got away with stealing several paintings from the Louvre? After planning the crime, getting in and out past security, he was captured only two blocks away when his SUV ran out of gas. When asked how he could mastermind such a crime and then make such an obvious error, he replied: "Monsieur, I had no Monet to buy Degas to make the Van Gogh!"

The cops lacked De Gaulle to bust him.

ONELINERS:

- Always keep several get well cards on the mantel. If unexpected guests arrive, they'll think you've been sick and unable to clean.
- NASA reports that galaxies are speeding away from earth at 90,000 miles a second. What do you suppose they know that we don't?
- I asked my mailman why my letters were all wet... he said "postage dew."
- Don't ever take a fence down until you know why it was put up.
- The only thing that wakes you up faster than coffee is spilled coffee.
- A good time to keep your mouth shut is when you're in deep water.
- Odd that when a house burns down, the only things left standing are the chimney and the fireplace.
- Only in America do we shop at places with limited parking, overpriced items, and long lines and insultingly, call them convenience stores.
- I went to see Pavarotti once and I'll tell you this much, he doesn't like it when you join in.
- How dangerous could a fax be, if the pen is mightier than the sword and a picture is worth a thousand words.
- My husband has suggested a candlelight dinner at home for our anniversary. Is he being romantic or just cheap?
- A perfect summer day is when the sun is shining, the breeze is blowing, the birds are singing and the lawn mower is broken. • There are two types of roads in our country. One is under construction and the other is under repair.
- The president has said that inflation has been arrested. He should check . . . I think it's out on bail.
- The next time you pay your property taxes, remember every local politician who went to Hawaii on your dime.
- Yesterday is experience, tomorrow is hope, today is getting from one to the other.
- When you get older, lack of pep is often mistaken for patience.
- A clean tie attracts the soup of the day.
- If something is confidential, it will be left in the copier machine.
- What will today's younger generation tell their children they had to do "without?"
- "Common sense is the collection of prejudices acquired by age eighteen." -- Albert Einstein

LOST IN DESERT

Two Mexicans, Luis and Pepe, have been lost in the desert for weeks. At death's door, they see a tree in the distance. As they get nearer, they see that it's draped with rasher upon rasher of bacon: smoked bacon, crispy bacon, life-giving nearly-raw juicy bacon, all sorts of bacon.

"Hey, Luis," says Pepe, the first Mexican, "'Ees a bacon tree! We're saved!!"

So Luis goes on ahead and runs up to the tree. As he gets to within five feet, he's gunned down in a hail of bullets.

His friend Pepe drops down on the sand and calls across to the dying Luis. "Luis!! Luis!! Que pasa, hombre?"

With his last breath Luis calls out, "Ugh, run, Pepe! Run, amigo, run! 'Ees not a bacon tree, 'ees a ham bush!!"

CLEAR INSTRUCTIONS

Before rushing to work, I prepared a casserole for that evening's dinner and put it in the fridge. As I turned to leave, I told my son to stick it in the oven when he got home from school. "Make sure to put it in at 350," I said.

"Sorry, can't," he replied. "I don't get home until quarter after four."

HOUSEHOLD APPLIANCE

The family had finally purchased their first dishwasher. The father liked to inspect every new thing that came into the house, so he stayed in the kitchen and watched the display count down all forty-four minutes of the dishwashing cycle.

Suddenly he called out for his wife, shouting, "It's useless, the dishwasher is useless!"

The wife was amazed that the newest appliance could be broken after only one use, but he insisted that because they had a water softener, the dishwasher was useless.

She decided to look for herself, and there it was, on the inside door, next to the detergent dispenser: "USE LESS WITH SOFT WATER."

FIRST DAY ON THE JOB

"So, how did you do?" the boss asked his new salesman after his first day on the road.

"All I got were two orders."

"What were they? Anything good?"

"Nope," the salesman replied. "They were 'Get out!' and 'Stay out!"

COLD CREAM

Little Johnny watched, fascinated, as his mother gently rubbed cold cream on her face. "Why are you rubbing cold cream on your face, Mommy?" he asked.

"To make myself beautiful," said his mother.

A few minutes later, she began removing the cream with a tissue.

"What's the matter?" asked Little Johnny. "Giving up?"

LITTLE JOHNNY ON THE PLAYGROUND

Finding one of her students making faces at others on the playground, Ms. Smith stopped to gently reprove the child. Smiling sweetly the teacher said, "Johnny, when I was a child, I was told if I made ugly faces I would stay like that."

Little Johnny looked up and replied, "Well, you can't say you weren't warned."

"QUICK TAKES"

- I saw that my low-fuel light was on, so I stopped and got $10 worth of gas. And when I was done, I saw that my low-fuel light was still on.
- Quitters never win, winners never quit. But those who never win and never quit are idiots.
- There can't be any life on Mars. They haven't asked the United States for any money.
- When thieves get caught stealing money, they go to jail. When politicians get caught, it's an honest mistake.
- My greatest fear is there is no such thing as PMS and this is really my wife's personality.
- Federal Express had a terrific obstacle to overcome: They had to convince people that anything with the word "Federal" in it could be speedy.
- Dr. Ruth says women should tell their lovers how to make love to them. My husband goes nuts if I tell him how to drive the car!
- After divorce, most men realize that poker isn't the only game that starts with holding hands and ends with an astounding financial loss.
- Your children weren't made to like you. That's what grandchildren are for.
- Some people grin and bear it. Others smile and change it.
- We know cellphones don't interfere with navigation equipment on airlines, but they sure do tick off the person sitting next to you.
- I've been counting calories for six months now. I don't know about my figure but, my arithmetic's improving.
- A vacation is a two-week-long experience where money and time race against each other, until both are totally exhausted.
- Nothing is real to you until you experience it. Everything else is just hearsay.
- A positive attitude may not solve all your problems, but it will annoy enough people to make it worth the effort.
- Grueling endurance tests: the marathon, the iron-man competition, the airport security line.

What do you call a fake noodle? An impasta.

PASSWORD PROTECTED

A new employee calls the Help Desk to complain that there's something wrong with her password. "The problem is that whenever I type the password, it just shows stars," she says.

"Those asterisks are to protect you," the Help Desk technician explains, "so if someone were standing behind you, they wouldn't be able to read your password."

"Yeah," she says, "but they show up even when there is no one standing behind me!"

PRESCRIPTION

The man told his doctor he wasn't able to do all the things around the house that he used to do. When the examination was complete, he said, "Now, Doc, I can take it. Tell me in plain English what's wrong with me."

"Well, in plain English," the doctor replied, "You're just a plain old lazy bum."

"Thank You." said the man. "Now give me the medical term, so I can tell my wife!"

"Alexander Hamilton started the U.S. Treasury with nothing - and that was the closest our country has ever been to being even." Will Rogers

"Trial by jury is the palladium of our liberties. I do not know what a palladium is, but I am sure it is a good thing!" Mark Twain

"No one appreciates the value of constructive criticism more thoroughly than the one who's giving it." Hal Chadwick

JUNK MAIL CAN BE FUN!

When you get advertisements enclosed with your phone or utility bill, return these ads with your payment.

Let the sending companies throw their own junk mail away.

When you get those "pre-approved" letters in the mail for everything from credit cards to 2nd mortgages and similar type junk, do not throw away the return envelope. Most of these come with postage-paid return envelopes. It costs the sender more than the regular 37 cents postage if and when they receive them back. It costs them nothing if you throw them away. The postage was approximately 50 cents before the last increase and it is according to the weight. In that case, why not get rid of some of your other junk mail and put it in these cool little, postage-paid return envelopes?

Here is one of Andy Rooney's (60 Minutes) ideas: Send an ad for your local chimney cleaner to American Express. Send a pizza coupon to Citibank. If you didn't get anything else that day, then Just send them their blank application back. If you want to remain anonymous, just make sure your name isn't on anything you send them. You can even send the envelope back empty if you want to just to keep them guessing.

A DEVOTED WIFE

A woman's husband had been slipping in and out of a coma for several months, yet she had stayed by his bedside every single day.

One day, he motioned for her to come nearer. As she sat by him, he whispered, eyes full of tears, "You know what? You have been with me all through the bad times. When I got fired, you were there to support me. When my business failed, you were there. When I got shot, you were by my side. When we lost the house, you stayed right here. When my health started failing, you were still by my side... You know what?"

"What dear?" she gently asked, smiling as her heart began to fill with warmth.

"I think you're bad luck!"

WE WILL ALL DIE SOMEDAY

A Bible study group was discussing the unforeseen possibility of their sudden death. The leader of the discussion said, "We will all die some day, and none of us really knows when, but if we did we would all do a better job of preparing ourselves for that inevitable event."

Everybody nodded their heads in agreement with this comment. Then the leader said to the group, "What would you do if you knew you only had 4 weeks of life remaining before your death, and then the Great Judgment Day?"

A gentleman said, "I would go out into my community and minister the Gospel to those that have not yet accepted the Lord into their lives."

"Very good!" said the group leader, and all the group members agreed, that would be a very good thing to do.

One lady spoke up and said enthusiastically, "I would dedicate all of my remaining time to serving God, my family, my church, and my fellow man with a greater conviction."

"That's wonderful!" the group leader commented, and all the group members agreed, that would be a very good thing to do.

But one gentleman in the back finally spoke up loudly and said, "I would go to my mother-in-law's house for the 4 weeks."

Everyone was puzzled by this answer, and the group leader asked, "Why your mother-in-law's home?"

Then the gentleman smiled and said, "Because, that would be the longest 4 weeks of my life!"

I COULDN'T DECIDE whether to go to Salt Lake City or Denver for vacation, so I called the airlines to get prices.
"Airfare to Denver is $300," said a cheery salesperson.
"And what about Salt Lake City?"
"We have a really great rate to Salt Lake -- $99.00, but there is a stopover."
"Where?" I asked.
"Denver."

POOR
One day a father of a very wealthy family took his son on a trip to the country with the firm purpose of showing his son how poor people can be.

They spent a couple of days and nights on the farm of what would be considered a very poor family.

On their return from their trip, the father asked his son, "How was the trip?"

"It was great, Dad."

"Did you see how poor people can be?" the father asked.

"Oh Yeah." said the son.

"So what did you learn from the trip?" asked the father.

The son answered, "I saw that we have one dog, and they had four. We have a pool that reaches to the middle of our garden, and they have a creek that has no end. We have imported lanterns in our garden, and they have the stars at night. Our patio reaches to the front yard and, they have the whole horizon. We have a small piece of land to live on, and they have fields that go beyond our sight. We have servants who serve us, but they serve others. We buy our food, but they grow theirs. We have walls around our property to protect us, they have friends to protect them."

With this the boy's father was speechless.

Then his son added, "Thanks Dad for showing me how poor we are."

A PRECIOUS LITTLE GIRL walks into a pet shop and asks, with the sweetest little lisp, between two missing teeth, "Excuthe me, mithter do you keep widdle wabbits?"

As the shopkeeper's heart melts, he gets down on his knees so that he's on her level and asks, "Do you want a widdle white wabbit, or a thoft and fuwwy bwack wabbit, or maybe one like that cute widdle bwown wabbit over there?"

She, in turn, blushes, rocks on her heels, puts her hands on her knees, leans forward and says, in a tiny quiet voice, "I don't think my python weally gives a dang."

MUSICIANS' HUMOR

A C, an E-flat, and a G go into a bar. The bartender says: "Sorry, but we don't serve minors."

So, the E-flat leaves, and the C and the G have an open fifth between them. After a few drinks, the fifth is diminished and the G is out flat. An F comes in and tries to augment the situation, but is not sharp enough.

A D comes into the bar and heads straight for the bathroom saying, "Excuse me. I'll just be a second."

An A comes into the bar, but the bartender is not convinced that this relative of C is not a minor. Then the bartender notices a B-flat hiding at the end of the bar and exclaims: "Get out now! You're the seventh minor I've found in this bar tonight."

The E-flat, not easily deflated, comes back to the bar the next night in a 3-piece suit with nicely shined shoes. The bartender (who used to have a nice corporate job until his company downsized) says: "You're looking sharp tonight, come on in! This could be a major development."

This proves to be the case, as the E-flat takes off the suit, and everything else, and stands there au natural. Eventually, the C sobers up, and realizes in horror that he's under a rest.

The C is brought to trial, is found guilty of contributing to the diminution of a minor, and is sentenced to 10 years of DS without Coda at an upscale correctional facility.

On appeal, however, the C is found innocent of any wrongdoing, even accidental, and that all accusations to the contrary are bassless.

The bartender decides, however, that since he's only had tenor so patrons, the soprano out in the bathroom, and everything has become alto much treble, he needs a rest - and closes the bar.

0-200 IN 4 SECONDS

The couple had been debating the purchase of a new auto for weeks. He wanted a new truck. She wanted a fast little sports-like car so she could zip through traffic around town. He would probably have settled on any beat up old truck, but everything she seemed to like was way out of their price range.

"Look!" she said. I want something that goes from 0 to 200 in 4 seconds or less. And my birthday is coming up. You could surprise me."

For her birthday, he bought her a brand new bathroom scale. Services are pending.

Will Rogers once said,
"Even if you're on the right track, you'll get run over if you just stand there."

PUN IN-TEN-DID

1. Evidence has been found that William Tell and his family were avid bowlers. However, all the Swiss league records were unfortunately destroyed in a fire. Thus we'll never know for Whom the Tells Bowled.

2. A man rushed into a busy doctor's office and shouted, "Doctor! I think I'm shrinking!!" The doctor calmly responded, "Now, settle down. You'll just have to be a little patient."

3. A marine biologist developed a race of genetically engineered dolphins that could live forever if they were fed a steady diet of seagulls. One day his supply of the birds ran out. He had to go out and trap some more. On the way back, he spied two lions asleep on the road. Afraid to wake them, he gingerly stepped over them. Immediately, he was arrested and charged with transporting gulls across sedate lions for immortal porpoises.

4. Back in the 1800s the Tates Watch Company of Massachusetts wanted to produce other products and, since they already made the cases for pocket watches, decided to market compasses for the pioneers traveling west. It turned out that although their watches were of finest quality; their compasses were so bad that people often ended up in Canada or Mexico rather than California. This, of course, is the origin of the expression, "He who has a Tates is lost!"

5. A thief broke into the local police station and stole all the toilets and urinals, leaving no clues. A spokesperson was quoted as saying, "We have absolutely nothing to go on."

6. An Indian chief was feeling very sick, so he summoned the medicine man. After a brief examination, the medicine man took out a long, thin strip of elk rawhide and gave it to the chief, instructing him to bite off, chew, and swallow one inch of the leather every day. After a month, the medicine man returned to see how the chief was feeling. The chief shrugged and said, "The thong is ended, but the malady lingers on."

7. A famous Viking explorer returned home from a voyage and found his name missing from the town register. His wife insisted on complaining to the local

civic official who apologized profusely saying, "I must have taken Lief off my census."

8. There were three Indian squaws. One slept on a deer skin, one slept on an elk skin and the third slept on a hippopotamus skin. All three became pregnant and the first two each had a baby boy. The one who slept on the hippopotamus skin had twin boys. This goes to prove that the squaw of the hippopotamus is equal to the sons of the squaws of the other two hides.

9. A skeptical anthropologist was cataloging South American folk remedies with the assistance of a tribal brujo who indicated that the leaves of a particular fern were a sure cure for any case of constipation. When the anthropologist expressed his doubts, the brujo looked him in the eye and said, "Let me tell you, with fronds like these, who needs enemas?"

10. A guy wrote 10 puns and entered them in a contest. He figured with ten entries he couldn't lose. As they were reading the list of winners he was really hoping one of his puns would win, but unfortunately, no pun in ten did.

MORE PUNS IN-TEN-DID
1. A VULTURE BOARDED a plane, carrying two dead raccoons. The stewardess stopped him and said, "Sorry sir, only one carrion per passenger."

2. NASA RECENTLY SENT a number of Holsteins into orbit for experimental purposes. They called it the herd shot round the world.

3. TWO BOLL WEEVILS GREW UP in S. Carolina. One took off to Hollywood and became a rich star. The other stayed in Carolina and never amounted to much-- and naturally became known as the lesser of two weevils.

4. TWO ESKIMOS IN A KAYAK were chilly, so they started a fire, which sank the craft, proving the old adage you can't have your kayak and heat it too.

5. A 3-LEGGED DOG WALKS into an old west saloon, slides up to the bar and announces, "I'm looking for the man who shot my paw."

6. DID YOU HEAR ABOUT the Buddhist who went to the dentist and refused to take Novocain? He wanted to transcend dental medication.

7. A GROUP OF CHESS ENTHUSIASTS checked into a hotel, and met in the lobby where they were discussing their recent victories in chess tournaments. The hotel manager came out of the office after an hour, and asked them to disperse. He couldn't stand chess nuts boasting in an open foyer.

8. A WOMAN HAS TWINS, gives them up for adoption. One goes to an Egyptian family and is named "Ahmal." The other is sent to a Spanish family and is named "Juan". Years later, Juan sends his birth mother a picture of himself. Upon receiving the picture, she tells her husband she wishes she also had a picture of Ahmal. He replies, "They're twins for Pete's sake!! If you've seen Juan, you've seen Ahmal!!"

9. A GROUP OF FRIARS opened a florist shop to help with their belfry payments. Everyone liked to buy flowers from the Men of God, so their business flourished. A rival florist became upset that his business was suffering because people felt compelled to buy from the Friars, so he asked the Friars to cut back hours or close down. The Friars refused. So, the florist then hired Hugh McTaggert, the biggest meanest thug in town. He went to the Friars' shop, beat them up, destroyed their flowers, trashed their shop, and said that if they didn't close, he'd be back. Well, totally terrified, the Friars closed up shop and hid in their rooms. This proved that Hugh, and only Hugh, can prevent florist Friars.

10. MAHATMA GANDHI, as you know, walked barefoot his whole life, which created an impressive set of calluses on his feet. He also ate very little, which made him frail, and with his odd diet, he suffered from very bad breath. This made him.... what? (This is sooo bad it's good...) --a super-callused fragile mystic hexed by halitosis.

THAT'S THE WAY, UH, HUH!

An elderly gentleman arrived in Paris by plane. At the French customs desk, the man took a few minutes to locate his passport in his carry-on bag. "You have been to France before, monsieur?" the customs officer asked, sarcastically.

The old man admitted he had been to France previously.

"Then you should know enough to have your passport ready!"

The American said, "The last time I was here, I didn't have to show it."

"Impossible. Americans always have to show your passports on arrival in France!"

The American senior gave the Frenchman a long hard look. Then he quietly explained. "Well, when I came ashore at Omaha Beach on D-Day in 1944 to help liberate this country, I couldn't find any Frenchmen to show it to.

NEWS BULLETIN!!!
The National Transportation Safety Board recently divulged they had "covertly" funded a project with the U.S. automakers for the past 5 years, whereby the automakers were installing black-box voice recorders in 4-wheel drive pickup trucks and SUV's in an effort to determine in fatal accidents, the circumstances in the last 15 seconds before the crash.

They were surprised to find in 38 of the 50 states the recorded last words of drivers in 61.2 percent of fatal crashes were, "Oh S _ _ t!"

Only the states of North Carolina, South Carolina, Virginia, Oklahoma, Tennessee, Kentucky, Arkansas, Alabama, Georgia, Mississippi, Louisiana, southern Missouri and Texas were different, where 89.3 percent of the final words were: "Hold my beer, I'm gonna try somethin."

ONE DARK AND GLOOMY NIGHT, a man is hitch-hiking for a ride. After several hours, he sees a ghost-like car creeping toward him. The car stops and he gets in to find no one behind the wheel. Frozen with fear, he can't jump or run away. The car moves forward and eventually approaches a sharp curve. The man prays for his life, sure the ghost car will crash and he'll plunge to his death.

Suddenly, a hand appears through the window and turns the wheel. Terrified, the man jumps out and runs to a nearby bar where he shares his supernatural experience.

As he finishes, two country boys walk into the bar. One laughs and says to the other, "Look Bubba, there's the idiot who rode in our car while we were pushing it."

("Thanks" to Kim Bircher)

A TRUCK DRIVER WAS DRIVING down a particularly icy road when he noticed a tollbooth ahead. He put on his brakes, but the truck failed to stop. The truck crashed into the tollbooth, smashing it. As he surveyed the damage, a second truck pulled up. Workers scrambled out and began reconstructing the tollbooth with a white putty. Before long it looked as good as new. Puzzled, he asked about the substance.

The worker said, "Oh, that's just tollgate booth paste."

YOU MIGHT BE A FARM WIFE IF...
Contributed by Tracy Stringfellow ... who IS a farm wife!
• If your name is taped to the side of a cakepan.
• If you call the implement dealer and he recognizes your voice.
• If the vet's number is on the speed dial of your phone.

- If you know how to change the flat on your car, but can't because the spare is being used on a flatbed.
- If your second vehicle is still a pickup.
- If the folks in the Emergency Room have a pool going for your kids and it involves the type of injury and when it will occur.
- If your husband has ever used field equipment to maintain your yard.
- If you're in the habit of buying foodstuffs in bulk.
- If a "night out" involves the local 4-H club.
- If the word "auction" makes you tingle.
- If you've ever washed your kids or the dishes with a pressure washer.
- If "picking rock" is considered a chance to get out of the house.
- If "wild game" reminds you of dinner and not the bedroom.
- If the "fresh ingredients" your recipe calls for reminds you to do the garden chores.
- If taking lunch to the field is as close as you get to a picnic.
- If that pail with a hole in it is a flowerpot in the making.
- If your rock garden was hand-picked.
- If you can mend a pair of pants and the fence that ripped them.
- If you're on the lookout for new uses for "Jell-O".
- If the shopping list in your purse includes the sizes of filters, tires, overalls, chains, belts, lights, cables, spark plugs or shotgun shells.
- If "Farm," "Ranch," "Country," "Cowboy," or "Antique" is in the name of your favorite magazine.
- If your tan lines are somewhere below your shoulder and above your elbow.
- If "Lacey" or "Frilly" refers to a farm animal but not your nightgown.
- If you ever went on a date to the rodeo.
- If you've ever been grateful for fingernail polish, because it hides the dirt under your nails.
- If you've ever called your husband to supper, using a radio.
- If you buy antiques because they match the rest of your furniture.
- If being taken out to dinner has ever included a talk by a farm seed dealer.
- If your driveway is longer than a stone's throw.
- If your mailbox looks like a piece of farm machinery.
- If your kids' wading pool has ever doubled as a stock tank, or vice versa.
- If the daily paper is always a day late.
- If you have a yard, but not a lawn.
- If you have lots of machinery and each piece is worth more than your house.
- If the leaky barn roof gets fixed, before the leaky house roof.
- If duct tape is always on your shopping list.
- If the neighbor's house is best viewed with binoculars.
- If the directions to your house include the words "miles," "silos,"

"last," or "gravel road."
• If the tractor and the combine have air conditioning and an FM radio but your car doesn't.
• If your storage shed is a barn.
• If you measure travel in miles not minutes.
• If your farm equipment has the latest global positioning technology and you still can't find your husband.
• If you consider "hot dish" a food group.
• If your husband says, "Can you help me for a few minutes?" and you know that might be anywhere from a few minutes to six hours.
• If you plan your vacations around farm shows.
• If grass stains are the least of your laundry problems.
• If your refrigerator contains medicine, livestock medicine.
• If your car's color is two-toned and one color is gravel road brown.
• If you knew everyone in your high school.
• If you've ever grown your own wall decorations.
• If you've entertained the romantic notion of living in an old, country farmhouse with a fireplace, but gave it up because firsthand experience tells you that it's cold, drafty, smoky and sooty.
• If you use newspapers to help keep the kitchen floor clean.
• If you've ever said, "Oh, it's only a little mud.".
• If you need a pair of vice grips to run a household appliance.
• If your husband gave you flowers, but you had to plant the seeds yourself.
• If you've used the loader to reach the windows when they needed washing.
• If you've ever used a broom to shoo a critter.
• If you've ever discovered a batch of kittens in your laundry basket.
• If dinner is at noon and lunch is before and after dinner.
• If you shovel the sidewalk, with a skidsteer loader.
• If you can find a use for that old tractor seat.
• If you've ever found mice in the underwear drawer.
• If quality time with your hubby means you'll have a flashlight in one hand and a wrench in the other.
• If you know the difference between field corn and sweet corn.
• If family "pets" include deer, coons, squirrels, foxes or birds.
• If you can make a meal that can be ready in six minutes and will still be ready in two hours.
• If your basement is really a cellar.
• If "sharing a cab" has nothing to do with a taxi and everything to do with getting across the field.

What did the tailor think of her new job? It was sew-sew.

THE GOSSIPY PASTOR

Carl and Sam were at odds with each other. They could not even remember the initial cause of friction. Their hostility had festered through the years.

Pastor Fred was deeply concerned, so he prayed that God would use him as a peacemaker.

Pastor Fred called on Carl. "What do you think of Sam?" he asked.

"He's the sorriest guy in town!" Carl growled

"But," Pastor Fred replied, "you have to admit that he's a hard-working man."

"No one can deny that," said Carl. "I've never known a person who worked harder."

The next day Pastor Fred visited Sam. "Do you know what Carl said about you?"

"No, but I can imagine his lies," Sam responded angrily.

"This may surprise you," said Pastor Fred, "but he said he's never known a harder worker."

"He said that?" Sam was stunned.

"By the way, what do you think of Carl?" Pastor Fred asked Sam.

"It is no secret that I have absolutely no use for him." Sam replied slowly.

"But you must admit he's honest in business," said Pastor Fred.

"There's no getting around that," said Sam grudgingly. "In business he's a man you can trust." The next day Pastor Fred met Carl again. "Do you know what Sam said about you? He claims you're absolutely trustworthy in business, that you are scrupulously honest."

"Well, how 'bout that," reacted Carl with a smile.

Soon the gossipy Pastor noticed Sam and Carl would cautiously nod to each other in a friendly sort of way. Before long they were shaking hands, talking, even visiting in each other's homes. Today they are best of friends.

Many people, even church folk, seem to delight in promoting a fight by carrying news of ill-will. Learn a lesson from Pastor Fred's tactic of positive-gossip. Let your "gossip" be to spread words of praise and healing. THAT's the only gossip that's worthy of a Christian.

LEATHER

When a woman wears leather clothing, a man's heart beats quicker, his throat gets dry, he goes weak in the knees, and he begins to think irrationally. Ever wonder why? ... Because she smells like a new truck.

WE ALL GET HEAVIER, as we get older, because there's a lot more information in our heads. So I'm not fat, I'm just really intelligent and my head couldn't hold any more, so it started filling up the rest of me! ... I must be REALLY smart!

A U.S. MARINE SQUAD was marching north of Basra when they came upon an Iraqi terrorist, badly injured and unconscious. On the opposite side of the road was an American Marine in similar but less serious state.

The Marine was conscious and alert and as first aid was given to both men, the squad leader asked the injured Marine what had happened.

The Marine reported, "I was heavily armed and moving north along the highway here, and coming south was a heavily armed insurgent. We saw each other and both took cover in the ditches along the road.

"I yelled to him that Saddam Hussein is a miserable, lowlife, scumbag, and he yelled back that Senator Ted Kennedy is a good-for-nothing, fat, left wing liberal drunk. So I said that Osama Bin Ladin dresses and acts like a frigid, mean spirited woman!"

He retaliated by yelling, "Oh yeah? Well so does Hillary Clinton!"

"And so, Sir, there we were, standing in the middle of the road shaking hands, when a truck hit us."

WHEN GEORGE FOUND OUT he was going to inherit a fortune when his sickly father died, he decided he needed a woman to enjoy it with.

So, one evening he went to a singles bar where he spotted the most beautiful woman he had ever seen. Her natural beauty took his breath away.

"I may look like just an ordinary man," he said as he walked up to her, "but in just a week or two, my father will die, and I'll inherit 20 million dollars."

Impressed, the woman went home with him that evening and, three days later, she became his stepmother. ... Smart girl.

DEAR LORD,

I pray for Wisdom to understand my man; Love to forgive him; And Patience for his moods. Because, Lord, if I pray for Strength, I'll beat him to death.

THINGS YOU WOULD NEVER HEAR
A SOUTHERNER SAY

• We don't keep firearms in this house. • Has anybody seen the sideburn trimmer? • You can't feed that to the dog. • I thought Graceland was tacky. • No kids in the back of the pick-up, it's not safe. • Wrasslin's fake. • Honey, did you mail that donation to Greenpeace? • We're vegetarians. • Do you think my hair is too big? • I'll have grapefruit instead of biscuits and gravy. • Honey, these bonsai trees need watering? • Who's Richard Petty? • Give me the small bag of pork rinds. • Deer heads detract from the decor. • Spitting is such a nasty habit. • I just couldn't find a thing at Wal-Mart today. • Trim the fat off that steak. • Cappuccino tastes better than espresso. • The tires on that truck are too big. • I'll have the arugula and radicchio salad. • I've got it all on a floppy disk. • Unsweetened tea tastes better. • Would you like your fish poached or broiled? • My fiancé, Paula Jo, is registered at Tiffany's. • I've got two cases of Zima for the Super Bowl. • Little Debbie snack cakes have too many fat grams. • Checkmate. • She's too old to be wearing that bikini. • Does the salad bar have bean sprouts? • Hey, here's an episode of "Hee Haw" that we haven't seen. • I don't have a favorite college team. • I believe you cooked those green beans too long. • Those shorts ought to be a little longer, Darla. • Elvis who? • Be sure to bring my salad dressing on the side. • Would you like hash browns instead of grits? • Hunting? No, I've already shot my limit. Maybe next time!

GUILTY DOG

It was the end of the day when I parked my police van in front of the station. As I gathered my equipment, my K-9 partner, Jake, was barking, and I saw a little boy staring in at me.

"Is that a dog you got back there?" he asked.

"It sure is," I replied.

Puzzled, the boy looked at me and then towards the back of the van. Finally he said, "What'd he do?"

BEARD

When a young announcer was raising funds on a local public television station, a woman called in and told the volunteer operator she would donate a hundred dollars if the announcer would shave off his beard. He agreed to help the cause and returned to work clean-shaven. The following day, the check arrived from his mother.

JOURNEY

A priest was preparing a dying man for his 'long day's journey into night.' Whispering firmly, the priest says, "Denounce the devil! Let him know how little you think of his evil."

The dying man says nothing. The priest repeats his order again. Still, the dying man says nothing. The priest asks, "Why do you refuse to denounce the devil and his evil?"

The dying man replies, "Until I know exactly where I'm headed, I don't think it's such a good idea to aggravate anybody just yet."

11 PEOPLE ON A ROPE

Eleven people were hanging on a rope under a helicopter, ten men and one woman. The rope was not strong enough to carry them all, so they decided that one has to leave, because otherwise they are all going to fall. They were not able to name that person, until the woman held a very touching speech. She said that she will voluntarily let go of the rope, because as a woman she is used to giving up everything for her husband and kids, or for men in general, and was used to always making sacrifices with little in return. As soon as she finished her speech, all the men started clapping their hands.

SICK LEAVE

Negotiations between union members and their employer were at an impasse. The union denied that their workers were flagrantly abusing their contract's sick-leave provisions. One morning at the bargaining table, the company's chief negotiator held aloft the morning edition of the newspaper. "This man," he announced, "Called in sick yesterday!" There on the sports page was a photo of the 'supposedly' ill employee, who had just won a local golf tournament with an excellent score.

The silence in the room was broken by a union negotiator. "Wow," he said. "Think of the score he could have had if he hadn't been sick!"

FATHER'S OPINION

4 years: My daddy can do anything. 7 years: My dad knows a lot, a whole lot. 8 years: My father doesn't know quite everything. 12 years: Oh, well, naturally Father doesn't know that, either. 14 years: Father? Hopelessly old-fashioned. 21 years: Oh, that man is out-of-date. What did you expect? 25 years: He knows a little bit about it, but not much. 30 years: Maybe we ought to find out what Dad thinks. 35 years: A little patience. Let's get Dad's assessment before we do anything. 50 years: I wonder what Dad would have thought about that. He was pretty smart. 60 years: My Dad knew absolutely everything! 65 years: I'd give anything if Dad were here so I could talk this over with him. I really miss that man.

THE NEW GO-FER

Freddie was eighteen years old, friendly, and eager to do things right. Unfortunately, he wasn't especially bright. He had just started his first job, as a delivery boy and general go-fer at a furniture warehouse. His first task was to go out for coffee. He walked into a nearby coffee shop carrying a large thermos. When the counterman finally noticed him, he held up the thermos. "Is this big enough to hold six cups of coffee?" he said. The counterman looked at the thermos, hesitated for a few seconds, then finally said, "Yeah. It looks like about six cups to me."

"Good," Freddie said. "Give me two regular, two black, and two decaf."

THE DRILL SERGEANT

One of my husband's duties as a novice drill instructor at Fort Jackson, S.C., was to escort new recruits to the mess hall. After everyone had made it through the chow line, he sat them down and told them, "There are three rules in this mess hall: Shut up! Eat up! Get up!" Checking to see that he had everyone's attention, he asked, "What is the first rule?"

Much to the amusement of the other instructors, 60 privates yelled in unison, "Shut up, Drill Sergeant!"

51 DAYS

A bartender is sitting behind the bar on a typical day, when the door bursts open and in come four exuberant Seattleite women. They come up to the bar, order five bottles of champagne and ten glasses, take their order over and sit down at a large table. The corks are popped, the glasses are filled and they begin toasting and chanting, "51 days, 51 days, 51 days!"

Soon, three more Seattle women arrive, take up their drinks and the chanting grows. "51 days, 51 days, 51 days!"

Two more Seattle women show up and soon their voices are joined in raising the roof. "51 days, 51 days, 51 days!"

Finally, the tenth woman comes in with a picture under her arm. She walks over to the table, sets the picture in the middle and the table erupts. Up jumps the others, they begin dancing around the table, exchanging high-fives, all the while chanting "51 days, 51 days, 51 days!"

The bartender can't contain his curiosity any longer, so he walks over to the table. There in the center is a beautifully framed puzzle of the Cookie Monster. When the frenzy dies down a little bit, the bartender asks one of the blondes, "What's all the chanting and celebration about?

The woman who brought in the picture pipes in, "Everyone thinks that Seattle women are dumb and they make fun of us. So, we decided to set the record straight. Ten of us got together, bought that puzzle and put it together. . . the side of the box said 2-4 years, but we put it together in 51 days!"

BIRD CALLS

For forty years we have studied bird calls . There are so many different species , and to make it more difficult they have territorial accents just like people do. The really amazing thing is, we have translated all of their calls. And the message is always they same . No matter the breed or the location, the message is always the same: "Yah yah yah! Cats can't fly!"

THE RIDDLE

"It's time to see how clearly you can think," the teacher said to his class. "Now, listen carefully, and think about what I'm saying. I'm thinking of a person who has the same mother and father as I have. But this person is not my brother and not my sister. Who is it?"

The kids in the class furrowed their brows, scratched their heads, and otherwise showed how hard they were thinking. But no one came up with the right answer.

When everyone in the class had given up, the teacher announced, "The person is me."

Little Jeffrey beamed at learning the answer. "That's a good one," he said to himself. "I'll have to try that on Mom and Dad."

At dinner that night, little Jeffrey repeated the riddle to his parents. "I'm thinking of a person who has the same mother and father as I have," he said. "But this person isn't my brother and isn't my sister. Who is it?"

His parents furrowed their brows, scratched their heads, and otherwise pretended that they were thinking hard. Then they both said, "I give up. Who is it?"

"It's my teacher!" Jeffrey said.

HONESTLY!

A woman stood before a judge in court for theft charges. She was charged for stealing a can of peaches.

The judge asked the woman, "Ma'am, did you steal that can of peaches?"

The woman replied, "I did, indeed, Your Honor."

The judge inquired, "And, how many peaches were in the can you stole?"

"There were 6 peaches, Sir." The woman confessed.

"Then, as your sentence, you will serve 6 days in jail. One day for each peach you stole."

At that moment, the woman's husband, who was sitting in the courtroom, raised his hand and spoke out, "Sir, Your Honor, may I say something?"

"Identify yourself and speak up so the court can hear you," responded the judge.

"Sir, I am this woman's husband. I just wanted you to know she also stole a can of peas."

SIMPLE RULES
1. You only need two tools: WD-40 and Duct Tape. If it doesn't move and should, use the WD-40. If it shouldn't move and does, use the duct tape.
2. Everyone seems normal until you get to know them.
3. Never pass up an opportunity to go to the bathroom.
4. Be really nice to your family and friends; you never know when you might need them to empty your bedpan.

IN LIVING COLOR
I was at the mall the other day eating at the food court.

I noticed an old man watching a teenager sitting next to him.

The teenager had spiked hair in all different colors: green, red, orange, and blue.

The old man kept staring at him. The teenager would look and find the old man staring every time.

When the teenager had enough, he sarcastically asked, "What's the matter old man, never done anything wild in your life?

The old man did not bat an eye in his response, "Got drunk once and an affair with a peacock. I was just wondering if you were my son."

LECTURE
"What are you doing out here at 2 A.M.?" said the officer.

"I'm going to a lecture." The man said.

"And who is going to give a lecture at this hour?" the cop asked.

"My wife," said the man.

7 AMAZINGLY SIMPLE HOME REMEDIES
1. If you are choking on an ice cube, don't panic. Simply pour a cup of boiling water down your throat and presto. The blockage will be almost instantly removed.
2. Clumsy? Avoid cutting yourself while slicing vegetables by getting someone else to hold them while you chop away.
3. Avoid arguments with the little woman about lifting the toilet seat by simply using the sink.
4. For high blood pressure sufferers: simply cut yourself and bleed for a few minutes, thus reducing the pressure in your veins. Remember to use a timer.
5. A mouse trap, placed on top of your alarm clock, will prevent you from rolling over and going back to sleep after you hit the snooze button.
6. If you have a bad cough, take a large dose of laxatives, then you will be afraid to cough.

7. Have a bad toothache? Smash your thumb with a hammer and you will forget about the toothache.

TWO GAS COMPANY SERVICEMEN, a senior training supervisor and a young trainee, were out checking meters in a suburban neighborhood. They parked their truck the end of the alley and worked their way to the other end. At the last house, a woman looking out her kitchen window watched the two men as they checked her gas meter. Finishing the meter check, the senior supervisor challenged his younger coworker to a foot race down the alley back to the truck to prove that an older guy could outrun a younger one. As they came running up to the truck, they realized the lady from that last house was huffing and puffing right behind them. They stopped and asked her what was wrong.

Gasping for breath, she replied, "When I see two men from the gas company running as hard as you two were, I figured I'd better run too!"

A MINISTER IN A LITTLE CHURCH had been having trouble with the collections. One Sunday he announced, "Now, before we pass the collection plate, I would like to request that the person who stole the chickens from Farmer Condill's henhouse please refrain from giving any money to the Lord. The Lord doesn't want money from a thief!"

The collection plate was passed around, and for the first time in months everybody gave.

PRE-NUPTIAL PROBLEMS

A young man called his mother and announced excitedly that he had just met the woman of his dreams. Now what should he do?

His mother had an idea: "Why don't you send her flowers, and on the card invite her to your apartment for a home-cooked meal?"

He thought this was a great strategy, and a week later, the woman came to dinner.

His mother called the next day to see how things had gone.

"I was totally humiliated," he moaned. "She insisted on washing the dishes."

"What's wrong with that?" asked his mother. "I think it's a wonderful gesture."

"We hadn't started eating yet."

MEMORY PROBLEMS

An elderly couple had dinner at another couple's house, and after eating, the wives left the table and went into the kitchen. The two gentlemen were talking, and one said, "Last night we went out to a new restaurant and it was really great. I would recommend it very highly." The other man said, "What is the name of the restaurant?" The first man thought and thought and finally said, "What is the name of that flower you give to someone you love? You know... the one that's red and has thorns." "Do you mean a rose?" "Yes, that's the one," replied the man. He then turned towards the kitchen and yelled, "Rose, what's the name of that restaurant we went to last night?"

HANG-GLIDING

Here in Kentucky, you don't see too many people hang-gliding. Bubba decided to save up and get a hang-glider. He takes it to the highest mountain, and after struggling to the top, he gets ready to take flight. He takes off running and reaches the edge-- into the wind he goes!

Meanwhile, Maw and Paw Hicks were sittin' on the porch swing talkin bout the good ol days when maw spots the biggest bird she ever seen! "Look at the size of that bird, Paw!" she exclaims. Paw raises up," Git my gun, Maw." She runs into the house, brings out his pump shotgun. He takes careful aim. BANG...BANG.....BANG.....BANG! The monster size bird continues to sail silently over the tree tops. "I think ya missed him, Paw," she says. "Yeah," he replies, "but at least he let go of Bubba!"

WHEELCHAIR RIDE

Hospital regulations require a wheelchair for patients being discharged. However, while working as a student nurse, I found one elderly gentleman already dressed and sitting on the bed with a suitcase at his feet who insisted he didn't need my help to leave the hospital. After a chat about rules being rules, he reluctantly let me wheel him to the elevator. On the way down I asked him if his wife was meeting him.

"I don't know," he said. "She's still upstairs in the bathroom changing out of her hospital gown."

SEATTLE LADY WITH A BABY

At a pharmacy, a Seattle woman asked to use the infant scale to weigh the baby she held in her arms. The clerk explained that the device was out for repairs, but said that she would figure the infant's weight by weighing the woman and baby together on the adult scale, then weighing the mother alone and subtracting the second amount from the first.

"It won't work," explained the woman. "I'm not the mother, I'm the aunt."

What has one horn and gives milk? The milk truck!

BIG EXCUSE

Our local newspaper ran several stories about a study that tied female obesity to a virus. One evening my sister came home exhausted from a long day at work. "Did you read the paper?" she asked. "I'm not going in to work tomorrow. I'm calling in fat."

DIPLOMA

A grandmother was pushing her little grandchild around Wal-Mart in a buggy. Each time she put something in the basket she would say, "And here's something for you, Diploma." or "This will make a cute little outfit for you, Diploma." and so on.

Eventually a bewildered shopper who'd heard all this finally asked, "Why do you keep calling your grandchild Diploma?"

The grandmother replied, "I sent my daughter to Virginia Tech and this is what she came home with!"

WHAT ARE THEY TEACHING YOU?

A fifth generation farmer has determined that his son will be the first in their family to go to college. So, he and the wife save every penny for years and when the big day comes for junior to leave for school, the old man is the proudest he's ever been. After the first semester junior comes home for Christmas break and the old man sits him down for a talk. "Well, boy, you been at school for three months now, I want you to tell me some of that fancy book learnin'."

So, junior says, "My favorite class is math, pa. Just last week we learned a new formula...Pi r squared."

At hearing this the old man screws up his eyes and smacks his forehead, "Dog gone-it! I spent all that money on schooling and all you can tell me is Pi r squared? Why everybody know pie are round...CORNBREAD are squared!"

WEEKEND PASS NEEDED

Although I knew our commanding officer hated doling out weekend passes, I thought I had a good reason. "My wife is pregnant and I want to be with her," I told the C.O.

Much to my surprise he said, "Permission granted."

Inspired by my success, a fellow soldier also requested a weekend pass. His wife wasn't pregnant, so when the C.O. asked why he should grant him permission, my friend re- sponded, "My wife is getting pregnant this weekend and I want to be with her."

Submitted by Patrick Linden, Wellpinit, WA:
Q: What do you call a bear with no teeth? A: A gummy bear.

Submitted by Patrick Linden, Wellpinit, WA:
Did you hear about the dyslexic, insomniac, athiest? He stayed up all night wondering if there really is a dog.

THE FOOTBALL HERO

Larry, a local football star, is jogging down the street when he sees a building on fire. A lady is standing on a third story ledge holding her pet cat in her arms. "Hey, lady," yells Larry, "Throw me the cat."

"No," she cries, "It's too far."

"I play football, I can catch him."

The smoke is pouring from the windows. Finally, the woman waves to Larry, kisses her cat goodbye, and tosses it down to the street. Larry keeps his eye on the cat as it comes hurtling down toward him. The feline bounces off an awning and Larry runs into the street to catch it. He jumps six feet into the air and makes a spectacular one handed catch.

The crowd that has gathered to watch the fire breaks into cheers. Larry does a little dance, lifts the cat above his head, wiggles his knees back and forth, then spikes the cat into the pavement.

OUT WITH THE BOYS

A man left for work one Friday afternoon. But, being payday, instead of going home, he stayed out the entire weekend hunting with the boys and spent his entire paycheck.

When he finally appeared at home Sunday night, he was confronted by a very angry wife and was barraged for nearly two hours with a tirade befitting his actions.

Finally his wife stopped the nagging and simply said to him. "How would you like it if you didn't see me for two or three days?"

To which he replied, "That would be fine with me."

Monday went by and he didn't see his wife. Tuesday and Wednesday came and went with the same results. Thursday, the swelling went down just enough where he could see her a little out of the corner of his left eye.

WILLING TO ADMIT IT

A husband and wife were involved in a petty argument, both of them unwilling to admit they might be in error.

"I'll admit I'm wrong," the wife told her husband in a conciliatory attempt, "if you'll admit I'm right."

He agreed and, like a gentleman, insisted she go first. "I'm wrong," she said. With a twinkle in his eye, he responded, "You're right!"

IT'S TAXING ...
A fine is a tax for doing wrong. A tax is a fine for doing well.

A FAIRY TALE

Once upon a time, in a land far away, a beautiful, independent, self-assured princess happened upon a frog as she sat contemplating ecological issues on the shores of an unpolluted pond in a verdant meadow near her castle.

The frog hopped into the princess' lap and said, " Elegant Lady, I was once a handsome prince until an evil witch cast a spell upon me. One kiss from you, however, and I will turn back into the dapper, young prince that I am. And then, my sweet, we can marry and set up housekeeping in your castle with my mother, where you can prepare my meals, clean my clothes, bear my children, and forever feel grateful and happy doing so. "

That night, as the princess dined sumptuously on lightly sautéed frog legs seasoned in a white wine and onion cream sauce,
she chuckled and thought to herself, "I don't freakin think so."

ON VACATION, A MAN AND HIS WIFE check into a hotel. The husband wants to have a snack at the restaurant, but his wife is extremely tired so she decides to go on up to their room to rest. She lies down on the bed. Just then, a train passes by very close to the window and shakes the room so hard she's thrown out of the bed. Thinking this must be a freak occurrence, she lies down once more. But just a few minutes later a train again shakes the room so violently, she's pitched to the floor. Exasperated, she calls the front desk and asks for the manager who says he'll be right up.

The manager is skeptical but the wife insists the story is true. "Look... lie here on the bed -- you'll be thrown right to the floor!"

So, he lies down next to the wife. Just then the husband walks in.

He takes one look at the manager lying in bed with his wife and yells, "Hey! What are you doing in here!?"

The manager calmly replies, "Would you believe I'm waiting for a train?"

A PROPERTY MANAGER of single-family residence was showing a unit to prospective tenants and asking the usual questions.
"Professionally employed?" he asked.
"We're a military family," the wife answered.
"Children?"
"Oh, yes, ages nine and twelve," she answered proudly.
"Animals?"
"Oh, no," she said earnestly. "They're very well behaved."

"**I ARISE IN THE MORNING** torn between a desire to improve the world and a desire to enjoy the world. This makes it hard to plan the day." --E. B. White

WHILE TAKING DOWN THE VITALS for a soon-to-be mom, I asked how much she weighed. "I really don't know," she said. "Well, more or less," I prompted. "More, I guess," she answered sadly.

POLICE TEST

A young man was taking a verbal test to join the local police force. The question asked, "If you were driving a police car, alone on a lonely road at night, and were being chased by a gang of criminals driving sixty miles an hour, what would you do?"

The young man answered without a second's thought: "Seventy!"

GLASSES FOR WORK

I came home from work last night exhausted. I said to my wife, "I need my glasses checked. I'm so nearsighted I nearly worked myself to death."

Perplexed, the wife asked, "What's being nearsighted got to do with working yourself to death?"

"I couldn't tell whether the boss was watching me or not, so I had to work the whole time!"

CANDY JAR

Where I used to work, we had a jar full of candy bars to give to children while their parents were filling out necessary paper work. After I was given permission by the mother to offer one to her daughter, I held the dish down for her to make her choice.

After choosing, the girl's mother gave the girl a stern look and asked, "What do you say to the nice lady?"

The little girl then looked sweetly at me and said, "May I please have two?"

WORKING SMARTER, NOT HARDER

Co-workers sympathized as my mother complained that her back was really sore from moving furniture.

"Why don't you wait till your husband gets home?" someone asked.

"I could," my mother told the group," but the couch is easier to move if he's not on it."

WHY DO PEOPLE constantly return to the refrigerator with hopes that something new to eat will have materialized?

JOE SMITH STARTED THE DAY early having set his alarm clock (MADE IN JAPAN) for 6 a.m. While his coffeepot (MADE IN CHINA) was perking, he shaved with his electric razor (MADE IN HONG KONG). He put on a dress shirt (MADE IN SRI LANKA), designer jeans (MADE IN SINGAPORE) and tennis shoes (MADE IN KOREA). After cooking his breakfast in his new electric skillet (MADE IN INDIA) he sat down with his calculator (MADE IN MEXICO) to see how much he could spend today. After setting his watch (MADE IN TAIWAN) to the radio (MADE IN INDIA) he got in his car (MADE IN GERMANY) (filled with GAS from Saudi Arabia) and continued his search for a good paying AMERICAN JOB. At the end of yet another discouraging and fruitless day checking his Computer (Made In Malaysia), Joe decided to relax for a while. He put on his sandals (MADE IN BRAZIL) poured himself a glass of wine (MADE IN FRANCE) and turned on his TV (MADE IN INDONESIA), and then wondered why he can't find a good paying job in America.

RULES KIDS WON'T LEARN AT SCHOOL

Unfortunately there are some things that children should be learning in school, but don't. Not all of them have to do with academics. Here are some basic rules that may not have found their way into the standard curriculum.

Rule #1. Life is not fair. Get used to it. The average teenager uses the phrase "it's not fair" 8.6 times a day. You got it from your parents, who said it so often, you decided they must be the most idealistic generation ever. When they started hearing it from their own kids, they realized Rule #1.

Rule #2. The real world won't care as much about your self-esteem as your school does. It'll expect you to accomplish something before you feel good about yourself. This may come as a shock. Usually, when inflated self-esteem meets reality, kids complain that it's not fair. (See Rule No. 1)

Rule #3. Sorry, you won't make $40,000 a year right out of high school. And you won't be a vice president or have a car phone either. You may even have to wear a uniform that doesn't have a Gap label.

Rule #4. If you think your teacher is tough, wait 'till you get a boss. He doesn't have tenure, so he tends to be a bit edgier. When you mess up, he is not going ask you how feel about it.

Rule #5. Flipping burgers is not beneath your dignity. Your grandparents had a different word for burger flipping. They called it opportunity. They weren't embarrassed making minimum wage either. They would have been embarrassed to sit around talking about Kurt Cobain all weekend.

Rule #6. It's not your parents fault. If you screw up, you are responsible. This is the flip side of "It's my life," and "You're not the boss of me," and other eloquent proclamations of your generation. When you turn 18, it's on your dime. Don't whine about it or you'll sound like a baby boomer.

Rule #7. Before you were born your parents weren't as boring as they are now. They got that way paying your bills, cleaning up your room and listening to you tell them how idealistic you are. And by the way, before you save the rain forest from the blood-sucking parasites of your parents' generation try delousing the closet in your bedroom.

Rule #8. Life is not divided into semesters, and you don't get summers off. Nor even Easter break. They expect you to show up every day. For eight hours. And you don't get a new lease on life every 10 weeks. It just goes on and on.

Rule #9. Television is not real life. Your life is not a sitcom, nor a soap opera. Your problems will not all be solved in 30 minutes, minus time for commercials. In real life, people actually have to leave the coffee shop to go to jobs. Your friends will not be perky or as polite as Jennifer Aniston.

Rule #10. Be nice to nerds. You may end up working for them.

Rule #11. Enjoy this while you can. Sure, parents are a pain, school's a bother, and life is depressing. But someday you'll realize how wonderful it was to be kid. Maybe you should start now.

THE WEDDING DRESS
Betty was soon to be married. More than anything, she wanted to wear the wedding dress her mother was married in. Betty's mother was beaming with pride as she gave her consent. Later in the evening, the family gathered in the living room to wait while Betty tried on the dress. When Betty entered the room, there was a chorus of approval. The dress fit perfectly and looked wonderful on her.

Betty's mother burst into tears.

Seeing this, Betty said, "Don't worry Mom, you're not losing a daughter, your gaining a son."

"Forget about that!" she said with a sob. "I used to fit into that dress!"

SITTING TOGETHER ON A TRAIN, traveling through the Swiss Alps, are a French guy, an American guy, an old Greek lady, and a young blonde Swiss girl.

The train goes into a dark tunnel and a few seconds later there is the sound of a loud slap.

When the train emerges from the tunnel, the Frenchman has a bright red hand print on his cheek. No one speaks.

The old lady thinks: The Frenchman must have groped the blonde in the dark, and she slapped his cheek.

The blonde thinks: That Frenchman must have tried to grope me in the dark, but missed and fondled the old lady and she slapped his cheek.

The Frenchman thinks: The American must have groped the blonde in the dark. She tried to slap him but missed and got me instead.

The American thinks: I can't wait for another tunnel, so I can smack that Frenchman again!

ONELINERS
• No more about Elvis, OK? Thankyouverymuch.
• To a worm, digging in the hard ground is more relaxing than going fishing.
• An alarming number of people suffer from seriousness.
• A wishbone has never taken the place of a backbone.
• When you have your head up your butt, 4 of the 5 senses do not work.
• Exaggeration is a billion times worse than understatement.
• Whenever I feel blue, I start breathing again.
• Whether it's landslides or our aging bodies, gravity always wins.
• I'll bet you can get a real good deal on 14 bridesmaid dresses right now on eBay.
• When gas prices reach $5 a gallon, it should include car insurance.
• The best antiques are old friends.
• So many journalists, so little real news.
• I wouldn't touch the Metric System with a 3.048m pole.

MISTAKES

A building contractor was being paid by the week for a job that was likely to stretch over several months. He approached the owner of the property and held up the check he'd been given.

"This is two hundred dollars less than we agreed on," he said.

"I know," the owner said. "But last week I overpaid you two hundred dollars, and you never complained."

The contractor said. "Well, I don't mind an occasional mistake. But when it gets to be a habit, I feel I have to call it to your attention."

DID YOU HEAR THE NEW California quarter's reverse side features a bear, a miner, a condor, a redwood, and poppies? The engraving depicts the bear observing the miner as he cooks the condor over a redwood fire he made after smoking a distillate of the poppies.

WE WENT TO THE MOVIE the other night. I sat in an aisle seat as I usually do because it feels a little roomier. Just as the feature was about to start a baby boomer from the center of the row got up and started working her way out.

"Excuse me, sorry, oops, excuse me, pardon me, gotta hurry, oops, excuse me."

By the time she got to me I was trying to look around her and I was a little impatient so I said, "Couldn't you have done this a little earlier?"

"No!!" she said in a loud whisper, "The TURN OFF YOUR CELL PHONE PLEASE message just flashed up on the screen and mine is out in the car."

DEBATE

Two Federal Way women were skiing at Snoqualmie when they got into a debate about the best way to ski down a particular hill.

"The best way is down the left side of the course, where it's nearly all powder," said the first woman.

"No, the best way is straight down the middle, where the snow is packed tight," argued the other.

"Look," said the first woman, "Let's get another opinion. There's a guy dragging a sled up the hill. Let's go ask him."

The second woman agreed, and in a few minutes the two caught up with the guy.

"Excuse me," said the first woman. "I say the best way to ski down this hill is to take the left side of the course, where it's nearly all powder, and my friend thinks the best way is straight down the middle, where the snow is packed tight. Can you tell us who's right?"

"Sorry, ladies," said the man, "but there's no use in asking me. I'm a tobogganist."

"Oh," said the second woman. "Well, in that case, can I get a pack of Marlboros?"

How do you communicate with a fish? Drop him a line!

RANSOM

A young corporate executive was sent a ransom note saying that he was to bring $50,000 to the 17th hole of the country club at 10 o'clock the next day if he ever wanted to see his wife alive again.

He didn't arrive until almost 12:30.

A masked man stepped out from behind some bushes and growled, "What took ya so long? You're over two hours late."

"Hey! Give me a break." whined the executive. "I have a 27 handicap."

The following is the philosophy of Charles Schultz, the creator of the "Peanuts" comic strip. You don't have to actually answer the questions. Just read the straight through, and you'll get the point.
1. Name the five wealthiest people in the world.
2. Name the last five Heisman trophy winners.
3. Name the last five winners of the Miss America.
4. Name ten people who have won the Nobel or Pulitzer Prize.
5. Name the last half dozen Academy Award winner for best actor and actress.
6. Name the last decade's worth of World Series winners.

How did you do? The point is, none of us remember the headliners of yesterday. These are no second-rate achievers. They are the best in their fields. But the applause dies. Awards tarnish. Achievements are forgotten. Accolades and certificates are buried with their owners.

Here's another quiz. See how you do on this one:
1. List a few teachers who aided your journey through school.
2. Name three friends who have helped you through a difficult time.
3. Name five people who have taught you something worthwhile.
4. Think of a few people who have made you feel appreciated and special.
5. Think of five people you enjoy spending time with.

Easier? The lesson: The people who make a difference in your life are not the ones with the most credentials, the most money, or the most awards. They are the ones that care.

"Don't worry about the world coming to an end today. It's already tomorrow in Australia." (Charles Schultz)

YOU KNOW YOU'RE A REDNECK IF ... you use the gap between your front teeth to gauge which weed eater line you need.

My Aunt
Joe says to Bill, "Want to see a picture of my Aunt?"
"Sure."
So Joe takes out a picture.
"What are you talking about?" Bill says, "That's not your aunt! That's a picture of a fish!"
Joe responds, "Well, sure it is... It's my Aunt Chovy!"

A WOMAN WENT INTO a hardware store to purchase a bale of peat moss. She gave a personal check in payment and said to the clerk, "I suppose you will want some identification."

He replied, without hesitation, "No ma'am, that won't be necessary."
"How come?" asked the woman.
"Crooks don't buy peat moss." answered the clerk.

AN OLD MAN STRODE in to his doctor's office and said, "Doc, my druggist said to tell you to change my prescription and to check the prescription you've been giving to Mrs. Smith."

"Oh, he did, did he?" the doctor shot back. "And since when does a druggist second guess a doctor's orders?"

The old man says, "Since he found out I've been on birth control pills since February."

NOISE ABATEMENT
"Flight 1234," the control tower advised, "turn right 45 degrees for noise abatement."

"Roger," the pilot responded, "but we're at 35,000 feet. How much noise can we make up here?"

"Sir," the radar man replied, "have you ever heard the noise a 727 makes when it hits a 747?"

A MAN IN ALABAMA had a flat tire, pulled off on the side of the road and proceeded to put a bouquet of flowers in front of the car and one behind it. Then he got back in the car to wait. A passerby studied the scene as he drove by and was so curious he turned around and went back.

He asked the fellow what the problem was.
The man replied, "I have a flat tare."
The passerby asked, "But what's with the flowers?"
The man responded, "When you break down they tell you to put flares in the front and flares in the back! I never did understand that neither."

PRE-FLIGHT CHECK
After an overnight flight to meet my father at his latest military assignment, my mother wearily arrived at Rhein-Main Air Base in Germany with my eight siblings and me -- all under age 11. Collecting our many suitcases, the ten of us entered the cramped customs area.

A young customs official watched our entourage in disbelief, ''Ma'am,'' he said, ''do all these children and this luggage belong to you?''

''Yes, sir,'' my mother said with a sigh, ''they're all mine.''

The customs agent began his interrogation: ''Ma'am, do you have any weapons, contraband or illegal drugs in your possession?''

''Sir,'' she calmly answered, ''if I'd had any of those items, I would have used them by now.'

AT A WEDDING I recently attended, the priest called for a moment of silence to remember the faithful dead.

As the church grew quiet, a little boy sitting in front of me turned to his father and said excitedly, "Dad, you have some of their albums!"

THE FOLLOWING COMMENTS WERE MADE IN THE YEAR 1957:
(1) "I'll tell you one thing, if things keep going the way they are, it's going to be impossible to buy a week's groceries for $20.00."
(2) "Have you seen the new cars coming out next year? It won't be long when $5,000 will only buy a used one."
(3) "If cigarettes keep going up in price, I'm going to quit. A quarter a pack is ridiculous."
(4) "Did you hear the post office is thinking about charging a dime just to mail a letter?"
(5) "If they raise the minimum wage to $1, nobody will be able to hire outside help at the store."
(6) "When I first started driving, who would have thought gas would someday cost 29 cents a gallon. Guess we'd be better off leaving the car in the garage."
(7) "Kids today are impossible. Those ducktail hair cuts make it impossible to stay groomed. Next thing you know, boys will be wearing their hair as long as the girls."
(8) "I'm afraid to send my kids to the movies any more. Ever since they let Clark Gable get by with saying 'damn' in 'Gone With The Wind,' it seems every new movie has either 'hell' or 'damn' in it."
(9) "I read the other day where some scientist thinks it's possible to put a man on the moon by the end of the century. They even have some fellows they call astronauts preparing for it down in Texas."

(10) "Did you see where some baseball player just signed a contract for $75,000 a year just to play ball? It wouldn't surprise me if someday that they will be making more than the President."

(11) "I never thought I'd see the day all our kitchen appliances would be electric. They are even making electric typewriters now."

(12) "It's too bad things are so tough nowadays. I see where a few married women are having to work to make ends meet."

(13) "It won't be long before young couples are going to have to hire someone to watch their kids so they can both work."

(14) "No one can afford to be sick any more, $35.00 a day in the hospital is too rich for my blood."

(15) "I'm just afraid the Volkswagen car is going to open the door to a whole lot of foreign business."

(16) "Thank goodness I won't live to see the day when the Government takes half our income in taxes. I sometimes wonder if we are electing the best people to Congress."

(17) "The drive-in restaurant is convenient in nice weather, but I seriously doubt they will ever catch on."

(18) "I guess taking a vacation is out of the question now days. It costs nearly $15.00 a night to stay in a hotel."

A GUY WAS HITCHHIKING on a very dark and stormy night. The night was getting on and no cars went by. Suddenly he saw a car roll slowly toward him and stop. Without thinking about it, the guy jumped into the back seat and closed the door when he suddenly realized there was nobody behind the wheel! Just then the car started slowly rolling forward again. He was beginning to get really freaked out when he noticed a curve in the road ahead. He was just thinking about climbing into the front seat when a hand mysteriously appeared through the window and moved the wheel. The guy, paralyzed in terror, watched how the hand appeared every time right before a curve. Gathering his courage, the guy finally jumped out of the car and ran to the nearest town. Wet and in shock, he went to a restaurant and started telling everybody about the horrible experience he just went through. About half an hour later, two guys walked into the same restaurant. They were looking around for a table when one said to the other, "Hey, look, isn't that the jerk who got in the car when we were pushing it?"

READ THE LABEL!
1. On a blanket from Taiwan - NOT TO BE USED AS PROTECTION FROM A TORNADO.
2. On a helmet mounted mirror used by US cyclists - REMEMBER, OBJECTS IN THE MIRROR ARE ACTUALLY BEHIND YOU.

3. On a Taiwanese shampoo - USE REPEATEDLY FOR SEVERE DAMAGE.
4. On the bottle-top of a (UK) flavored milk drink - AFTER OPENING, KEEP UPRIGHT.
5. On a New Zealand insect spray - THIS PRODUCT NOT TESTED ON ANIMALS.
6. In a US guide to setting up a new computer - TO AVOID CONDENSATION FORMING, ALLOW THE BOXES TO WARM UP TO ROOM TEMPERATURE BEFORE OPENING. (Sensible, but the instruction was INSIDE the box.)
7. On Sainsbury's peanuts - WARNING - CONTAINS NUTS. (Really? Peanuts contain nuts?)
8. In some countries, on the bottom of Coke bottles - OPEN OTHER END.
9. On a packet of Sunmaid raisins - WHY NOT TRY TOSSING OVER YOUR FAVORITE BREAKFAST CEREAL?
10. On a Sears hairdryer - DO NOT USE WHILE SLEEPING.
11. On a bag of Fritos - YOU COULD BE A WINNER! NO PURCHASE NECESSARY. DETAILS INSIDE. (The shoplifter special!)
12. On a bar of Dial soap - DIRECTIONS - USE LIKE REGULAR SOAP. (And that would be how?)
13. On Tesco's Tiramisu dessert (printed on bottom of the box) - DO NOT TURN UPSIDE DOWN. (Too late! You lose!)
14. On Marks & Spencer Bread Pudding - PRODUCT WILL BE HOT AFTER HEATING. (Are you sure? Let's experiment.)
15. On a Korean kitchen knife - WARNING: KEEP OUT OF CHILDREN. (DANG! Who are they to tell me what to do with my kids?)
16. On a string of Chinese-made Christmas lights - FOR INDOOR OR OUTDOOR USE ONLY. (As opposed to use in outer space?)
17. On a Japanese food processor - NOT TO BE USED FOR THE OTHER USE. (Now, I'm curious).

A MAN AND HIS WIFE had been debating the purchase of a new auto for weeks. He wanted a new truck. She wanted a fast little sports car so she could zip through traffic around town. He would have settled on a used truck, but everything she seemed to like was way out of their price range.

"Look!" she said. "I want something that goes from 0 to 200 in 4 seconds or less. And my birthday is coming up. You could surprise me!"

For her birthday, he bought her a brand new bathroom scale.

... Assault charges are pending.

Where do sheep go to get haircuts? To the Baa Baa Shop!

JESUS AND THE REDNECK

An Irishman in a wheelchair entered a restaurant one afternoon and asked the waitress for a cup of coffee.

The Irishman looked across the restaurant and asked, "Is that Jesus sitting over there?"

The waitress nodded "yes," so the Irishman told her to give Jesus a cup of coffee on him.

The next patron to come in was an Englishman with a hunched back. He shuffled over to a booth, painfully sat down, and asked the waitress for a cup of hot tea. He also glanced across the restaurant and asked, "Is that Jesus over there?"

The waitress nodded, so the Englishman said to give Jesus a cup of hot tea, "my treat."

The third patron to come into the restaurant was a redneck on crutches.

He hobbled over to a booth, sat down and hollered, "Hey there, sweet thang. How's about gettin' me a cold glass of Coke!"

He, too, looked across the restaurant and asked, "Is that God's boy over there?"

The waitress once more allowed as how it certainly was, so the redneck said to give Jesus a cold glass of Coke, "on my bill."

As Jesus got up to leave, he passed by the Irishman, touched him and said, "For your kindness, you are healed."

The Irishman felt the strength come back into his legs, got up, and danced a jig out the door.

Jesus also passed by the Englishman, touched him and said, "For your kindness, you are healed."

The Englishman felt his back straightening up, and he raised his hands, praised the Lord and did a series of back flips out the door.

Then Jesus walked towards the redneck. The redneck jumped up and yelled, "Don't touch me... ... I'm drawin' disability!"

A LADY IN REDMOND called 9-1-1 from her cellphone and said, "Someone broke into my car and stole everything out of it! They stole the steering wheel, the brake and gas pedals, the radio, and all the gauges! You need to send a policeman over here right now!"

A police car arrived on the scene and as he was waiting for a backup unit to show up, he got out of his patrol car to take a look at the Redmond lady's car.

He called the back up unit on the radio and said, "Unit 54 to Unit 75, you don't need to come out to the auto burglary on Elm Street."

Unit 75 responded, "Copy that, but why?"

Unit 54 replied, "Because the lady was calling from the back seat of her car."

ALL IN A DAY'S WORK

A farmer and his recently hired hand were eating an early breakfast of biscuits and gravy, scrambled eggs, bacon and coffee that the farmer's wife had prepared for them. Thinking of all the work they had to get done that day, the farmer told the hired man he might as well go ahead and eat his dinner too.

The hired man didn't say a word, but filled his plate a second time and proceeded to eat. After awhile the farmer said,

"We've got so much work to do today, you might as well eat your supper now too."

Again, the hired man didn't respond but refilled his plate a third time and continued to eat.

Finally, after eating his third plate of food, the hired man pushed back his chair & began to take off his shoes.

"What are you doing?" the farmer asked.

The hired man replied, "I don't work after supper."

THREE WOMEN FROM KING COUNTY were hiking. The first woman said, "Oh, look! Bear tracks!"

The second woman said, "Those aren't bear tracks! Those are moose tracks!"

The third woman said, "You two don't know anything! I can tell you don't get outdoors very often! Those aren't bear tracks OR moose tracks! Those are DEER tracks!"

As the two woman stood there arguing, a train came by and ran them over.

GITTIN' 'R DONE

A Marine was attending a college course between missions in Iraq and Afghanistan. The professor, an avowed atheist, shocked the class one day when he walked in, looked toward the ceiling, and said loudly, "God, if you are real, then I want you to knock me off this platform. I'll give you exactly 15 minutes."

The lecture room fell silent and the professor began his lecture. Ten minutes went by and the professor proclaimed, "Here I am God - still waiting."

It got down to the last minute when the Marine stood up, walked toward the professor and threw his best punch, knocking him off the platform and out cold. The Marine went back to his seat and sat down. The other students were shocked and stunned and sat there looking on in silence. The professor came to, noticeably shaken, looked at the Marine and asked, "What is the matter with you? Why did you do that?"

The Marine calmly replied, "God is busy today protecting America's soldiers who are protecting your right to behave like an idiot. So He sent me."

WORSE THAN A BROKEN HEART!

I stopped at a florist shop after work to pick up roses for my wife. As the clerk was putting the finishing touches on the bouquet, a young man burst through the door, breathlessly requesting a dozen red roses.

"I'm sorry," the clerk said. "This man just ordered our last bunch."

The desperate customer turned to me and begged, "Please I'll pay you twice what you paid for those roses?"

"What happened?" I asked. "Did you forget your wedding anniversary?"

"It's even worse than that," he confided. "I broke my wife's hard drive!"

WOULD OR WOULDN'T DO

Cassie walked into a gift shop that sold religious items. Near the cash register she saw a display of caps with "WWJD" printed on all of them. She she asked the clerk what the letters were supposed to mean, and the clerk replied that the letters stood for "What Would Jesus Do" and was meant to inspire people to not make rash decisions, but rather to imagine what Jesus would do in the same situation.

Cassie thought a moment and then replied, "Well, I don't think Jesus would pay $14.95 for one of these caps."

PARTY ENTERTAINMENT

A lady is throwing a party for her granddaughter, and had gone all out with a caterer, band, and a hired clown. Just before the party started, two bums showed up looking for a handout. Feeling sorry for the bums, the woman told them that she would give them a meal if they would help chop some wood for her out back. Gratefully, they headed to the rear of the house.

The guests arrived, and all was going well with the children having a wonderful time. But the clown hadn't shown up. After a half an hour, the clown finally called to report that he was stuck in traffic, and would probably not make the party at all.

The woman was very disappointed and unsuccessfully tried to entertain the children herself. She happened to look out the window and saw one of the bums doing cartwheels across the lawn. She watched in awe as he swung from tree branches, did midair flips, and leaped high in the air.

She spoke to the other bum and said, "What your friend is doing is absolutely marvelous. I have never seen such a thing. Do you think your friend would consider repeating this performance for the children at the party? I would pay him $100!"

The other bum says, "Well, I dunno. Let me ask him. HEY WILLIE! FOR $100, WOULD YOU CHOP OFF ANOTHER TOE?"

Among Friends

Two elderly ladies had been friends for many decades. Over the years they had shared all kinds of activities and adventures. Lately, their activities had been limited to meeting a few times a week to play cards.

One day they were playing cards when one looked at the other and said, "Now don't get mad at me, I know we've been friends for a long time. But, I just can't think of your name! I've thought and thought, but I can't remember it. Please tell me what your name is."

Her friend glared at her. For at least three minutes she just stared and glared at her. Finally she said, "How soon do you need to know?"

Points to Ponder

- A bus station is where a bus stops. A train station is where a train stops. On my desk I have a work station...

- If they arrested the Energizer Bunny, would they charge it with battery?

- I believe five out of four people have trouble with fractions.

- How come you never hear about gruntled employees?

- If a tin whistle is made out of tin (and it is), then what, exactly, is fog horn made out of?

- If quitters never win, and winners never quit, what fool came up with, "Quit while you're ahead?"

- Okay, who stopped the payment on my reality check?

- What hair color do they put on the driver's licenses of bald men?

- What WAS the best thing before sliced bread?

Q: What do prisoners use to call each other?
A: Cell phones.

Q: What has four legs, is big, green, fuzzy, and if it fell out of a tree would kill you?
A: A pool table.

A Hunting Story

Having shot a moose, two men from Seattle began dragging it by the tail to their pick-up.

On the way they were stopped by a game warden. "Let me see your hunting licenses boys," he said.

When he saw that everything was in order he asked if he could give them some advice.

"Sure!'" the hunters agreed.

"Well boys, I think that you would find it a lot easier to drag that moose by the horns and not by the tail."

"O.K. and thanks," said the hunters.

After about five minutes one said to the other, "Boy, dragging by the horns is sure a lot easier, eh?"

"Yeat, you're right," said the friend, "but have you noticed that we are getting further away from the truck?"

Wife's Cat

A man hated his wife's cat and he decided to get rid of it. He drove 20 blocks away from home and dropped the cat there. The cat was already walking up the driveway when he approached his home.

The next day, he decided to drop the cat 40 blocks away but the same thing happened.

He kept on increasing the number of blocks but the cat kept on coming home before him. At last he decided to drive a few miles away, turn right, then left, past the bridge, then right again and another right and so on until he reached what he thought was a perfect spot and dropped the cat there.

Hours later, the man calls his wife at home and asked her, "Jen is the cat there?"

"Yes, why do you ask?" answered the wife.

Frustrated, the man said, "Put that cat on the phone, I am lost and I need directions."

Promise

It was the day after Christmas at a church in Spokane. The pastor of the church was looking over the cradle when he noticed that the baby Jesus was missing from among the figures. Immediately he turned and went outside and saw a little boy with a red wagon, and in the wagon was the figure of the little infant, Jesus.

So, he walked up to the boy and said, "Well, where did you get Him, my little friend?"

The little boy replied, "I got him from the church."

"And why did you take him?"

The boy said, "Well, about a week before Christmas I prayed to the little Lord Jesus and I told him if he would bring me a red wagon for Christmas I would give him a ride around the block in it."

On the Wrong Note

Like many cello players, I sometimes get an odd buzz on one of the strings. A rubber cylinder helps damp the troublesome tone. One of these was mixed in with my pocket change, which I had pulled out while at the coffee machine.

"What's that?" the woman standing next to me asked.

"If you put it on your G-string," I explained without thinking, "you won't hear any wolf notes."

What's Up, Doc?

I sat there waiting for my new doctor to make his way through the file that contained my very extensive medical history.

After he finished all 17 pages, he looked at me and said, "You look better in person than you do on paper."

Where Am I?

Bob was driving to work when a truck ran a stop sign, hit his car broadside, and knocked him cold.

Passersby pulled him from the wreck and revived him. Bob began a terrific struggle and had to be tranquilized by the medics.

Later, when Bob was calm, they asked him why he struggled so much.

Bob said, "I remembered the impact. Then, nothing. I woke up on a concrete slab in front of a huge, flashing sign. Turns out somebody was standing in front of the 'S' on the 'Shell' sign."

Spread some laughter, share the cheer.
Let's be happy, while we're here!

CPSIA information can be obtained
at www.ICGtesting.com
Printed in the USA
FSHW021047151121
86209FS